THE HAWAIIAN JOURNAL OF HISTORY

Devoted to the History of Hawai'i, Polynesia, and the Pacific Area
Volume 38 • 2004

ARTICLES

ON THE COVER

Class of 1899, Kamehameha School for Girls, in graduation dresses they designed and sewed as part of their manual and industrial education: *(left to right)* Maria Maby, Louise Aoe Wongkong, Jane Nahiwa, and Ellen Pearce. Kamehameha Schools Photo Archives, Luryier Diamond, photo archivist.

Abbreviations

ABCFM	American Board of Commissioners for Foreign Missions
AH	State Archives of Hawai'i
BH	Board of Health, AH
BHL	Board of Health Letters, AH
BHM	Board of Health Minutes, AH
BPBM	Bernice Pauahi Bishop Museum
BPRO	British Public Record Office
CCM	Cabinet Council Minutes, AH
DB	*Daily Bulletin*
DPI	Department of Public Instruction, AH
EB	*Evening Bulletin*
F	*The Friend*
FO & Ex	Foreign Office and Executive File, AH
FOLB	Foreign Office Letter Book, AH
HA	*Honolulu Advertiser*
HAA	*Hawaiian Almanac and Annual;* also called Thrum's *Annual*
HBC	Hawai'i State Bureau of Conveyances
HG	*Hawaiian Gazette*
HHS	Hawaiian Historical Society
HJH	*Hawaiian Journal of History*
HMCS	Hawaiian Mission Children's Society
HSB	*Honolulu Star-Bulletin*
ID	Interior Department, AH
IDLB	Interior Department Letter Book, AH
IDLF	Interior Department Land File, AH
IDM	Interior Department Miscellaneous, AH
MH	*Missionary Herald*
P	*Polynesian*
PCA	*Pacific Commercial Advertiser*
PCR	Privy Council Records, AH
PP	*Paradise of the Pacific*
RHAS	Royal Hawaiian Agricultural Society
SIG	*Sandwich Islands Gazette*
SIN	*Sandwich Islands News*
SSB & A	*Sunday Star-Bulletin and Advertiser*

CARL KALANI BEYER

Manual and Industrial Education for Hawaiians During the 19th Century

Introduction

The purpose of this article is to make the case for the importance of the use of manual and industrial education in educating Hawaiians in the history of this curricular practice. The term manual and industrial education refers to either the manual labor system and/or manual training system in vogue during the 19th century. Charles Bennett, the most prolific researcher of this form of education, coined this term. Manual and industrial education emphasized a curriculum where learning was accomplished by both the hands and the mind. After becoming institutionalized in Europe, it next took root in the United States.[1]

When one investigates the history of manual and industrial education in the U.S., there is little mention of its use in educating Hawaiians during the 19th century.[2] Since the primary sponsors of education for Hawaiians were either American Protestant missionaries or their children, who usually returned to the U.S. for their college education, it is apparent that Hawaiian education had an American influence. My research reveals substantial evidence, demonstrating that

Carl Kalani Beyer, Ph.D., is an associate professor in the Teacher Education Department at Concordia University, River Forest, Illinois. Dr. Beyer is a graduate of the Kamehameha Schools and Beloit College, has masters' degrees from Northern Illinois University and Benedictine University, and a doctorate from the University of Illinois at Chicago. He has published widely in this field, including in The Hawaiian Journal of History *in 2003.*

The Hawaiian Journal of History, vol. 38 (2004)

especially in the use of manual and industrial education the efforts of the missionaries deserve a major place in the history of American education. Not only did the use of manual and industrial education mirror what was taking place in the United States, it anticipated and even influenced American use of this curricular practice. Moreover, it is the intention of this article to prove that in using manual and industrial education, the educators in Hawai'i deserve to be recognized as not mere borrowers but innovators. Most of the implementation of manual and industrial education in Hawai'i was based on local conditions and, as such, anticipated on their own some of the same elements of this educational system in the United States. Furthermore, the missionary educators in Hawai'i began to use manual and industrial education in the 1830s as one of several curricular alternatives; after mid-century, they began to steer all of the schools they controlled or influenced towards some form of this educational system. By the early years of the 20th century, it was the preferred curriculum in both the private and public schools of Hawai'i. As a result, in terms of length of time and continuity, it was more preponderant than what was practiced in the U.S.

The organization of this paper consists of three sections. The first section identifies the foundations of manual and industrial education in Europe and its use in the United States. The second section investigates the use of manual and industrial education in Hawai'i before the 1880s. The final section examines the arrival in Hawai'i of a more systematic form of manual and industrial education, known as manual training, during the latter two decades of the 19th century.

The Early History of Manual and Industrial Education

Manual and industrial education resulted as a reaction to the formal study of Latin and Greek grammar that predominated as the major form of education through the 18th century. Most scholars credit Johann Pestalozzi for fathering this form of education.[3] Pestalozzi was a Swiss education reformer who in the last quarter of the 18th century came to advocate both manual labor and manual training systems. While the manual labor system involved the inclusion of working with the hands as part of the curriculum, the manual training system involved instruction of the hands through the specific use of tools. Both systems combined their special focus with moral and intellectual instruction. In Pestalozzi's thinking, neither system should lead to vocational education, which was a form of education that trained students for profitable employment. He preferred an education where industry became a means to providing a general education.[4] According to Bennett, "Pestalozzi believed that children in school should learn to work, not only because of the economic value of skill and habit of labor, but because it was the basis of knowledge. He recognized the fact that 'doing leads to knowing'."[5]

Philip Emanuel von Fellenberg, an associate of Pestalozzi, organized and conducted the first manual and industrial education schools based on his mentor's philosophy. He contributed three types of institutions: the agricultural school, the industrial reform school, and the manual labor school. At his academy in Hofwyl, Switzerland, he organized and conducted a variety of educational activities. He brought together upper and lower class students. The Academy was intended for the sons of rich families; the Farm and Trade School provided instruction for poor children.[6] Fellenberg wanted to bring together young people of different social strata. Nevertheless, the education for each class was different. Manual labor was used as a means to provide physical training for his upper class students, and a means of paying for instruction and living expenses for his lower class students. The curriculum for the upper class students was a classical education; the curriculum for the lower class was agricultural, technical, with a common school academic education. This action combined both the manual labor and manual training systems.[7]

Pestalozzi's manual and industrial education first made its way to the United States in 1809, when the first Pestalozzian school was opened in Philadelphia through the philanthropy of William Maclure. The philanthropist had been in Paris when he met Francis Joseph Nichols Neef, who had trained under Pestalozzi. Maclure convinced Neef to come to America and help establish a school. In 1820, after moving this school several times, Neef and Maclure collaborated to help organize a manual labor movement.[8] In 1826, Neef and Maclure formed a partnership with Robert Dale Owen. At that time, they joined their philosophies in developing the education system at the commune in New Harmony, Indiana.[9] The school they developed was organized along the lines suggested by Pestalozzi; physical labor was combined with moral and intellectual culture.[10]

Manual and industrial education was a curriculum that also developed in the United States independent of Pestalozzi's influence. The first system in the U.S. to use any form of manual and industrial education were the schools for Native Americans. Colonial Indian education aimed to make converts, to train missionaries, and to produce laborers skilled in European work techniques. Academic instruction was reserved for students training for the ministry. One of the schools practicing an early form of manual and industrial education was Moor's Charity School for Indians. In 1755, Reverend Eleazer Wheelock founded this school at Lebannon, Connecticut; in 1769, he moved it to Dartmouth College. The purpose of the school was to train Native American men to become missionaries. The curriculum included reading, writing, arithmetic, English, Greek, and Latin. The use of a manual labor system was minimized to having the boys do some work around the school. Indian girls lived in homes in the neighborhood to learn housekeeping and sewing, and went to school one day a week to learn to read and write. It was the intent of the educators that the girls would also become missionaries and that the education of both genders would prevent them from reverting to tribal ways when they returned to their people.[11]

After the American Revolution, mission schools began to stress inculcating Native American students in industriousness. Little success occurred until the newly established American Board of Commissioners for Foreign Missions (ABCFM) introduced the Lancastrian system. In 1798, Joseph Lancaster had introduced this system in England. According to Ronald Raymond, "the fundamental premise of Lancaster's system revolved around mass public education utilizing older or more advanced students, or 'monitors', as instructors."[12] Located in Tennessee, Brainerd School for Native Americans was the first school where the ABCFM sponsored the Lancastrian system. The school also used the manual labor system. Through the influence of Cyrus Kingsbury, secretary of ABCFM, other schools were eventually established based on both these systems. In subsequent years, the reliance on the Lancastrian system waned while the use of the manual labor system grew.[13]

After 1835, due to the insistence of the federal government, the manual labor model was introduced into all Native American schools financed by the federal government and operated by missionaries. By mid-century, education at Indian schools consisted of common school academic subjects (English, arithmetic, history, geography, religion) and manual labor appropriate to proper gender roles. Boys learned such skills as blacksmithing, woodwork, and agriculture. The girls learned civilized cooking, dressmaking, and other domestic arts.[14] These manual labor schools would be the predominate institution to educate Native Americans until the 1880s.[15]

Even while manual labor was being established among Native American schools, Fellenberg's Academy was furnishing as well the inspiration for a manual labor movement among Whites in America. According to Bennett, it began in the years from 1825 to 1830, reached its height about 1834, and in less than 10 years had spent its force as an educational movement. In certain schools, it left a type of work, which grew and became permanent. He delineates the way Fellenberg's system was used in the United States.

> In Fellenberg's academy for the upper classes of society, manual labor was used as a means of physical training. In Fellenberg's farm and trade school, manual labor was a means of paying for instruction and living expenses. In democratic America these two aims were combined.[16]

Bennett purports that the theological seminaries took the lead in this movement. The rise of the American Education Society in 1815 helped promote the use of manual labor among the theological seminaries.[17] David Allmendinger provides the motivation for this move. This organization wanted to tap young men from lower class Protestant families to fill an increasing number of vacant pulpits. Manual labor was deemed as a means of helping to support these students at seminaries.[18] Bennett discovers that up to 1829, the most successful manual labor experiment was the one at the Andover Theological Seminary at Andover, Massachusetts. Its voluntary program based upon mechanical labor became the model for other seminaries. In many other schools, it was largely agricultural, and, in the most successful schools, it was compulsory. Maine Wesleyan Seminary went one step further by uniting manual labor with academics. The purpose was to help three classes of young men: the "worthy poor" who wanted an education; the "idle well-to-do" who needed proper motives to industry to keep them from dissipation; and the "especially talented" students who needed exercise for the good of their health.[19] Other locations for theological seminaries that used manual labor included the following: Auburn, New York; Maryville, Tennessee; South Hadley, Massachusetts; Lane, Ohio; Bowdoin, Maine; and Middlebury, Vermont.[20]

Manual and industrial education was also used to educate Blacks in the United States. During the period from 1830 to 1860, Northern philanthropists started manual and industrial education schools for free Blacks. These schools were established for the following reasons: opposition from White skilled mechanics to apprentice Blacks; as a way to offer Blacks a common school education; and to make it possible for Black students to support themselves by working at an occupation while attending classes. While the program at these schools had a vocational focus, they also relied on both manual labor and manual training systems.[21]

The general aim of the manual and industrial education programs in Black institutions was to dignify labor, to train skilled workers, and to prepare industrial teachers. The majority of the students at these institutions paid a part of their school expenses by working at their trade for wages while at school. The main reason for the failure of these schools was their being located in rural areas, which did not afford markets for the students to either sell their trade or the products of their labor. Two schools were more successful. Begun in 1834, the Peterboro Manual Labor School in Madison County, New York, provided a common school education along with manual training. This training was used not to learn a trade but to support the students at school. At the Institute for Colored Youths, begun in 1852, instruction was provided in mechanic arts. This instruction was free to persons of good moral character who were 16 years of age or older. All pupils were first instructed in the use of tools, materials, simple operatives, and then they advanced by progressive stages until all operations in their trade were thoroughly mastered.[22]

Manual and Industrial Education in Hawai'i Prior to 1880

The American Protestant missionaries, who arrived in Hawai'i in 1820, were the primary curriculum developers who introduced this form of education. In this study, the term "missionary" refers to ordained ministers, men and women who were not ordained but served the mission, the ministers' wives and children, those men who resigned from the mission but stayed in Hawai'i, and missionary allies. Throughout this study the word missionary refers to all the people in this group.[23]

The missionaries were sent by the ABCFM, a Calvinist organization developed after the Great Awakening of 1800, to spread their brand of Christianity. For these missionaries, Hawai'i became one of many frontiers for their religion and culture. Their adherence to an aggressive brand of Calvinism and New England values led to a twofold mission: converting Hawaiians to Christianity and remolding the Hawaiian society into the image of New England.

Over the next 20 years, the missionaries implemented an educational program in five steps. The first step was developing English schools for the *ali'i* (chiefs, nobility). The second step was to translate reading material into the Hawaiian language once it became clear how difficult it was to teach literacy in the English language. As *ali'i* gave the missionaries permission to approach the *maka'āinana* (commoners) and required that they attend to the *palapala* (the act of learning to read), the task of making over 50,000 adults literate seemed more surmountable if the instruction was in the vernacular. The third step was to send the best students from the school for *ali'i* to act as teachers at schools for commoners throughout the district. This system involved some training of *ali'i* teachers. At most of the mission stations, the plan brought teachers together from all parts of the district for a period of several weeks or months to receive special instructions designed to make them more effective teachers.[24] The annual report of the ABCFM for 1832 demonstrates that they understood the Lancastrian monitorial system.[25] The process was highly successful in making a large number of people literate in a very short time. From the point of view of the missionaries, education was playing an important part in the transformation of Hawai'i.

Between 1824 and 1827, nearly the entire adult population of the Hawaiian Islands went to school. This missionary educational system reached the peak of its development in 1832, when more than 53,000 pupils were enrolled in 900 schools, the equivalent of 40 percent of the total Hawaiian population. But few of the students were children.[26]

The establishment of Lahainaluna High School in 1831 as a teacher-training center resolved the dilemma posed by inadequately prepared teachers. This was the fourth step in the development of an educational system by the missionaries during the early years. The purpose of the school was to prepare young men to become teachers in the common schools or assistant teachers of religion. It was also determined that the school would use the manual labor system as far as possible.[27] Thus, manual and industrial education began in Hawai'i.

During the second decade of the missionaries' presence in Hawai'i, they reorganized their educational endeavors by shifting from adult to child education and by improving the training of teachers. In 1833, when the school system for adult Hawaiians began to fall apart, the missionaries at most of the stations began to create select schools for adolescents. Select or station schools were day schools developed for the best students from the district common schools. In order to enhance the development of select schools, the missionaries voted at the 1836 general meeting to erect as soon as practical one model school house at each station at the expense not exceeding $200 and appropriated $100 to $150 to pay graduates of Lahainaluna High School as teachers at these schools.[28] In addition, in 1837, the American board sent its next company of missionaries, eight qualified teachers, to help with these schools. This was the fifth, and final, step in the missionaries educational program.[29] When an economic depression hit the United States, the American Board could no longer finance all the endeavors of the Hawaiian mission. As a consequence, the Hawaiian government was given control over the common schools and most of the select schools to form the public school system.

Coinciding with the development of select schools was the beginning of the special schools. Special schools were those select schools receiving sufficient financial support to remain independent from the public school system and boarded their students. Boarding students provided more opportunities for the educators to experiment with some form of manual and industrial education. The rationale to create these boarding schools was to provide an education for select students under the continuous influence of the missionary educators. This decision arose as the result of arguments made by Reverends Richard Armstrong and David Lyman at the general meeting of 1835. Both men believed that education needed to be both practical and delivered in an isolated environment away from the bad influences of other White men and the Hawaiian culture. As a result, it was agreed to board students at the Hilo select school begin a boarding school for girls at Wailuku, Maui, and shift from educating adults in a day situation to children as boarders at Lahainaluna High School.[30] All these innovations were considered to be experimental.

Initially, all three schools had a common school curriculum in addition to using some form of manual and industrial education. When Armstrong and Lyman spoke about wanting a "practical" education at all the select schools, they were referring to using some form of manual and industrial education. Consequently, it was hoped that the select schools would also implement this meaning of "practical" into their curriculum. Even though the curriculum at the high school included manual labor, in time its academics became formal. In contrast to a common school curriculum, a formal school curriculum was at this time the equivalent of a high school or academy curriculum. Eventually, students desiring to enter into the ministry were provided training in the classics after they had finished the required four-year course of instruction.[31]

Lahainaluna High School was the premier educational institution for Hawaiians for over 40 years.[32] Education provided at the high school level was a very new phenomenon, even in the United States. The first high school in the U.S. was founded in Boston in 1821. By the time Lahainaluna was begun, there were no more than 10 high schools in the whole country. But Lahainaluna High School was also a teacher training school. In that regard, it preceded the first American normal school by eight years.[33]

The founder of Lahainaluna High School, Reverend Lorrin Andrews, arrived in Hawai'i in 1828. He was educated at Jefferson College and Princeton Theological Seminary, schools that required manual labor of their students.[34] In a letter to the ABCFM, he summarizes the expectations the missionaries had for the school: "Here in almost savage ignorance, without the least vestige of civilization, are the future lawyers and doctors and school masters and preachers of the Sandwich Islands."[35] These expectations were warranted because students admitted to the high school were the best teachers from the various station schools. They were also for the most part *kaukau ali'i,* a class of Hawaiians who were used to serving and following the orders of the *ali'i nui* (high chiefs). When the *ali'i nui* wanted the *palapala* to be successful, they ordered their servers to go to Lahainaluna to learn. This group of men, who were thoroughly educated in the knowledge of the traditional culture and the select among students of the missionary station schools, represented the educated elite of the Hawaiian Kingdom.[36] By necessity, the school was a day school since all the students were adults, many with wives and children. The students and their families were given plots of land to build shelters and raise food. Although the education during the first year was rudimentary due to the lack of materials, Andrews reports that attendance was good, the scholars were obedient and well behaved, and evinced an anxious desire to learn.[37]

By intention and due to lack of funds, the scholars at the school were expected to do manual labor to provide for their housing and food. In fact, every scholar entered the school with full understanding that manual labor was part of the business of the school. The general meeting of 1832 agreed that Andrews should start a manual labor department and voted $150 for the purpose of procuring tools and materials. At this time, tools and turning lathes were donated. The lathe allowed the manufacture of other tools. Andrews hoped to hire an artisan to help create a manual labor department, and this employee's wife would run a school for the wives of the scholars.[38]

Until the general meeting of 1834, Lahainaluna High School was an experiment. The progress made under Andrews' leadership convinced the missionaries that they needed to enlarge the school and give it permanent status.[39] They acquired a printing press—a hand-operated model that could print about 100 sheets per hour—and machinery for binding books.[40] In addition, they designated a place for a distinct library, built a church on campus, again requested an instructor of manual arts, and charged a tuition of one dollar per month with manual labor canceling the tuition. By this time, the American Board had agreed that the school should be placed on a permanent basis.[41]

While training teachers was the initial purpose for founding the high school, ultimately the American Board intended it to be a seminary. Thus, in 1837, the board insisted the name of the school be changed to Lahainaluna Seminary.[42] As such, its graduates would be trained as preachers of the gospel for Hawaiians and other islands of the Pacific Ocean. In keeping with this design, Andrews began to teach the Greek language to a select group of students. Both the general meeting of that year and the American Board approved this action. Primarily, Andrews' action was motivated by his desire to have his scholars read the Bible in its original language. But Andrews was not content in just having the school be a seminary. He envisioned that with more funds, the school could be a college or university. This vision was based on his observation that at least half of the scholars were already equivalent to sophomores in colleges in the United States. The mission decided that in the 1836–1837 school year, all new students would be boys between the ages of seven and 17, and they would be boarders. As the result of this new policy, for the next three years there were two distinct schools: one for the adults who were day students, and another for boys who were boarders. While the adults who performed manual labor did so voluntarily to cover the tuition expense, the boys were required to labor three hours a day as part of their curriculum.[43]

With government help and finances in order, the attention of the school turned towards raising its standards. In the general meeting of 1844, the missionaries now believed the school could produce legislators, judges, secretaries, and other government agents and be more likely to furnish clergymen, lawyers, and physicians for Hawaiian society.[44] The report of the minister of public instruction for 1846 summarizes the results of the first 15 years of the school's existence: out of the total number of students enrolled at Lahainaluna, 297 had left the institution, 42 had died, 108 were employed as teachers, 45 were in government service, and 31 in other useful services. The ABCFM had contributed $68,500 towards the school through this 15-year period.[45]

In spite of the commitment of the ABCFM, in 1846 the mission transferred the seminary to the government due to the inability of the American Board to continue financing the school.[46] The government assumed its maintenance, including salaries, and agreed not to interfere with religious teaching. Even though the school was technically a public school—the only high school among the public schools—it continued to provide the American Protestant churches in Hawai'i with ministers and missionaries as well as training the most prominent and influential members of the kingdom.[47] Graduates of Lahainaluna Seminary served as school superintendents, principals, and teachers, licensed preachers and ordained ministers, choir leaders, legislators (leading members in both the House of Nobles and the House of Representatives), cabinet officials, privy councilors, governors, circuit and district judges, lawyers, surveyors, tax assessors and collectors, historians, writers, orators, translators, journalists, compilers, various governmental officers, and civil servants.[48]

While Lahainaluna Seminary was primarily a formal school using manual labor to help defray the costs of the school, Hilo Boys' Boarding School epitomized Pestalozzi's model as it combined manual labor and manual training in its curriculum. More than any other person, David Beldon Lyman was the heart, hands, and mind behind the Hilo Boarding School. He arrived in Hawai'i in 1832. He was the oldest of eight children born to a New England farm family. His household was religious and industrious. He graduated from Williams College and from Andover Theological Institute, where he experienced manual labor as a part of his education. Within three months after the American Board selected him, he married Sarah Joiner and headed for Hawai'i. Upon his arrival in Hawai'i, he spent two months in Honolulu before assignment to Hilo. During his four years of preaching and teaching in the Hilo District, he decided it would be best to develop a boarding school for young students so that habits of Christianity and industry might be inculcated at an early age.[49] Mildred Gordon says he "was very practical, reserved in personality, a good farmer and carpenter who enjoyed seeing the practical results of his work."[50] Consequently, he did not follow the scholastic traditions of his day. His main goal was to fit the education to the ability of his students. Based on his leadership for over 50 years (fig. 1), Hilo Boarding School proved to be unique, not only in Hawai'i, but worldwide; it was an early innovator in preparing students for a trade, in making the training of the hands as important as the training of the mind, and in introducing music as an important and natural part of school work.[51]

The objective of the school was to develop good teachers and preachers with both piety and good character. "Habits of industry, thrift, and morality based on the principles of the Gospel were considered" by missionaries at the school "as most essential for these fun-loving, easy-going Hawaiians."[52] A pamphlet on the Hilo Boarding School summarizes its mission:

> It aimed to take Hawaiian youth in their natural uncultured state and by dint of unsparing painstaking effort to impart to them such mental and moral furnishing as they were able to receive and appropriate in combination with a wholesome physical training in the ways of social and civilized life.[53]

Throughout the entire history of the school, manual and industrial education played a prominent role. Agriculture was included in the curriculum from the beginning to help the school be self-sufficient. The boys' involvement in raising their own food cut down on the expenses of the school, which often led to the school making money. In 1884, Reverend William Oleson, the principal, reported that

FIG. 1. David Lyman, Sarah Lyman and children, Hilo, in 1853. Lyman introduced Western manual and industrial education into the Hilo Boarding School. Hawaiian Mission Children's Society Library.

$3,500 was raised annually from the sale of farm products. But it was also believed that laboring in the fields was good education for the students. Even when the boys and/or their parents asked to be released from manual labor, the instructors refused their request. They were "convinced that such work was valuable not only for the health of the students, but contributed to the good discipline of the school, as well as being valuable in forming habits of thrift and industry."[54] The curriculum kept the boys busy from morning until night (fig. 2). Francis Lyman, one of David Lyman's sons, portrayed just how exacting the curriculum was:

> From the beginning of the school up to the present time, the scholars have raised the kalo, bananas, sugar cane, and other vegetables for their living, making their own poi, and doing all the work on their farm, and keeping the school premises in order, working morning and evening. Besides being taught in the class-room in books and in vocal and instrumental music, from four to five hours each day, for five days in the week, they were taught to be self-supporting youth while at school,

FIG. 2. Students in the Hilo Boarding School Shop, Class of June 1901, displaying their work. Courtesy of Lyman Museum.

> by the work of their hands, farming, tailoring, house painting, stone work, cooking, etc, and to become good reliable Christian men, and loyal citizens, not ashamed to work.[55]

Using his experiences from his farm background and education, David Lyman developed an educational system that mirrored the connection Pestalozzi made between both learning by the hands and the mind and the use of manual labor and manual training. According to Levi Lyman, another son of David and Sarah Lyman, the following are the six values of the manual and industrial education system that his father instituted at Hilo Boys' Boarding School:

> First, there was the need to solve the daily food. D. Lyman made food production a condition of entrance into the Hilo Boarding School. If a boy did not work, he did not eat. He soon learned by experience, the value of industry. Second, he learned further that his work must be productive, that he should not only put in time, but that the larger quantity of food he helped produce, the better his table was supplied. Third, work must be up to a certain standard of perfection or it will not pass. Fourth, they learn that when an order is taken to be filled at a certain time, this must be ready on time. Fifth, by their extra labor many of the boys earn enough to cover their school fee, and some enough to buy in addition all their books, clothing and incidentals, and the more thrifty are able to open up a bank account. This provided early life lessons in self-reliance. Sixth, each one must do his part, and do it well, whether interested in it or not.[56]

As Lyman was able to acquire tools, he instituted a form of manual training that involved designing and using tools to complete a project. The school was still primarily interested in training teachers for the common schools and, when it switched to English instruction, its graduates were also being trained for the English select schools. In 1840 and 1844, tailoring and dairying were added to the manual and industrial education curriculum. Furthermore, drawing on the Hawaiian love of music, the instructors made singing in the European manner a requirement, and, as they acquired instruments, orchestral music became a regular part of the curriculum. The school struggled financially after 1850, when the American Board withdrew its financial support.[57] The school's instructors devised and furnished an all-around training much like growing up on a farm in order to compensate for the lack of funds to acquire machines and tools. This was done through short courses offered by the home crafts department, a curriculum entirely distinct from the school's manual labor courses. It included training in knot-making and splicing of ropes, window glazing, soldering, general repair work, care of horses, wagons and farm implements, leather work, sharpening tools, concrete work, laying water pipes, repairing faucets, and installing and repairing electrical lines.[58]

In 1860, a transfer of the school to the government was proposed. The trustees stipulated that instruction be given by men who would be approved by the American Board and by the HEA and that it continue as a school of high caliber to qualify men for teaching, the ministry, and professional and business life. It is unclear why, but the transfer never took place. As a consequence, the missionaries were able to continue experimenting with manual and industrial education for male students.[59]

The work being done at Hilo Boys' Boarding School did not go entirely unnoticed. The Hilo school influenced the way Samuel Chapman Armstrong approached industrial education when he began Hampton Institute in 1865. Armstrong was born in Hawai'i to the missionary couple, Reverend Richard and Clarissa Chapman Armstrong. His education and experience in Hawai'i prepared him well for the work he implemented at Hampton Institute. Of primary importance was his accompanying his father, who as the minister of public instruction made official tours of various schools of the Islands. Among all the schools observed by Samuel Armstrong, the work being done by Reverend Lyman at Hilo Boys' Boarding School impressed him the most.[60] In practice, the manual and industrial education system at Hampton Institute was much like what Lyman had instituted at the Hilo Boys' Boarding School; it used manual labor to give students a chance to meet bills for board and clothing, to develop high standards of discipline, and to enhance students' energy level. This system also helped students to meet the mental rigors of the curriculum.[61]

Lahainaluna Seminary and Hilo Boys' Boarding Schools were not the only schools using some form of manual and industrial education before the 1880s. The boys' schools at Waialua on the island of O'ahu, Kohala on the island of Hawai'i, and Waioli on the island of Kaua'i were select schools whose founders continued to operate independently of the public school system with little support from the Sandwich Islands Mission (SIM). Their education mirrored that of Hilo Boys' Boarding School since they used a common school academic curriculum along with manual and industrial education. However, while they developed the same reliance on the manual labor system as the Hilo school, they never did incorporate the manual training system. Even though these schools never had the same impact as Hilo Boys' Boarding School, they demonstrate the wide use of manual and industrial education among the missionary special schools.[62]

In addition, early in the promotion of select schools, there were two female schools: Wailuku Female Seminary and Hilo Girls' School; founded in 1835 and 1838 respectively. Even though both schools were closed by 1850, beginning in the 1860s, four new female seminaries were established: Waialua and Kawaiaha'o on the island of O'ahu, Kohala on the island of Hawai'i, and Mauna'olu on the island of Maui. The latter three survived well into the 20th century. All of these female schools included common school academics and relied upon manual labor to help develop industriousness in the students and defray the costs of operating the school.[63]

While the missionary special schools were heavily involved in some aspect of manual and industrial education, the public schools were primarily involved in training their students just to be literate. After 1850, as few Hawaiians were acquiring parcels of land under the *Māhele* land division, missionary and Hawaiian leaders agreed that in order to help Hawaiians become self-sufficient, independent, and economically successful, they also needed to be educated in the skills of agriculture and industry. In the minutes of the meeting of the HEA for 1855, the missionaries spelled out their understanding of the importance of manual labor to this endeavor:

> The connexion [sic] therefore between our schools and labor is most intimate and important. The two must go together. It is too often the case . . . that our native youth, both male and female, acquire some intelligence at school, and then at the age of fourteen or fifteen leave

> school only to live in idleness and vice. What is wanted is to introduce them to the useful trades; to induce them to engage in the cultivation of the soil, or some branch of regular and useful labor.[64]

This interest translated into both chiefs and missionaries encouraging the merits of manual labor even in government schools. An editorial in a Hawaiian journal exemplifies this belief when it proclaims, "it would be hardly possible to overestimate the importance of manual labor in all schools for Hawaiians. We believe that the scholars in all Government schools should be obliged to 'mahi ai' [work] vigorously two or three hours a day."[65] Samuel T. Alexander, a second-generation missionary, echoed these sentiments. He admonished the government to provide each school with a small plot of land for each pupil to "mahi ai for two to three hours each day and have girls learn sewing or braiding mats and hats."[66]

As the minister of public instruction and former missionary, Richard Armstrong greatly influenced both the government schools and the missionary special schools. He stressed vocational experience and the lessons of manual labor in both roles. Armstrong imposed manual labor in the curriculum of the public schools well ahead of schools in the United States. Whenever Principal Lyman was in Honolulu, he was sure to meet with Armstrong at his home. They discussed the advantages of manual labor and worked on ideas that could be implemented at the Hilo school.[67]

As the result of Richard Armstrong's untimely death and the missionaries being at odds with the Hawaiian monarchs after 1854, the missionaries had less and less influence over decisions involving the public schools. However, when H. Rexford Hitchcock, the son of missionaries, replaced Abraham Fornander as inspector general of the schools in 1870, and when Charles R. Bishop assumed the presidency of the board of education in 1874, missionary influence over the public schools began to return.[68]

One of the first innovations under this new leadership was the establishment of the Haleakala Boys' School. The school's principal and main teacher were missionaries Robert W. Andrews and Mrs. Samuel A. Thurston. It represented one of the few schools attempting to provide instruction in both the English and Hawaiian languages. While the academic curriculum was common school, its main focus was agriculture. Eventually, it concentrated on the dairy industry. In the 1874 biennial report, Charles R. Bishop states "no school under the control of government posseses so great advantages, as this institution, for development into a practical, industrial school, at which the mechanical trades in common demand may be taught to the youth of this Kingdom."[69] Due to the rising expenses of the school and inadequate government finances and dairy profits, the school closed in 1880.[70]

In 1878, based upon the initial experience at Haleakala Boys' School, the Legislature made it lawful for the board of education to include agricultural and industrial education in public school instruction.[71] The law provided that the teachers receive four-fifths and the students receive one-fifth of the net profits from the work. Where manual labor was practiced, Bishop relates, it involved two to five hours of daily agricultural labor. The proceeds helped pay the expenses of books and gave the pupils habits of industry.[72]

Manual Training in the United States and Hawai'i

In the 1880s, a new form of manual and industrial education spreading throughout the U.S. made its way to Hawai'i. This version of manual and industrial education was a more systematic form. It was called manual training and was a form of curriculum based on providing manipulative experiences. It emphasized developing students through instruction based on handwork, and providing general industrial training to meet the rapidly changing demands brought on by industrialization.[73] In part, this curriculum was intended to offer an alternative to the almost exclusively academic education common at this time in the United States. Calvin Woodward, one of its supporters, was particularly concerned that the usual method of education steered students away from employment requiring hard labor.[74] Teaching character was an important component of manual training, as was the idea that schools provide real-life experiences and modify student conduct in accordance with predetermined aims and ideals.[75]

At this time, the missionaries shifted from the manual labor form of manual and industrial education to the manual training form. All the missionary female seminaries introduced industrial departments.[76] Probably because they were incapable of making the transition, Kohala and Waioli Boys' School were released to join the other government English select schools.[77] Waialua Boys' School had closed in 1845.[78]

When Reverend William Oleson became the principal of the Hilo Boys' Boarding School, manual and industrial education took on a more systematic form. Although Oleson was new to the Islands, he was knowledgeable of the manual training curriculum beginning to take hold in the United States. Under his leadership (1879–1887), the school began a new era. He increased the endowment fund and added new industrial courses. The first major new education building in 10 years was erected and a house for the principal was built. A paved roadway was begun and completed by 1880. An iron cookhouse and a student bathhouse were constructed. In 1884, a classroom and two dormitories were completed. In 1886, a two-story building was completed that contained a floor for a dining hall and another floor for a dormitory.[79] In essence, Hilo Boys' Boarding School, the guiding light for manual training in Hawai'i, was being re-organized to be more like the new manual training schools in the United States.

During the latter two decades of the 19th century, as the missionaries began to pursue a more systematic form of manual training, Hilo Boarding School truly became an industrial school. In 1886, William W. Hall gave the school carpenter tools. A year later, a printing press and a wood lathe were donated and the government appropriated $1,500 for an industrial arts building. In 1890, funds for a blacksmith shop and three sewing machines were acquired. In 1892, Charles C. Kennedy donated a steam boiler and another party donated an engine lathe. That same year a 15-light dynamo was purchased for lighting, making the school buildings the first to have lights in all of Hilo. In 1894, the school started an ice plant. In 1895, the school added a coffee huller and pulper. Finally, after years of farming done entirely by hand, a plow and mower were purchased.[80] Gordon highlights the advances that Hilo Boarding School promoted and the good it provided for Hilo:

> In many ways the Hilo Boarding School was the advance guard for new industries in the community, such as printing, the making of ice, dairying, and the manufacture of electricity. The boys trained to take part in

> these new industries. When the community could take over an industry as a regular business enterprise, the school relinquished the project as a community enterprise.[81]

Hilo Boarding School was unique in many regards. It is one of the oldest schools in Hawai'i. Its agricultural curriculum began 26 years before the Congress of the United States made federal land grants available to found similar schools in 1862. Its elementary tool work and industrial training began 40 years before the founding of the first manual training school in the United States at Boston in 1878.[82] The school was credited for "serving well in the early days in educating leaders among the Hawaiian race, producing what was most needed among them, teachers, preachers, and intelligent agriculturalist, and homemakers".[83] In tribute to its founder, Reverend Oleson states, "it was a well-deserved tribute paid to a notable educator when General (Samuel) Armstrong said that, when he wished to make Hampton the best kind of school for the freedman, he took Father Lyman's Hilo School as his pattern."[84]

During the latter two decades of the 19th century, manual training spread from its base at Hilo Boys' Boarding School to encompass two new manual training schools for boys, the inclusion of manual training at all the female seminaries, and the spread of this form of curriculum to the public schools. The first effort in the diffusion of manual training was the establishment of the Kamehameha School for Boys (fig. 3).

Before her death in 1884, Bernice Pauahi Bishop, heir to the vast lands of the Kamehameha dynasty, established through her will the design to create two private schools, one for boys and one for girls. The students were to be Hawaiians by preference. Instruction was to be in English. As per her wishes, the course of study required several hours of manual labor every day.[85] Even though the school was not officially a missionary school, since most of the people connected with it were members of the missionary party, including its founders, board of directors, first president, and first and second principals, it was considered an extension of the education work being done by the missionaries. Once it was decided that the principal and his associates were to be chosen according to how well they knew the Hawaiian character and could provide religious and moral training, Reverend Oleson was chosen to be the school's first principal. He was sent to the United States to study current educational methods, particularly those used at Hampton Institute.[86] While Oleson was doing this work, Samuel Armstrong was recruiting staff members for the school. He discovered Theodore Richards at Camp Chocarun for Boys in New Hampshire. Richards would later become the second principal of the Kamehameha School for Boys.[87]

Thirty-seven boys passed the entrance examinations to become the first class at the Kamehameha School for Boys. The school was commonly known as the Manual Department or "The Manual." Several of the boys came over from Hilo Boarding School with their principal to provide a nucleus of boys familiar with his program. The academic department offered a common school curriculum, with special emphasis on language training. The six-year program included written and mental drill in arithmetic, algebra, and geometry, language exercises in dictation, original composition, oral and written use of

FIG. 3. Students working in the Carpentry Shop, Kamehameha School for Boys, 1890, *(right)* Rev. Wm. Oleson, Principal, *(far left)* Charles E. King. Kamehameha Schools Photo Archives, Luryier Diamond, photo archivist.

idioms, synonyms, business forms, orders, bills, and accounts. Other academic pursuits included physical geography, historical narratives, reading, and penmanship. There was also an emphasis on moral instruction. The industrial programs included free-hand drawing and designing, mechanical drawing, source and manufacture of useful articles, and machine use. In addition, daily instruction was given in vocal music. Finally, the manual training department furnished a complete course of instruction in carpentry, black-smithing, piping, wood turning, and press work. (Figs. 4 and 5)[88] By the 1890s, the school added a Normal department due to the need for preparing Hawaiian teachers for positions in country districts where the need for teachers was the greatest.[89]

At about the same time that the Kamehameha School for Boys was being established, second generation missionaries were beginning the Kaua'i Industrial School. This school was originally conceived as a coeducational industrial school, near the city of Līhu'e, on the

FIG. 4. Carpentry Shop students building a school cottage 1902–1903, Kamehameha School for Boys. *(left to right, first row)* Charles Brickwood Lyman (1904), Kaumu Hanchett (1904); *(second row)* Mr. Ira Eskew, Instructor, David Desha (1905), Arthur Arnold (1905); *(third row)* Stephen Desha (1903). Kamehameha Schools Photo Archives. Luryier Diamond, photo archivist.

island of Kaua'i, because this island did not have any school providing an industrial education like the rest of the major islands. Juliette Smith and her brother Jared Smith were the founders of the school.[90]

The plans for the school included cultivating 30 acres of land to yield part of the food necessary for 75 pupils. Besides the principal and the two teachers, the staff included a matron and a superintendent of the Manual and Mechanical Shop. Benefactors like William Waterhouse, George Wilcox, and Abner Wilcox each paid the salary of one of the teachers. Tuition for the students was $25 per year. The average number of pupils was 24 although there were accommodations for 40 pupils. Other benefactors paid the tuition for three-fourths of the pupils.[91] Once the school was in operation, the boys worked in the schoolroom for five hours each day; one-and-a-half hours were spent in the shop and three and one-half hours were spent working on the grounds. The latter time was spent chiefly in raising sweet potatoes, bananas, papayas, and sorghum. The main mechanical industries were blacksmithing and carpentry. By 1891, the school

FIG. 5. Kamehameha School for Boys Print Shop, 1897. Kamehameha Schools Photo Archives. Luryier Diamond, photo archivist.

followed a more detailed curriculum for the three classes enrolled. Each class took courses in English, arithmetic, music, and recitations. The First Class added courses in physics and algebra, the Second Class added courses in printing and physiology, and the Third Class added a course in physiology. After school, all classes participated in baseball, croquet, or tennis.[92] Due to economic hardships to the sugar planters, the main philanthropists funding the school, and Jared Smith's death in 1898, the school closed in 1899.[93]

During the same time period that manual training was being systematized at Hilo Boys' Boarding School and instituted at Kamehameha School for Boys and Kaua'i Industrial School, the three surviving female seminaries and, after 1894, the Kamehameha School for Girls were adding industrial departments for the purpose of offering manual training to Hawaiian girls. Whereas education for females once focused on preparing wives for the educated Hawaiian men, it was becoming important to the leaders of Hawai'i that there was a need to train Hawaiian women for careers in the emerging plantation economy.[94]

Once the monarchy was overthrown in 1893 and the missionaries gained ultimate political power, more missionaries became administrators and teachers in the public schools. Eventually, missionary sons controlled all the major positions in the public school system. With this power, they began to introduce manual training there as well. In 1894, William R. Castle became the first missionary son to serve as president of the board of education. In his report for that year, he discusses the effort to introduce manual training into the public schools.[95] By 1898, Minister of Public Instruction William D. Alexander (another missionary son), directed the public schools to follow a more extensive curriculum for manual training. He developed a five-year manual training curriculum. Similar to Castle, he preferred the course work of manual training, rather than a full-blown manual training program as was being followed at the female seminaries, Hilo Boys' Boarding School, the Kamehameha Schools, Kaua'i Industrial School, and Lahainaluna Seminary. This curriculum involved Hawaiian male students making and using weather vanes, seed envelopes, and agricultural tools and Hawaiian female students weaving baskets and sewing clothing. The purpose of the curriculum was to prepare its pupils for industrial or agricultural occupations.[96]

The best example of missionary adherence to the manual training curriculum was the conversion of Lahainaluna Seminary from a formal school into a manual training school like the Kamehameha School for Boys. When the missionaries regained control of the public schools, manual training was introduced at Lahainaluna Seminary. In 1899, William D. Alexander, pronounced that the school was a manual training school. Money was appropriated to rebuild the school since the original buildings were in disrepair and to construct the necessary shops to provide a top-notch manual training program. The new buildings were dedicated in 1904, and the school was officially renamed as Lahainaluna Technical High School. The once formal curriculum of the school was altered to include courses in bookkeeping, typewriting, mechanical and architectural drawings, sanitation and civics, commercial arithmetic and business English. In the past, its best graduates were expected to become leaders, but now they were being steered by their education to serve as bookkeepers or technicians. Charles MacDonald says, "the object of the manual training was to fit the lads to earn a living in the conditions obtaining in Hawaii."[97] Alatau Atkinson, former inspector general of the public schools, best exemplifies the alteration of the training when he delivered the address at the formal opening of Lahainaluna Technical High School in 1904:

> Lahainaluna is essentially the training place for the poor man. . . . To train a man we must not merely train his intellect, we must train his hand with equal care. We must make him understand the dignity of labor. We must teach him not theoretically, we must teach him practically.[98]

Conclusion

This study establishes the important role played by missionary use of manual and industrial education for Hawaiians both to the history of Hawaiian and American education. One of the most important points is the fact that Samuel Chapman Armstrong borrowed his initial ideas for his industrial education system at Hampton Institute from the Hilo model. What was practiced at the Hilo school and designed by Reverend David Lyman in the 1830s was unique in comparison to what was being done at this time in the United States. Until Hampton Institute was begun in 1865, no other experiments in the United States even came close to matching the work being accomplished at Hilo Boys' Boarding School. In addition, the symbiotic relationship of preparing the best *maka'āinana* students at the Hilo school to be further trained at Lahainaluna Seminary was also unique in comparison to what was being done at this time in the United States. In fact, it was more like what Fellenberg had introduced in Hofwyl, Switzerland. The experiments with manual labor, manual training, and a common school curriculum at Hilo Boys' Boarding School for *maka'āinana* (equivalent to the lower class) and the experiments with manual labor and a formal curriculum at Lahainaluna Seminary for *kaukau ali'i* (equivalent to the upper class) mirrored Fellenberg's schools for the lower and upper classes. Furthermore, Lahainaluna Seminary was like Moor's Charity School for Indians, the first Indian academy. At both institutions, formal education was combined with a manual labor system to train its brightest members to serve as missionaries.

During the 19th century, the missionaries' use of manual labor in schools for Hawaiians paralleled how it was used among Native Americans. Since members of the American Board were involved with both educating Indians and Hawaiians, this is not surprising. Many of the missionaries had experienced manual labor at the colleges or seminaries they attended. There they experienced manual labor as exercise, to lessen their expenses, and as a means to enhance morals, promote habits of industry, and independence of character and originality. Initially, the financial needs of the schools for Hawaiians warranted using manual labor to defray the expenses. The missionaries did not have to be told by the government to use manual labor, as was the case with educating Native Americans in the United States. It was apparent to them that manual labor combined goals of Christianity and civilization by developing virtues of labor, industry, and economy—all essential in a person with good character and "civilized" deportment. As a consequence, manual labor was a requirement of all students. The Hawaiian and Native American schools were also very similar in their common school curriculum and the manual training skills that each taught: blacksmithing, wood working, and agriculture for boys, and cooking, dressmaking, and domestic arts for girls.

Manual training arrived in Hawai'i many years before it began to spread throughout the United States in the 1880s. However, the new version of manual training arrived in Hawai'i at about the same time. The systematizing of manual training at Hilo Boys' Boarding School, the establishment of manual training at both the Kamehameha School for Boys and the Kaua'i Industrial School, the addition of manual training departments at the female seminaries and the Kamehameha School for Girls (fig. 6), the shift in curriculum that led to formation of the Lahainaluna Technical High School, and the introduction of manual training into the public schools are examples of this diffusion. Through all these efforts, the educators borrowed ideas solicited by reading literature, visiting schools, or communicating with the practitioners of manual training in the United States.

Compared to most school systems in America, the program in the Islands was implementing a more extensive use of manual training. Even when some American school districts were committed to man-

FIG. 6. Kamehameha School for Girls sewing class, late 1890s. Kamehameha Schools Photo Archives. Luryier Diamond, photo archivist.

ual training, at most, they only had one high school offering that curriculum. In 1899, Hawai'i could claim six manual training schools among the special schools: two male schools (Kamehameha School for Boys and the Hilo Boys' Boarding School) and four female schools (Kawaiaha'o, Kohala, and Mauna'olu female seminaries and the Kamehameha School for Girls). The Kamehameha Schools were the best financed and made the most extensive use of the manual training model current in the United States. All these schools were private schools. It is apparent how more advanced this curricular practice was in Hawai'i when Lahainaluna Technical High School, a public school, is added to the six private schools, and one takes into account the use of manual training among all the other public schools.

Notes

1 See Charles A. Bennett, *History of Manual and Industrial Education up to 1870* (Peoria, IL: Charles A. Bennett Co., 1926).

2 See Melvin L. Barlow, *History of Industrial Education in the United States* (Peoria, IL: Chas. A. Bennett Co., 1967); Charles A. Bennett, *The Manual Arts* (Peoria, IL: The Manual Arts P, 1917); Bennett, *History of Manual and Industrial Education;* Stuart H. Comings, *Industrial and Vocational Education: Universal and Self Sustaining, 2nd ed.* (Boston: Christopher Publishing House, 1915); Clyde W. Hall, "A Survey of Industrial Education for Negroes in the United States up to 1917," (Ph.D. diss, Bradley U, 1953); Charles H. Ham, *Manual Training: The Solution of Social and Industrial Problems* (New York, NY: Harper & Brothers, 1896); Frank J. Keller, *Principles of Vocational Education* (Boston, MA: D.C. Heath and Co., 1948); F. Theodore Struck, *Foundations of Industrial Education* (New York, NY: John Wiley and Sons, 1930); Samuel J. Vaughn and Arthur B. Mays, *Content and Methods of the Industrial Arts* (New York, NY: Century Co., 1924); Calvin M. Woodward, *Manual Training in Education* (London: Walter Scott, 1890).

3 Barlow, *History of Industrial Education* 128; Bennett, *History of Manual and Industrial Education* 106–107; Charles H. Ham, *Manual Training* 245; Vaughn and Mays, *Content and Methods* 22–23.

4 Barlow, *History of Industrial Education* 22.

5 Bennett, *History of Manual and Industrial Education* 120.

6 Barlow, *History of Industrial Education* 31–32.

7 Keller, *Principles of Vocational Education* 5–11.

8 Bennett, *History of Manual and Industrial Education* 120; Keller, *Principles of Vocational Education* 5–11; Struck, *Foundations of Industrial Education* 16.

9 Bennett, *History of Manual and Industrial Education* 120.

[10] Barlow, *History of Industrial Education* 31–32.

[11] Evelyn C. Adams, *American Indian Education* (Morningside Heights, NJ: King's Crown P, 1946) 19–23.

[12] Ronald Raymond, "Joseph Lancaster's Monitorial System of Instruction and American Indian Education, 1815–1838," *History of Education Quarterly* XXI, Winter (1981) 395.

[13] Raymond, "Joseph Lancaster's Monitorial System" 395; Joel Spring, *The Cultural Transformation of a Native American Family and Its Tribe 1763–1995* (Mahwah, NJ: Lawrence Erlbaum Associates, 1996) 28–36.

[14] Michael C. Coleman, *American Indian Children at School, 1850–1930* (Jackson, MS: U P of Mississippi, 1993) 16–17.

[15] Adams, *American Indian Education* 51.

[16] Bennett, *History* 183.

[17] Ibid.

[18] David F. Allmendinger, Jr., "The Strangeness of the American Education Society: Indigent Students and the New Charity, 1815–1840," *History of Education Quarterly* XI, no. 1 (1971) 3.

[19] Bennett, *History* 185.

[20] Barlow, *History of Industrial Education* 26–27.

[21] Hall, "A Survey of Industrial Education" 8–12.

[22] Hall, "A Survey of Industrial Education" 15.

[23] This meaning of the term missionary relates to its common use by *kama'aina* (Hawaiian Islands born). Reverend Sereno Bishop, a missionary, confirms this usage of the term missionary. He says, "that was the name for all among the whites who represented the active Protestant Evangelical Christianity planted here [Hawai'i], and by more latitude was applied to all who stood for morality and decorum against prevalent lewdness, obscene *hula* dances, drunkenness, opium and the lottery, as espoused by the Royal court and reckless whites." Sereno E. Bishop, "Are Missionaries' sons tending to America a stolen Kingdom?," *F*, 52, no. 1 (1894) 2.

[24] William D. Alexander, "The Development of Education in Hawaii," *F*, LIX (December 1902) 22–24; William D. Alexander and Alatau T. Atkinson, *An Historical Sketch of Education in the Hawaiian Islands* (Honolulu, HI: Board of Education of the Hawaiian Kingdom, 1888) 1–21; William Westervelt, "The First Twenty Years of Education in the Hawaiian Islands," (Honolulu: Annual Report of the H H S (19th), 1911) 16–26.

[25] *Annual Report and Minutes of the ABCFM, 1832* (Boston, MA: ABCFM, 1832) 77.

[26] Walter P. Frear, *A Century of Achievement* (Honolulu, HI: Hawaiian Mission Association, 1920) 12–13.

[27] Frear, *A Century of Achievement* 22–33; Westervelt, "First Twenty Years" 16–26.

[28] *Extracts from the Minutes of the General Meeting of the SIM, 1835* (Honolulu, HI: SIM, 1835) 10–11.

[29] Alexander, "Development" 24; Alexander and Atkinson, *Historical Sketch* 21; Westervelt, "First Twenty Years" 26.

[30] *Extracts, 1832* 14–16.

[31] Bernard O. Wist, "American Foundations of Public Education in Hawaii: The Socio-Economic Factors Which Were Influential in the Shaping of an American Public School System in Hawaii" (Ph.D. diss, Yale U, 1937) 32–34.

[32] George T. Lecker, "Lahainaluna" (Ph.D. diss, U of Hawaii, 1938) xii.

[33] Wist, "American Foundations" 32–34.

[34] *Missionary Album: Portraits and Bibliographical Sketches of the American Protestant Missionaries to the Hawaiian Island,* (Honolulu, HI: HMCS, 1969) 24–25; Barlow, *History of Industrial Education* 26–27.

[35] "Unpublished Letters from Members of the Sandwich Islands Mission to the American Board of Commissioners for Foreign Missions, Volume I," in *SIM, HMCS* (Honolulu, HI: 1838) 185.

[36] George Kanalu Young, a descendent of *kaukau ali'i,* reports this connection that previous studies had omitted. According to other studies, the most talented Hawaiian men were sent to the high school. Young investigated the geneology of the students to discover their class connections. See George T.K. Young, "Mo'olelo Kaukau Ali'i: The Dynamics of Chiefly Service and Identity in 'Oiwi Society" (Ph.D. diss, U of Hawai'i, Mānoa, 1995).

[37] *Annual Report and Minutes of the ABCFM, 1835* (Boston, MA: ABCFM, 1835) 27–35.

[38] *Extracts from the Minutes of the General Meeting of the SIM, 1832* (Honolulu, HI: SIM, 1832) 28.

[39] Henry P. Judd, "The Founders of Lahainaluna," *F,* CL, no. 7 (1931) 150–152.

[40] On February 14, 1834, the school's printing presses published the Kingdom's first newspaper, the *Kalama Hawai'i (The Hawaiian Luminary).* The objectives for this publication were to show scholars how information of various kinds was circulated through the medium of a periodical, to communicate to them ideas on many subjects directly and indirectly, and to give them the experience of communicating their own opinions freely on any subject they chose. The newspaper was printed only for circulation within the school, but, in fact, it was the first newspaper within the confines of the United States west of the Missouri River. Lecker, "Lahainaluna" 66–72.

[41] *Extracts from the Minutes of the General Meeting of the SIM, 1834* (Honolulu, HI: SIM, 1834) 17–19.

[42] *Annual Report and Minutes of the ABCFM, 1837* (Boston, MA: ABCFM, 1837) 7–8; *Extracts from the Minutes of the General Meeting of SIM, 1837* (Honolulu, HI: 1837) 276–277.

[43] Ephraim W. Clark, "The Origin, Progress and Importance of the Mission Seminary at Lahainaluna, Maui," *Hawaiian Spectator* I, October (1838) 337–351.

[44] *Extracts from the Minutes of the General Meeting of SIM, 1844* (Honolulu, HI: SIM, 1844) 15–16.

45 Richard Armstrong, *Report of the Minister of Public Education to the Legislature of 1846* (Honolulu, HI: Hawaiian Government, 1846) 52–53.

46 Armstrong, *Report of 1846* 52–53.

47 Andrews, "Lahainaluna Seminary" 24

48 Lecker, "Lahainaluna" 483–485.

49 *Missionary Album,* 142–143; Mildred O. Gordon, "A History of the Hilo Boarding School" (M.A. thesis, U of Hawaii, 1936) 153.

50 Gordon, "A History of the Hilo Boarding School" 18.

51 Gordon, "A History of the Hilo Boarding School" 59.

52 Gordon, "A History of the Hilo Boarding School" 24.

53 *Hilo Boarding School for Boys: Seventy Five Years of Progress* (Hilo: HHS, 1911) 8.

54 Gordon, "A History of the Hilo Boarding School" 61.

55 Francis S. Lyman, "The Hilo Boys' Boarding School," *F,* LIX (December 1902): 25.

56 Levi Lyman, "Industrial Training," *F,* LXXVII, no. 5 (1920) 115.

57 William S. Terry, "The Financial Side of Hilo Boarding School," in *Hilo Boarding School for Boys: Seventy Five Years of Progress,* ed. HHS (Hilo, HI: HHS, 1911) 21–25.

58 Lyman, "Industrial Training" 114–115.

59 *Minutes of the Meeting of the HEA for 1860* (Honolulu, HI: HEA, 1860) 5–6.

60 Talbot, *Samuel Chapman Armstrong* 42.

61 Armstrong and Ludlow, *Hampton and Its Students* 22–23, 38–39; Francis G. Peabody, *Education for Life; the Story of Hampton Institute* (Garden City, NY: Double Day, Page & Co., 1918) 89, 181–183; Talbot, *Samuel Chapman Armstrong* 34–36, 42.

62 Henry T. Cheever, *Life in the Sandwich Islands: The Heart of the Pacific as it was and is* (New York, NY: A. S. Barnes & Co., 1856) 273; Ethel M. Damon, "Father and Mother Bond," *F,* XCIII, no. 7 (1923) 164.; Ethel M. Damon, *Father Bond of Kohala* (Honolulu, HI: F) 87–88; Ethel M. Damon, "The Story of Waioli Mission," *F,* XC (1921): 254–264; Sheldon Dibble, *History of Sandwich Islands* (Honolulu, HI: T. G. Thrum, 1854) 352.

63 For a more in depth discussion of these female seminaries, see Carl Kalani Beyer, "Female Seminaries in America and Hawai'i During the 19th Century," *HJH,* 37 (2003) 91–118.

64 *Minutes of the Meeting of the HEA for 1855* (Honolulu, HI: HEA, 1855) 5.

65 "Manual Labor," *P,* XVI, no. 43 (1860): 2.

66 Samuel T. Alexander, "President's Address before the HMCS on Hawaiians and Their Educational Needs, Twelfth Annual Report (June 20, 1864)," (Honolulu, HI: 1864) 112.

67 Damon, "Father and Mother Bond" 164.

68 Charles R. Bishop, *Biennial Report of President of the Board of Education to Legislature of 1874* (Honolulu, HI: Hawaiian Government, 1874) 1–18; Samuel Kamakau, *Biennial Report of President of the Board of Education to Legislature of 1870* (Honolulu, HI: Hawaiian Government, 1870) 1–14. Although Charles Bishop

was not a member of the ABCFM, he was considered by both the missionary and anti-missionary factions as a nominal member of the missionary group.

69 Bishop, *Biennial Report of 1874* 24.

70 Charles R. Bishop, *Biennial Report of President of the Board of Education to Legislature of 1880* (Honolulu, HI: Hawaiian Government, 1880) 10.

71 Bernice E. Nichols, "The History of Public Education of the Hawaiian Islands During the Period of the Monarch" (M.A. thes, U of Southern California, 1923) 24.

72 Charles R. Bishop, *Biennial Report of President of the Board of Education to Legislature of 1882* (Honolulu, HI: Hawaiian Government, 1882) 5–8.

73 Struck, *Foundations of Industrial Education* 63–67.

74 Woodward, *Manual Training in Education* 5.

75 Vaughn and Mays, *Content and Methods of the Industrial Arts* 4.

76 Beyer, "Female Seminaries" 11–112, 114.

77 Damon, "Father and Mother Bond" 164; Damon, *Father Bond of Kohala* 87–88; Damon, "Story of Waioli" 263–264; *Reports of Kohala Boys' School, 1865–1870,* Unpublished ms., Schools-Hawaiian-Kohala, HMCS Collection; *Reports of Waioli Boys' School, 1861–1868,* Unpublished ms., Schools-Hawaiian-Waioli, HMCS Collection.

78 Armstrong, *Report of 1846* 54.

79 Gordon, "A History of the Hilo Boarding School" 58–59.

80 Gordon, "A History of the Hilo Boarding School" 58–59.

81 Gordon, "A History of the Hilo Boarding School" 59.

82 Ethel M. Damon, "Hilo Boarding School," *F,* XCIII, no. 7 (1923): 168–170; William B. Oleson, "A Notable Educator," in *Hilo Boarding School for Boys: Seventy Five Years of Progress,* ed. HHS (Hilo, HI: HHS, 1911) 13–15.

83 *Hilo Boarding School for Boys* 15.

84 Oleson, "Notable Educator" 17.

85 "Kamehameha's Memorial," PP (1895): 69–70.

86 "Kamehameha's Memorial" 69–70.

87 Uldrich Thompson, *Reminescences of Kamehameha Schools* (Honolulu, HI: Bishop Museum P, 1922) 33–34.

88 Uldrich Thompson, "Argument for Enlarged Studies," *Handicraft* IV, no. 9 (1892): 1–4; Uldrich Thompson, "On Manual Training and Apprenticeship," *Handicraft* V, no. 6 (1893): 1–4.

89 Uldrich Thompson, "Normal Department," *Handicraft* VII, no. 4 (1895): 1–4.

90 *Statement of Kauai Industrial School Board to the President of the Hawaiian Board,* Unpublished ms., Smith Papers, HMCS Collection.

91 *Report of the Kauai Industrial School,* Unpublished ms., Smith Papers, HMCS Collection.

92 Jarett Smith, *Closing Exercises of Kauai Industrial School,* Unpublished ms., Smith Papers, HMCS Collection.

93 William D. Alexander, *Report of the Minister of Public Instruction of 1898* (Honolulu, HI: Territory of Hawaii, 1900) 61–64.

94 Beyer, "Female Seminaries" 111–112, 114.

95 William R. Castle, *Biennial Report of President of the Board of Education to Legislature of 1894* (Honolulu, HI: Republic of Hawaii, 1894) 87–90.

96 William D. Alexander, *Report of the Minister of Public Instruction of 1898* (Honolulu, HI: Territory of Hawaii, 1898) 50–52.

97 Charles A. MacDonald, "The Vocational-Trade School," in *Ka Lama Hawaii: The Centennial Yearbook of the Lahainaluna Technical High School* (Lahaina, HI: Territory of Hawaii, 1931) 44.

98 Alatau T. Atkinson, *Address Delivered at the Formal Opening of the New Lahainaluna School* (Lahaina, HI: Lahainaluna P, 1905) 2–3.

JEFFREY K. LYONS

Memoirs of Henry Obookiah: A Rhetorical History

Introduction

Memoirs of Henry Obookiah by Edwin W. Dwight is the story of a young Hawaiian man from 19th century Hawai'i who lived for only 26 years, and yet whose brief existence changed the course of a nation and the people of Hawai'i (fig. 1). The first edition of the book was published in New Haven, Connecticut, in 1818. *Memoirs of Henry Obookiah* and a slightly different title, *Memoir of Henry Obookiah,* have been published numerous times. A Sunday school edition was printed in 1830, a Hawaiian language translation edition was published in 1867 by the American Tract Society, and other translations were printed in Greek and the language of the Choctaw Indians.[1] The *Memoirs* were published once again in 1968, on the 150th anniversary of the life of Henry Obookiah[2], and most recently, in 1990, by the Women's Board of Missions for the Pacific Islands. The 1990 edition includes research notes by Margaret S. Ehlke which aid in the understanding of the context of the text. There is also an updated introduction by missionary descendant and author Albertine Loomis.[3]

The significance of the text *Memoirs of Henry Obookiah* is not the fact that this tiny book—which measures approximately four inches in

Jeffrey K. Lyons was born and raised in Hawai'i. He attended Punahou School and graduated with a B.B.A. from the University of Hawai'i in 1979. In 1985, he graduated from Regent University with an M.A. in Communication and is pursuing a doctorate there in communication. Lyons has wide-ranging interests in communications and is a faculty member at Hawai'i Pacific University. He is married with three children and lives in Mililani.

The Hawaiian Journal of History, vol. 38 (2004)

width and six inches in height, with a little over 100 pages—has been published numerous times over the last 150 years and continues to be read today. Its true significance is to be found in the remarkable life of Henry Obookiah (the Hawaiian spelling is Opukaha'ia), and how his short life inspired a missionary movement, which affected not only the nation of Hawai'i but other nations as well. David Forbes, author of the *Hawaiian National Bibliography 1780–1900, Volume I 1780–1830,* writes regarding the *Memoirs:* "This book did more than any other work to interest the general public of New England in supporting a

FIG. 1. Portrait of Henry Obookiah, undated, frontispiece in *Memoir of Henry Obookiah* (American Tract Society, rev. ed., no date.) Courtesy of Eleanor C. Nordyke.

mission to the Hawaiian Islands proposed by the American Board of Commissioners for Foreign Missions."[4] (fig. 2) Historians Kuykendall and Day state in *Hawaii: A History From Polynesian Kingdom to American Statehood:* "The beginnings of the Sandwich Islands Mission movement can be traced to the story of a young Hawaiian named Opukahaia (called Obookiah in New England), who was brought to the United States by a Captain Britnall in 1809 . . .".[5] Ruth A. Tucker is a missiologist[6] who studies the worldwide Evangelical Christian movement. Regarding the life of Henry Obookiah, Tucker writes, "He

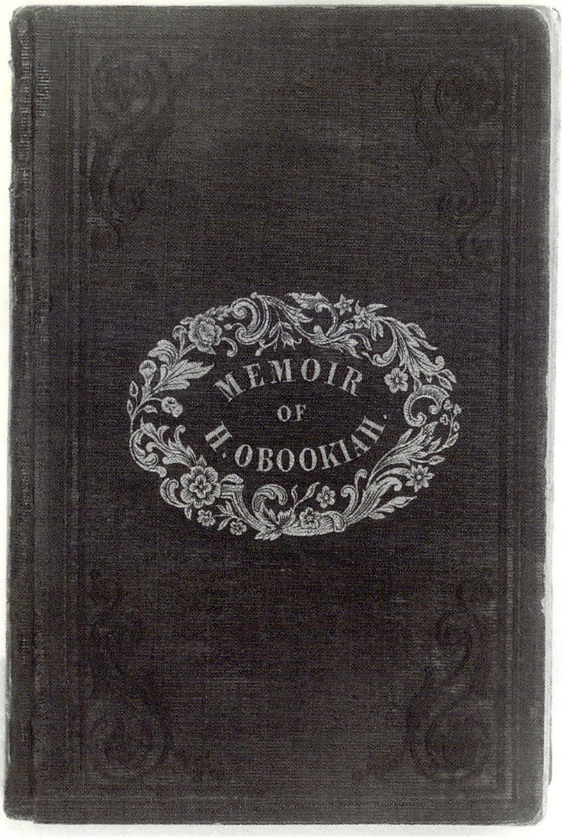

FIG. 2. Republished many times over two centuries, this little book changed history. Courtesy of Eleanor C. Nordyke.

stirred more hearts in death than he had in life, and scores of New Englanders turned their attention to bringing the gospel to Hawaii."[7]

Further, it could be argued that the effects of the Protestant missionaries who came to Hawai'i, beginning in 1820 with the first company, left a lasting impression upon the Hawaiian Islands. For they reduced the unwritten language of Hawaiian into its first orthography, printed primers, taught a nation literacy, printed the Bible and hymns in Hawaiian, established schools on every major island in the Hawaiian archipelago, educated many members of the Hawaiian monarchy, printed the first newspapers in the Hawaiian language, and encouraged scholarly publications such as David Malo's *Hawaiian Antiquities.*[8]

Rhetorical history as a methodology will be applied in this essay as a means to delve deeper into the text of *Memoirs of Henry Obookiah.* Kathleen J. Turner, the editor of *Doing Rhetorical History: Concepts and Cases,* discusses the importance of analyzing historical documents (letters, journals, memoirs, internal memos, published speeches, books, newspapers, and others) which are a reflection of the historical contexts from which they are written. By analyzing historical documents in this way, scholars are able to "contribute to historical, critical, and theoretical knowledge about both rhetoric and history."[9]

Although the original 1818 version of *Memoirs of Henry Obookiah* is extremely rare, the book was reprinted in 1990 and is readily available in public libraries in Hawai'i. It is the hope of this writer that readers of this essay who have not read the *Memoirs* will do so—and that this essay will add to their understanding and appreciation of the text.

How could such a tiny book containing the biography of a young Hawaiian who died at the age of 26, in 1818, so compel a foreign nation to send its young people thousands of miles to a distant land to be committed to missionary service? Who was the author of this book, and what motivated him to complete his task? Who were the people in New England who mentored and so generously expressed charity upon this orphan Hawaiian, thousands of miles from his homeland of Hawai'i? What was the state of Protestant Christian missions in the early 19th century in New England?

In this essay, we will first examine the birth of 19th century Protestant missions both in England and in America. Next we will examine the formation of the American Board of Commissioners for Foreign Missions (ABCFM), along with the establishment of the Foreign Mission School. The remainder of this essay will then be devoted to a rhetorical criticism of the final chapter of the *Memoirs of Henry Obookiah*. Particular attention will be given to the audience for which the book was written, the rhetoric chosen, and the intended message and claim presented by the author of the *Memoirs.*

Protestant Missions in England and America

William Carey is considered the father of modern Protestant missions. Carey was the pastor of a Baptist church in England. He was attracted to the cause of foreign missions by reading the accounts of Captain James Cook's voyages. According to Tucker, Carey "developed a biblical perspective on the subject, and he became convinced that foreign missions were the central responsibility of the church."[10] The Christian community in England was not ready for his ideas, and so in 1792 Carey published his *An Enquirey [sic] Into the Obligation of Christians to Use Means for the Conversion of the Heathens.*[11] As a result of Carey's book, which gave a compelling argument for the cause of foreign missions, the Baptist Missionary Society was formed. In 1793, Carey himself arrived in India in order to begin what became 40 years of foreign missionary service. By the year 1818, the same year that Henry Obookiah died, the Baptist mission, led by the Englishman Carey had completed 25 years of service in India. The work in India had produced some fruit: "there were some six hundred baptized converts and a few thousand more who attended classes and services."[12] In Susan Thorne's *Congregational Missions and the Making of an Imperial Culture in Nineteenth-Century England,* she discusses how the "'missionary spirit' was a defining characteristic of nineteenth-century England."[13]

The English on the other side of the Atlantic had a clear head start in the work of foreign missions. In the early 19th century, England had sent missionaries to India, Africa, Tahiti, and the South Pacific. Ironically, the English had sent no missionaries to Hawai'i—the very islands that the English explorer Captain James Cook landed on in 1778.[14] The Reverend Daggett, who preached at Obookiah's funeral in 1818, recognized the fact that the English were far ahead of the Americans in foreign missions, with the exception of the islands of Hawai'i.

> The Sandwich Islands are now the only important cluster of Islands in the great Southern ocean where the gospel has not been published, At the *Society Islands,* particularly at Otaheite and Eimeo, the triumphs of the cross have been great and glorious. . . . Proceeding westward we find Missionaries at the Friendly Isles, at New Zealand and New Holland. These include all the important Islands in the Southern Pacific, and these have been supplied with the bread of life from the liberality of Christians from England.[15]

It was not until 1812 that the first missionaries from America participated. Adoniram and Ann (Nancy) Judson departed from America, sponsored by the ABCFM, headed for India, and finally settled in Burma.[16] Obookiah himself even boarded for a brief time at the family home of Judson's wife.[17] As providence would direct, this same Judson was stricken by missionary zeal as a student at Andover Seminary, partly through his friendship with Samuel Mills.[18] This is the same Samuel Mills Jr. who was a benefactor of Henry Obookiah in whose father's house Henry Obookiah lived.[19] Samuel Mills Jr. was inspired by the writings of William Carey and led what became known as the "Haystack Prayer Meeting" in 1806. As a result of that prayer meeting, the ABCFM was founded in 1810.[20] One of the principle board members of the ABCFM was Dr. Reverend Timothy Dwight, who was president of Yale College. Henry Obookiah lived in the home of Dr. Dwight for a short time in 1809, having being introduced to him by Edwin W. Dwight, the author of *Memoirs of Henry Obookiah.* Edwin Dwight was a distant relative of Timothy Dwight.[21]

Birth of the ABCFM and the Foreign Mission School

The brief life of Henry Obookiah was attributed to his being a catalyst for the founding of the Foreign Mission School in Cornwall, Connecticut. "The interest he [Henry Obookiah] aroused led the American Board of Commissioners for Foreign Missions, of Boston, to establish a Missionary School at Cornwall, Conn., for 'the education of heathen youth'."[22] The gravestone of Henry Obookiah reads: "In Memory of HENRY OBOOKIAH a native of OWHYHEE [sic]. His arrival in this country gave rise to the Foreign mission school, of which he was a worthy member."[23] As a direct result of that school, 12 companies of missionaries were sent from New England to the far away nation of Owhyhee (modern Hawai'i), between the years of 1820 and 1848.[24]

What is clearly remarkable about the life of Henry Obookiah is that as a young Hawaiian in a foreign land he was instrumental in befriending the very agents who became the cornerstone for the modern Protestant missions movement in America. What had started on the other side of the Atlantic, through the persuasive works of William Carey and the formation of the Baptist Missionary Society in 1792, had now spread to America through a student-led movement by Samuel Mills Jr. and others, culminating in the formation of the ABCFM in 1810.[25] The ABCFM was founded the same year that Edwin W. Dwight, Samuel Mills Jr., and Dr. Timothy Dwight met Henry Obookiah.[26]

> In June, 1810, The General Association of Congregational churches met in Bradford, Massachusetts, in annual meeting. Samuel Mills (then studying at Andover Theological Seminary), with several fellow students, including Adoniram Judson, presented a petition requesting the formation of a society which could send them out as foreign missionaries.[27]

According to the Cornwall Historical Society, the Foreign Mission School was established in 1816 as a vehicle of the ABCFM. Accordingly, the purpose of the Foreign Mission School was:

> For the education of foreign youth, designing to fit them to become missionaries, school-masters, interpreters and physicians among heathen nations; and to communicate such information in agriculture and the arts as should tend to the promotion of Christianity and civilization.[28]

Obookiah, along with five other young men from Hawai'i, were part of the impetus in the establishing of the Foreign Mission School, which Obookiah was attending up until the time of his death. A tract called *A Narrative of Five Youths from the Sandwich Islands* was published in 1816, and it featured Obookiah along with five other young men from Hawai'i.[29] The purpose of the tract was to raise finances for the new Foreign Mission School, which opened in 1817. The school had as part of its purpose the training of Hawaiian youths to be sent back to Hawai'i as part of a missionary team.[30]

Henry Obookiah was clearly seen as the most promising of the five Hawaiian young men in New England among the Protestant Congregationalists. As such, Henry was taken along on "tour" with ministers in order to champion the cause for world missions, and to help raise money for the new Foreign Mission School. Obookiah's effectiveness as both a speaker and a reflection of Christian character is noted in the *Memoirs:*

> Obookiah's visit to this part of the country was of essential service to the cause of Foreign Missions. It has silenced the weak but common objection against attempting to enlighten the heathen, that they are too ignorant to be taught. This sentiment has prevented much exertion. It had a wicked origin. . . . But the appearance of Obookiah has done much in this region to wipe off this disgrace thrown upon the heathen, and to remove the objection so often made.[31]

Thus it can be seen that a Hawaiian youth by the name of Henry Obookiah had befriended and impressed the president of Yale College, along with Samuel Mills Jr. and other key agents, which helped to inspire the formation of the first American missionary society, the ABCFM. It was no surprise then that at the time of Obookiah's death, great and profound sadness had come over the Protestant congregational community, the leaders of the ABCFM, and the members of the Foreign Mission school in Cornwall, Connecticut. It was only fitting that Edwin W. Dwight, Obookiah's first teacher and also his teacher at the Foreign Mission School, would assemble a collection of letters, personal accounts, interviews, and his own recollections into a biography of the life of the young Hawaiian who arrived in New England, converted to Christianity, showed profound promise as being an evangelist to his own people, and then suddenly died of typhus fever at the age of 26.

Obookiah meets Dwight, his Biographer

Henry Obookiah was a young Hawaiian man who at the estimated age of 15 had witnessed the brutal death of his parents and chose to flee Hawai'i, the land of his birth, in search of a better life, in 1808. He befriended an American sea captain named Britnall, and secured passage to New England, departing from Kealakekua Bay on the Big Island of Hawai'i.[32] It was only 29 years prior, in 1778, that Captain Cook first arrived in the Hawaiian Islands and opened them to the outside world.[33]

Obookiah comments about his arrival in New England, "Within a few days we left our ship and went home with Captain Britnall to New-Haven, the place where he lived. There I lived with him for some time."[34] Apparently, Captain Britnall was becoming anxious to be relieved of the responsibility of caring for the youth. Henry continues:

> The captain was willing that I might take leave of this country and go home, if I wish. But this was disagreeable to my mind. I wished to continue in this country a little longer, I staid [sic] another week—saw Mr. E. W. Dwight, who first taught me to read and write. . . . the next morning I mentioned all this matter to the captain. He was pleased. And he wished me to go to school to Mr. Dwight. Thus I continued in school with him for several months.[35]

The story is told of a group of students who encountered the young Henry Obookiah on the steps of Yale College "weeping because of his ignorance."[36] One of those who met him that day was Edwin W. Dwight, who agreed to teach Obookiah how to read and write. After successfully pursuing studies with Dwight for a number of months, Obookiah expressed his desire to move out of the living quarters with Captain Britnall in order to further pursue his studies and also to work. Henry then moved in with the Dr. Dwight, the President of Yale College and a distant relative of Edwin Dwight. At this time, Edwin Dwight continued to tutor young Henry. In the year 1810, Henry moved to the home of Reverend Samuel J. Mills and continued to study and work.[37] Mills had a son, also named Samuel, who first met Obookiah and was one of the members of the famous "Haystack Prayer Meeting," which missiologists such as Ruth Tucker, and Ralph

Winter,[38] founder of the U.S. Center for World Mission, point to as being a critical point of inception in the modern missions movement, from which later sprang the ABCFM.[39]

Here we see that it was Edwin Dwight who was the first teacher of the Hawaiian youth. It was also Dwight who was instrumental in helping Henry to stay in America by introducing him to the president of Yale College.

Curiously, there is not a lot of other information published about Edwin Dwight. *The Christian spectator* [sic] published a review of *Memoirs of Henry Obookiah* in 1819. The reviewers wrote, "On the whole, we cordially recommend this little volume to the public, believing, that if it is extensively read, it will be extensively beneficial to the cause of Missions."[40] Oddly there is no discussion of Edwin W. Dwight in the review.

The first publication of the *Memoirs* included two sermons and a dedication message for the Foreign Mission School. The first sermon was preached at Obookiah's funeral on February 18, 1818, by the Yale-educated Presbyterian minister, Reverend Lyman Beecher. Beecher was a well-known minister and evangelist living in Litchfield, Connecticut, at the time of Henry's passing. Beecher later became president of Lane Theological Seminary in Cincinnati.[41] The second sermon and the dedication message were both given the same day on the occasion of the inauguration of the Foreign Mission School. The Reverend Joseph Harvey, a Congregational minister who lived in Goshen, preached a sermon, and the Reverend Herman Daggett, the first principal of the Foreign Mission School, gave a dedication address.[42] Later publications of the *Memoirs* did not include these sermons or the inauguration address.

The review in *The Christian spectator* is quite favorable. It deals, however, only with the content of the work and makes no mention of the author. As to intent of the work the reviewers wrote:

> . . . we should regret that the title page does not repeat the following assurance, contained in the proposals: 'The profits of the work will be applied to the benefit of the Foreign Mission School.' The omission, we have no doubt, was merely an oversight.[43]

In this, we can conclude that one of the purposes for writing the *Memoirs* was to help raise funds for the tiny struggling Foreign Mission

School, which was established in 1817, one year prior to the death of Obookiah, its most promising student.

Although there is little published information regarding Edwin W. Dwight, we do know that he was Obookiah's teacher at the time that Obookiah was attending the Foreign Mission School and then passed away. Prior to teaching at the Foreign Mission School in Cornwall, Connecticut, Dwight attended the Divinity School at Yale College.

> Dwight was in Litchfield, Connecticut, studying for the ministry under the Rev. Dr. Lyman Beecher when he was asked to take charge of 'Owhyhee boys at the Heathen School' in April 1817. Dwight later was a minister of a Congregational Church in Richmond, Massachusetts.[44]

Rhetorical Analysis of the Text

The text under examination is the final chapter of *Memoirs of Henry Obookiah,* (hereafter referred to as simply *Memoirs*) entitled, Chapter VII Connection With Foreign Mission School-Character-Sickness-Death. A table of contents and chapter divisions were added in the 1837 revised edition published by the American Tract Society.[45] However, the text is identical to the first printing of the *Memoirs* in 1818, with the exception of the conclusion, which was added in 1837 and is included in all subsequent publications of the *Memoirs.* The conclusion section was added to the original 1818 text. It gives a progress report of the ABCFM's missionary involvement in Hawai'i, which began in 1820 when the first company of Protestant missionaries arrived in the Hawaiian Islands. This rhetorical criticism will focus on the original 1818 text, which does not include the conclusion.

The *Memoirs* tell of the life of Henry Obookiah, how his family was killed by tribal warfare in Hawai'i, and how his life was miraculously saved. The *Memoirs* go on to describe Obookiah departing from Hawai'i at the age of 16 and arriving in New England. The major portion of the *Memoirs* traces young Obookiah's progress and chronicles the fact that he studied and boarded with a succession of Congregational ministers in New England. The effect of his studies and the living arrangements with such pious Christians had a most profound effect upon Obookiah, leading to his conversion to the Christian faith. At the opening of the final chapter of the *Memoirs,* young Obookiah is a model student at the Foreign Mission School and the hope of the mission to the Hawaiian Islands.

The final chapter of the *Memoirs* is an oxymoron. It is, in short, a tragedy of hope. Obookiah, the central character of the *Memoirs* dies just short of his goal of returning to his homeland of Hawai'i in order to share the good news of his Christian faith. Tragedy befalls the central character, but in the midst of tragedy hope springs forth through reliance upon providence—the mysterious interaction of a benevolent God in the affairs of men.

If it were not for the Calvinistic influence of Congregational doctrine, perhaps the *Memoirs* would never have been written, and the cause of the Foreign Mission School would have been lost. One of the core teachings of Calvinism was predestination, the belief that an omnipotent God has pre-established all future events and outcomes for each human being.[46] Calvinism was embraced in America, and one of its most prolific adherents was Jonathan Edwards. Edwards was a graduate of Yale in 1720, continued there in graduate studies, and was ordained as a Congregational minister in 1727. Through his powerful preaching and writings and a friendship with British minister George Whitefield, he started a revival that continued for the next 60 to 70 years in America.[47] Edwards was also a staunch adherent to Calvinistic doctrine,[48] and his influence was still felt at Yale and the Congregational churches of New England when Henry Obookiah arrived.

Upon examination of the text, one can see the influence of Calvinism and the doctrine of predestination in Obookiah's remarks, just moments before his death, "I've lost my time—I've lost my time." Again we see the influence of Calvinism upon Obookiah's faith as he delivers a final discourse to a group of Hawaiians who are by his deathbed. Obookiah proclaims to them, "I am willing to die when the voice of my Savior call me hence—I am willing, God design [sic] to take me."

The theme of a tragedy of hope, founded upon a belief that God is in control of everything and that He has predestined the length of the lives of men and women, is echoed throughout the final chapter of the *Memoirs*. Dwight writes these last words after describing the death of Obookiah: "The spirit had departed—but a smile, such as none present had ever beheld—an expression of the final triumph of his soul, remained upon his countenance."[49] In Dwight's view, Obookiah's death was not a tragedy, but an acceptance of God's providential will, ultimately culminating in *triumph.* Hope thus springs from the tragedy.

This theme of triumph through death, or tragedy of hope, was also reflected at the sermon delivered at the funeral of Henry Obookiah by the Reverend Lyman Beecher on February 18, 1818. The reader should also note Beecher's reference to providence and once again the hope that springs from reliance upon it.

> And to some it may seem, as if God were frowning upon this Institution [the Foreign Mission School], and was warning us after so much needless expense, and labor lost in the education of this youth, to cease from our vain expectation of sending the gospel to Owhyhee [sic], and give up our labor of love. But we do not thus interpret the voice of his Providence which speaks to us this day, but rather hear him saying to us, more audibly than ever, 'Go forward.'[50]

The Reverend Herman Daggett, the principal of the Foreign Mission School, echoed similar sentiments, as he also spoke regarding the life of Henry Obookiah.

> Thus has God led us, and thus has he blessed us in this undertaking. True he has taken from us the dear lamented Obookiah—but not until he had finished the work which God have him to do . . . he was to be the instrument of laying the foundation of this Seminary; of exciting a spirit of prayer and liberality in our churches in behalf of his native Island; and of convincing us what his countrymen might be and what they might enjoy, under the culture of Christian love. Having finished this work . . . God took him away, to be with Christ, which is far better.[51]

In both of these funeral passages by Beecher and Daggett, we see the Calvinistic themes of predestination, God being in control and choosing to call Obookiah back unto himself. We also see the message of hope in the midst of the tragedy, that of the laying of a foundation of the Foreign Mission School and the determined spirit to not give up the mission to Hawai'i, but instead to go forward.

The gravestone of Henry Obookiah, in Cornwall encapsulates the

Calvinistic teaching of 19th century New England, and underscores the tragedy of hope that summarizes the life of Obookiah:

> In Memory of HENRY OBOOKIAH a native of OWHYHEE [sic]. His arrival in this country gave rise to the Foreign mission school, of which he was a worthy member. He was once an Idolater, and was designed for a Pagan Priest; but by the grace of God and by the prayers and instructions of pious friends, He became a Christian. He was eminent for piety and missionary Zeal. When almost prepared to return to his native Isle to preach the Gospel, God took to himself. In the last sickness, he wept and prayed for Owhyhee, but was submissive. He died without fear with a heavenly smile on his countenance and glory in his soul. Feb. 17, 1818; aged 26.[52]

Memoirs of Henry Obookiah was published within a year of his death. The intended audience was the Christian community in New England. The Foreign Mission School which Obookiah was attending at the time of his death was dependent upon the continuing charity of Christians for financial support. According to the Cornwall Historical Society, the Foreign Mission School owned 30 acres of land and several buildings. The principal building was a schoolhouse that had been donated by the town for the school and moved to the site.[53]

Since the school was only one year old at the time of Obookiah's passing, and Obookiah himself had been the most promising student in attendance, there is little doubt that there was concern regarding the school's future viability. In a review of the *Memoirs,* published in 1819, the reviewer mentions that "the profits of the work will be applied to the benefit of the Foreign Mission School."[54] The *Memoirs* seemed to have contributed positively towards keeping the doors of the Foreign Mission School open since in 1825 donations remained abundant. In June of that year, cash donations were received from Connecticut, Massachusetts, and New York, along with articles of food and clothing sent to the students.[55]

In 1820, the first missionary company departed from New England to begin its work in the Hawaiian Islands. Nine members of that first company were students from the Foreign Mission School.[56] In 1819, the following was written regarding the *Memoirs,* "On the whole, we cordially recommend this little volume to the public, believing, that if it is extensively read, it will be extensively beneficial to the cause of Missions."[57] Thus we see that the intended audience of the *Memoirs* was the Christian community of New England, and that part of the book's purpose was to stir the hearts of New Englanders towards the cause of missions in order that they would give both financially and materially to the Foreign Mission School.

The final chapter of the *Memoirs* is divided into three sections. The first section establishes Henry Obookiah as the most promising student at the Foreign Mission School and a model of both scholarship and Christian character. The second section is short and is comprised of two letters written by Obookiah himself. The third section is an account of the sickness and death of Obookiah. The first and the last sections of the chapter are about eight pages in length, while the second section is much shorter, consisting of only two letters. What follows is a detailed description of these three sections along with the underlying theme of tragedy of hope.

In section one, Dwight describes Obookiah's character and Christian devotion, and as being "a little less than six feet in height."[58] The original 1818 edition contains a stunning engraving of Henry Obookiah, which appears in other editions and is featured on the cover of the 1990 edition. He is dressed in the attire of New England featuring a dress shirt and a double breasted jacket. The engraving depicts Obookiah as dignified, with a bright and yet determined countenance. The engraving placed at the beginning of the *Memoirs* is significant in that it depicts in visual form the effects of Christianity upon a youth from a foreign land. It is likely that the engraving was designed to quell New England prejudice against people of color.[59]

The first section goes on to describe Obookiah's many virtues including his "amiable and affectionate" disposition and his love for his friends. Dwight refers to Obookiah's journal and mentions his "expressions of affection and gratitude to those who had been his benefactors."[60] The reader is shown a young man with a love of life and an appreciation for friendships, as well as acts of kindness bestowed upon him.

Dwight then gives considerable attention to the state of Obookiah's mind and particularly to the success of his studies. This is important because past prejudice had led New Englanders to believe that the heathen were incapable of being raised to a higher state of education. Just prior to the final chapter in the *Memoirs,* Dwight addresses past prejudice against people of color. Obookiah seemed to have a most profound effect upon combating such prejudices. What follows is Dwight's description of Obookiah's tour of various Congregational churches for the cause of missions—just prior to his death.

> Obookiah's visit to this part of the country was of essential service to the cause of Foreign Missions. It has silenced the weak but common objection against attempting to enlighten the heathen, that they are too ignorant to be taught . . . and because, under these circumstances, people of color are devoid of knowledge, we have hastened to the irrational conclusion that all the heathen are a race of idiots . . . But the appearance of Obookiah has done much in this region to wipe off this disgrace thrown upon the heathen, and to remove the objection so often made.[61]

Aware of the deep underlying prejudices that existed in New England society as a whole against people of color, Dwight in the final chapter of the *Memoirs* gave a great deal of attention to the scholarly successes of Obookiah. Dwight sums up Obookiah's intellect in stating: "His mind was not of a common cast. It was such that, with proper culture, it might have become a mind of the first order."[62] Dwight backs up this claim by citing the fact that Obookiah, after learning English, began to reduce the unwritten Hawaiian language to a written form. Obookiah was said to have "made considerable progress towards completing a Grammar, A Dictionary, and a Spelling-book [in Hawaiian]."[63] Obookiah's grammar exists today, although the translation of Genesis has not been found.[64] According to Dwight, who was his teacher at the Foreign Mission School, Obookiah was also studying Hebrew and Latin. Dwight noted that Obookiah found a great deal of similarity between Hebrew and Hawaiian and that he found it easier to translate the Bible from Hebrew (instead of English) into Hawaiian.

The later part of section one deals with Obookiah's Christian faith. Dwight states, "Obookiah was a decided and consistent *Christian.*" After making his statement, Dwight backs up his claim by offering "additional proof of his [Obookiah's] piety."[65] Dwight then cites

Obookiah's habit of attending a weekly religious meeting on Saturday evening, along with other students. Dwight quotes from a letter written by the Reverend Perkins which describes Obookiah's habit of fervent daily prayer. Other instances of Christian devotion include requesting a time of prayer with a minister prior to speaking at a church, and Obookiah's persistence to share the good news of Christ "with persons whom he supposed to be destitute of grace."[66]

To summarize the two parts of the first section of the final chapter of the *Memoirs,* Dwight discusses Obookiah's character and Christian devotion. In discussing both of these topics, Dwight begins by making a claim and then backs it up with facts that warrant his conclusion to be true. Dwight cites as evidence not only his own recollections of Obookiah, but Obookiah's diary, accounts from others, letters from ministers, and public meetings which Obookiah attended. Dwight the teacher was no doubt trained in the art of rhetoric and persuasive discourse. His text displays compelling evidence that Obookiah was both an outstanding student and that his character reflected evidence of the transforming nature of the gospel.

The second section of the final chapter of the *Memoirs* is only half as long as the first. It consists of two letters written by Obookiah, selected by Dwight to demonstrate a unique insight into this remarkable Hawaiian youth. The letters were both written to New Englanders of prominence, as each has the title of Esq. following their names.

Both of the letters are responses to letters which Obookiah had received. They represent an ongoing correspondence and a deep gratitude of friendship and support. Obookiah's command of the English language is quite advanced, and it is difficult to detect that English is his second language. Both letters also quote scriptures and are a reflection of Obookiah's strong commitment to the Christian faith. The majority of the content of each letter regards spiritual matters. To Mr. S.W. Esq. Obookiah concludes his letter with these encouraging words, "Let us not neglect the duty which we owe to God to love him with our hearts, souls, and strength—and let us *pray without ceasing* [original emphasis]."[67] To Mr. A.S. Esq. Obookiah replies, and he rejoices in hearing news from his friend that additional converts have come to Christ in Amherst. Obookiah's zeal for sharing the gospel is evident as he writes, "We cannot expect to see a single soul coming out of the kingdom of Satan into the kingdom of Christ, unless we see one or more faithful and humble Christians running forward in spirit without any doubt. . . ." Obookiah concludes the letter by giving a brief progress report of the Foreign Mission School and mentioning that one of its members recently converted to Christ.

In the third and final section, Dwight dedicates the remainder of the chapter to Obookiah's sickness and death. Dwight sets the stage of the closing scene of the tragedy as he writes, "About the commencement of the year 1818, Obookiah became seriously indisposed, and was obliged wholly to abandon his studies."[68] The pacing of this final section of the *Memoirs* is rapid, as Dwight quotes numerous eyewitness accounts of Obookiah's encounters with friends as he spoke to them from his deathbed. There are also many quotes from Obookiah himself, and his last words that he spoke, both in English and in Hawaiian, which is translated for the benefit of the reader. The last few pages of the *Memoirs* are especially compelling reading as the reader has become acquainted with many promising aspects of this Hawaiian youth and is now faced with the harsh reality that Obookiah's sickness will soon lead to death. In section three, Obookiah's story is written more in the style of a novel than a biography—since almost half of the text is in first person narrative. Dwight, in his ample use of quotes and dialogue, draws the reader into the scene of the bedroom where Obookiah lies dying of typhus fever. The tragedy of a life so young, so promising, and now departing must have been enthralling reading for the New England public of the early 19th century.

Obookiah's words and response to his impending death are a beacon of hope in the midst of tragedy. He calls his countrymen to his side and he speaks to them in Hawaiian. One of the Hawaiian youth later translated the speech back into English for inclusion in the *Memoirs.* To his countrymen, Obookiah spoke on his deathbed:

> My dear countrymen, I wish to say something to you all—you have been very kind to me . . . above all things make your peace with God—you must make Christ your friend—you are in a strange land— . . . but God will be your friend if you put your trust in him—he has raised up friends here for you and for me. . . . I am willing to die when the voice of my Savior call me hence—I am willing, if God design to take me.[69]

Dwight describes the circumstances of Obookiah's last address to his countrymen in this way, "the address being continued until his strength was entirely exhausted—rendered the scene literally overwhelming—loud sobbing was heard throughout the room; and from persons little accustomed to weep."

What is further striking about the final words of Obookiah is what he did not say. There is not recorded a single word of anger or of doubting the will of God in his life. Obookiah never questions God's will nor pities his dire circumstance. In the midst of the tragedy, Obookiah continues to display his love for his countrymen, his friends and benefactors, and his deep commitment to Christ. Moments before his passing Obookiah spoke the Hawaiian words *Aloha o'e,* the phrase that was later made famous in the song written by Queen Lili'uokalani of Hawai'i. The phrase was translated in the *Memoirs* as "my love be with you."[70]

The closing words of the *Memoirs* reflect the tragedy of hope that underscores the life of Henry Obookiah. Dwight recounts:

> No alarm was given, until one of his countrymen, who was standing by his bed-side, exclaimed, *"Obookiah's gone."* All sprang to the bed. The spirit had departed—but a smile, such as none present had ever beheld—an expression of the final triumph of his soul, remained upon his countenance.[71]

Thus Dwight concludes the telling of the story of the life of Henry Obookiah, the orphan from Hawai'i, who died among friends in a foreign land. Dwight leaves us with the impression of hope as he refers to the "final triumph of his soul." Indeed for the Protestant Congregationalists of New England, death was not a defeat for the Christian; death was a promotion to a new heavenly home.

It is not inconceivable that many readers of the *Memoirs* have been moved to tears. The first two sections of the final chapter give evidence as to Obookiah's character and Christian piety. These sections use a more formal claim, evidence, and warrant format, laying out the facts in a logical and orderly manner. The final section plays like a scene in a movie or a tragic play. It is emotional in its approach, and yet it is sensitive and respectful of its subject matter. Dwight shows that he is both skillful in presenting the reader with the facts and also in writing a captivating, and heart-felt narrative. The result is a work which has a broad appeal to both the cognitive and the affective reader. Dwight, the teacher, has done justice to the life of Henry Obookiah and to the cause of the Foreign Mission School. The school was only in operation for nine short years,[72] and yet the effect of the school changed the destination of the nation of Hawai'i and began an American Protestant missionary movement, encouraging the formation of multiple mission agencies, many of which continue to this day.[73]

Albertine Loomis, the descendant of Elisha Loomis who was a member of the first missionary company to the Hawaiian Islands, sums up *Memoirs of Henry Obookiah* in the introduction to the 1990 edition:

> A few months after his [Henry Obookiah] death a book appeared in New England—a thin, brown-covered volume of a hundred small pages. It told in his own words and the words of those who had known him, the story of the boy's life and death . . . because they felt his vibrant presence in the *Memoirs,* men and women who never knew Opukaha'ia [Obookiah] in the flesh volunteered to carry his message after his death . . . among the church people of its day the book was a best seller. Men read it and sent generous gifts to the American Board to help finance a mission to the Sandwich Islands [modern Hawai'i]. Women read it and let it be known that they would go gladly to the Pacific if only young missionaries who needed 'companions' would look their way. . . . Slender and simple as it was, this book shaped the future of Hawai'i.[74]

Memoirs of Henry Obookiah is a truly significant work in relation to both the history of the nation of Hawai'i, which later was annexed by the United States, and the profound impact that it had upon American evangelical Protestant missions. It is rare that an individual such as Henry Obookiah would be a vessel chosen to affect two nations so profoundly. One might ask, would the effect have been the same if Dwight had not taken it upon himself to write Obookiah's *Memoirs?* Doubtless someone else would have written the story, but who else would have been so intimately acquainted with Obookiah as Dwight? Perhaps Samuel Mills Jr. could have undertaken the task, yet he had departed for missionary service in Africa three years prior to Obookiah's passing.[75] Just as Obookiah was chosen to be that grain of wheat which fell to the ground to die and bear fruit, Dwight, the teacher, seemed destined to be Dwight, the biographer, and because of his obedience the course of history changed.

Notes

1 Edwin W. Dwight, *Memoirs of Henry Obookiah* (Honolulu: Woman's Board of Missions for the Pacific Islands, 1990) 96.

2 Eric Cavaliero, "Young Hawaiian's Mission Life Noted," *HA,* Oct. 28 1967:A18.

3 Dwight, 1990 ed., xiii.

4 David Forbes, *Hawaiian National Bibliography 1780–1900 Volume I 1780–1830* (Honolulu: U of Hawai'i P, 1999) 332.

5 Ralph S. Kuykendall and A. Grove Day, *Hawaii: A History From Polynesian Kingdom to American State.* Revised Edition. (Englewood Cliffs, N.J: Prentice-Hall, 1976) 43.

6 Dr. Ruth A. Tucker is associate professor of missiology at Calvin Theological Seminary. The term *missiologist* refers to the science of *missiology,* the study of the worldwide evangelical Christian movement. Master degrees and doctorates are offered in missiology at institutions such as Fuller Theological Seminary and Asbury Theological Seminary.

7 Ruth A. Tucker, *From Jerusalem to Irian Jaya* (Grand Rapids: Zondervan Publishing House, 1983) 203.

8 David Malo, *Hawaiian Antiquities* (Honolulu: BPBM, 1980).

9 Kathleen J. Turner, *Doing Rhetorical History: Concepts and Cases* (Tuscaloosa: U of Alabama P, 1998) 8.

10 Tucker 114–115.

11 Ralph D. Winter and Steven C. Hawthorne, *Perspectives On The World Christian Movement—A Reader.* Revised ed. (Pasadena: William Carey Library, 1992) B-94.

12 Tucker 118.

13 Alison Twells, "Congregational Missions and the Making of an Imperial Culture in Nineteenth-Century England (Book)" *Church History* 71.4 (2002): 905.

14 Kuykendall and Day 14.

15 Dwight, Edwin W. *Memoirs of Henry Obookiah* (New Haven: Office of the Religious Intelligencer, 1818) 27.

16 Tucker 122.

17 Dwight, 1990 ed. 102.

18 Tucker 122.

19 Dwight, 1990 ed. 101.

20 Winter and Hawthorne B-65.

21 Dwight, 1990 ed. 101.

22 Oscar E. Maurer, *How the Gospel Came to Hawaii* (Honolulu: Central Union Church, nd) 8.

[23] Dwight, 1990 ed. ix.

[24] *Missionary Album Sesquicentennial Edition 1820–1970* (Honolulu: HMCS, 1969) 7–12.

[25] Winter and Hawthorne B-82.

[26] Dwight, 1990 ed. 17.

[27] Winter and Hawthorne B-82–83.

[28] Paul H. Chamberlain Jr., *Foreign Mission School* (Cornwall, CT: Cornwall Historical Society, Inc., 1968) 4.

[29] Dwight, 1990 ed. 99.

[30] Chamberlain Jr. 5.

[31] Dwight, 1990 ed. 71.

[32] Dwight, 1990 ed. 13.

[33] Kuykendall and Day 14.

[34] Dwight, 1990 ed. 12.

[35] Dwight, 1990 ed. 13.

[36] Kuykendall and Day 43.

[37] Dwight, 1990 ed. 17.

[38] Winter and Hawthorne, B-34.

[39] Tucker 122.

[40] *The Christian spectator (sic), Conducted by an Association of Gentlemen for the year 1819 Volume I* (New Haven: Howe & Spalding, 1819) 43.

[41] Sandra Roff. "An American Family: The Beecher Tradition" William and Anita Newman Library. Baruch College, New York, NY. 19 Mar. 2004 <http://newman.baruch.cuny.edu/digital/2001/beecher/lyman.htm>

[42] Dwight, 1990 ed. 96.

[43] *The Christian spectator* 43.

[44] Dwight, 1990 ed. 98.

[45] The 1837 edition of the *Memoirs,* published by the American Tract Society, is not dated. This author owns a copy. The 1837 publication date was established by obtaining a copy of the: *Twelfth Annual Report of the American Tract Society: Presented at New York, May 1837.* (New York: American Tract Society, 1837) 14.

[46] Louis B. Weeks, "John Calvin." III D, *Microsoft Encarta Reference Library 2002.* CD-ROM. Redmond: Microsoft (2001).

[47] "Jonathan Edwards," *Microsoft Encarta Reference Library 2002.* CD-ROM. Redmond: Microsoft (2001).

[48] John P Fitzgibbons, "A Towering Clergyman" *America* 189:14 (2003) 25–27.

[49] Dwight, 1990 ed. 91, 89, 92.

[50] Dwight, 1818 ed. 29.

[51] Dwight, 1818 ed. 14–15.

[52] Dwight, 1990 ed. ix.

[53] Chamberlain Jr. 6.

[54] *The Christian spectator* 43.

[55] Chamberlain Jr. 6.

[56] Dwight, 1990 ed. 98.

[57] *The Christian spectator* 43.
[58] Dwight, 1990 ed. 76.
[59] Chamberlain Jr. 8.
[60] Dwight, 1990 ed. 76.
[61] Dwight, 1990 ed. 71.
[62] Dwight, 1990 ed. 76.
[63] Dwight, 1990 ed. 78.
[64] Dwight, 1990 ed. 104.
[65] Dwight, 1990 ed. 79, 80.
[66] Dwight, 1990 ed. 79.
[67] Dwight, 1990 ed. 83.
[68] Dwight, 1990 ed. 84.
[69] Dwight, 1990 ed. 89.
[70] Dwight, 1990 ed. 89–90.
[71] Dwight 1990 ed. 92.
[72] Chamberlain Jr. 20.
[73] Tucker 186–187.
[74] Dwight, 1990 ed. xiii–xv.
[75] Otto G. Reuman, *The Influence of One Man—Henry Obookiah.* (Cornwall: The First Church of Christ in Cornwall, nd) Not paginated. "At Goshen."

BARBARA E. DUNN

William Little Lee and Catherine Lee, Letters from Hawai'i 1848–1855

"HONOLULU, HAWAIIAN ISLANDS, October 1st, 1848. My dear 'Kitty Scott.' Not long since my clerk brought me a newspaper, which upon opening I found to bear the inscription, 'with the respects of Miss Caroline Scott.' Dropping my head in an inquiring mood, I whispered to myself 'Caroline Scott? who is Caroline Scott?' When of a sudden up sprung from the floor beneath me, the dear little witch of my boyhood 'Kitty Scott,' and seating herself on my table sat smiling upon me in all the sweetness of her early youth."

Thus begins a seven-year correspondence between William Little Lee in Honolulu and his boyhood friend, Caroline "Kitty" Scott of Buffalo, New York. After Lee's marriage to Catherine Newton in 1849, she also wrote to Kitty. There are 11 letters in this collection. William wrote five of the letters and Catherine wrote six. The Lees covered such topics as the California Gold Rush, the French Admiral de Tromelin threatening the Hawaiian government and ransacking Honolulu, the smallpox epidemic of 1853, Līhu'e Sugar Plantation on Kaua'i, Lee's work on the Land Commission, and descriptions of Washington Place where the Lees boarded. One letter contains William Lee's account of the harrowing voyage on the *Henry* from Boston to Hawai'i in 1846 with Charles Reed Bishop. [fig. 1]

Barbara E. Dunn is the administrative director and librarian for the Hawaiian Historical Society.

The Hawaiian Journal of History, vol. 38 (2004)

William Little Lee did not plan to go to Hawai'i, let alone spend his life there. Born in Sandy Hill, New York, in 1821, and trained as a lawyer at Harvard Law School, he began to suffer from tuberculosis at age 25 and sought to find a better climate for his health. In February 1846, he sailed for the Oregon Territory with his friend and fellow adventurer, Charles R. Bishop. After a long and stormy voyage, their ship, the *Henry,* arrived in Honolulu harbor October 12, 1846, needing extensive repairs. Soon after arriving, Lee caught the attention of officials in the Hawaiian kingdom and was recruited by Attorney General John Ricord and Dr. Gerrit Judd, the minister of finance for Kamehameha III. Lee, then 26 years old, was only the second trained attorney in the Islands (after Ricord). The kingdom urgently needed legal assistance, and the king and government officials urged Lee to stay. He accepted and was appointed a judge in the newly organized

FIG. 1 William L. Lee *(left)* with Charles R. Bishop, Newburyport, Mass., 1846, before embarking for Hawai'i. Daguerreotype, Bishop Museum.

court system by Governor Mataio Kekūanaō'a. Lee, in turn, convinced his traveling companion Bishop to remain in Hawai'i as well.

Bishop stayed for 50 years. He married a Hawaiian royal princess, Bernice Pauahi, became a well-known financier and philanthropist, and founded the Bishop Museum.

In 1847, William Little Lee was elected Chief Justice of the Hawai'i Supreme Court, appointed to the privy council, and appointed president of the Board of Commissioners to Quiet Land Titles (the Land Commission), a volunteer post. In 1851, he was elected to the Legislature and became Speaker of the House of Representatives.

The legislature assigned Lee the task of drafting criminal and civil codes for the kingdom. Lee wrote many important laws that governed society throughout the monarchy period including the Masters and Servants Act of 1850. This law provided the basis of contract labor for both Hawaiians and immigrant workers on the sugar plantations. The legislature also asked Lee to draft a new constitution which was adopted in 1852. Lee essentially set up an American legal system for the Hawaiian kingdom. Kamehameha V annulled Lee's 1852 constitution in 1864 for being too liberal for a monarchical government.

Lee became physically ill while assisting in the care of the sick during the 1853 smallpox epidemic, and the tuberculosis reasserted itself. His health was never restored. He and his wife returned to the United States in 1855 to seek medical advice. But Hawai'i drew him back where he died May 28, 1857.

Catherine Newton Lee (ca. 1819–1894), from Albany, New York, was courted by William Lee before he left New York. Accepting a proposal from Lee by mail, Catherine sailed around the Horn with missionaries Dr. Charles H. and Lucy Wetmore and married Lee on board the *Leland* in Honolulu harbor on Sunday, March 11, 1849. She and her husband boarded for several years at Washington Place with Mrs. Mary Dominis, widow of Capt. John Dominis, who was lost at sea on the brig *Wm. Neilson* in 1846. Catherine N. "Kate" Lee was active in Honolulu social circles. She was known to be a clever, literary woman with interests in the women's issues of the day and noted for her advanced thinking.

After Lee's death, she returned to New York. On November 4, 1861, in Saratoga, New York, she married professor Edward L. Youmans, editor of *Popular Science Monthly*. Lee had left her considerable property, including an interest in Līhu'e Plantation on Kaua'i, and she used her wealth to support the magazine and establish her home as a favorite meeting place of literary people. She also continued Lee's work in actively promoting the sugar reciprocity treaty through influential friends in New York and Washington, D.C. She died August 29, 1894, seven years after her second husband. The obituary notice in the *Hawaiian Gazette,* September 21, 1894, says, "She was regarded by her friends as an example of a woman who knew how to reach and control public men without destroying their peace of mind."

Because William Little Lee is writing to a family friend, the letters give us some insight into his character and personality. He even offers a description of himself in his first letter to "Miss Kitty." He lived with the Scott family at Sandy Hill, New York, when he was 11 or 12 years old and befriended Kitty, one of the daughters. They apparently lost touch and became reconnected by happenstance after Lee arrived in Honolulu. Catherine Lee also writes to Miss Kitty giving her own insights on life and activities in Hawai'i and her husband's work. Several of the letters are written together on the same sheets of paper as "joint letters." In two letters, November 23, 1850, and April 16, 1854, Catherine employs crossways writing: that is, writing over her husband's words at a right angle. She refers to it in the April 16, 1854 letter, saying, "Crossing letters I abominate and hoping you will excuse me if I have made either William's or my own writing illegible." This crossways writing, today called "crossed" letters, was not uncommon prior to the introduction of postage stamps in the mid-19th century. It was done to save on postage. Two sheets of paper cost double the postage of a single sheet of any size. The letters end with Catherine Lee writing a short note to Miss Kitty in 1855 while she and William are visiting friends in New York and Boston. [fig. 2]

Mark Blackburn of Kamuela, Hawai'i, a private collector of Polynesian art and artifacts, brought these letters to the attention of the Hawaiian Historical Society. Mr. Blackburn purchased the letters from a rare book dealer in upstate New York who knew of his interest in Hawaiian history. He has kindly allowed the Society to publish these letters in this issue of *The Hawaiian Journal of History.*

William Little Lee to Caroline Scott of Buffalo, N.Y., from Honolulu, October 1, 1848

Honolulu
Hawaiian Islands
October 1st 1848

My dear "Kitty Scott,"

Not long since my clerk brought me a newspaper, which upon opening, I found to bear the inscription, "with the respects of Miss Caroline Scott." Dropping my head in an inquiring mood, I whispered to myself "Caroline Scott? who *is* Caroline Scott?" When of a sudden up sprung

FIG. 2 Crossways writing by Catherine Lee, written across her husband's words to save on postage costs. Courtesy Mark Blackburn.

from the floor beneath me, the dear little witch of my boyhood, "Kitty Scott," and seating herself on my table sat smiling upon me in all the sweetness of her early youth. Oh, you little wizard you, I see you this very moment—yes, just as I did fifteen long years ago, and I cannot, for the life of me, realize that you are grown up to be any thing else than the same little girl that once filled so much of my youthful brain. Kitty, (pardon my familiarity) the thought of you makes me feel like a little boy again, and as I travel back to the days when we played together in all the innocence of little children, a deep feeling comes over me that makes me wish I had the *real* Kitty Scott by my side, rather than her shadow. How much I *would* give, could I only seat you in the empty chair beside me, and talk over the funny times and little freaks that we have had together, in and around your old homestead at Sandy Hill. The picture of my life, when a little boy, 11 or 12 years of age I lived in your father's family, stands out from the canvass of youth in bold colors, and often do the figures therein portrayed step forth and speak to me of the pleasures that clustered so thickly around the path of my boyhood. There, in the back room, sits "Grandpa Scott," all swallowed up in the last whig newspaper, while the old clock ticks loud in the corner, and the mug of cider sits mulling and simmering away on the stove in perfect harmony with the old man's thoughts and tastes. This scene reminds me of how much pleasure I took in drawing his cider, cutting his tobacco, listening to his stories, and in doing a thousand little things for him, which he always repaid with kindness. "Netty" [Antoinette, Kitty's sister] and myself were his pets, and he would allow *me* to tease him in many ways, when for the same liberties he would knock another boy heels over head. But the old man has gone the way of all the living, and I trust rests in the Lord. He was eccentric but kind, irritable but warm hearted, and I loved him. He has gone, and may the earth lie light upon his grave.

The scene changes, and I go to the kitchen. Ugh! how cold I am as I feel the keen wind of the cold winter mornings, when a little boy I used to jump out of bed before daylight and run from Grandpa's room to the kitchen and build a fire. Soon, however, the stove was red hot, the tea kettle began to sing, and then I went to the foot of the chamber stairs and cried out at the top of my voice, "Antoinette! Antoinette!" "Yes"—was the answer, and in another breath down came the dear good girl who had jumped from the bed into her dress with one bound, and with another stood before me with the back of her dress all open ready to be hooked up. I loved that good girl with all the fondness of a little boy, and I love her *now,* for my memory is crowded with a multitude of kindnesses that she has bestowed upon me. God bless her! I say, from the bottom of my heart, God bless her!

Soon after "Netty" came down, the door of Mother's bedroom invariably opened, and out slipped a little girl, who sitting down on the floor before the stove, pulled the bottom of her long white night gown close around her feet, and looking into the stove hearth, sat purring away like a little kitten. That little girl was Kitty Scott, now "Miss Caroline Scott of Buffalo." And well do I remember, that same Kitty Scott in those days used to have a severe pain in the instep of one foot, and how often of a cold morning have I seated myself on the floor beside her and bathed that little white foot with Opodeldoc [camphorated soap liniment]. Don't kick Kitty, I pray you don't, at this pedal allusion of mine, but tell me all about that little foot,—the paths it has been treading for so many years—the obstacles it has surmounted—the burning sands it has crossed in the journey of life,—the thorns it has trod upon,—the cool streams it has laved in,—the flower banks it has pressed,—the nets and pits it has avoided, and whither its steps now tend. Oh my dear girl, may God keep that little foot and its twin companion from the ways of sorrow, and lead you onward and upward through life and death to the gates of Heaven.

Kitty, I have often tried to picture you as "Miss Caroline Scott," and see you just as you are at the present day, but that little girl in the long night gown disturbs my vision, and I can form no conception of the sweet lass of twenty one. I think, however, that you must look much as Netty did, but perchance my reckoning is all wrong, and I beg you to give me a picture of yourself drawn by your own fair hand. How tall—how broad, how weighty are you. What the color of your hair, your eyes, your cheeks etc. etc.? The *"Tout Ensemble"* I ken is lovely, but I would know what goes to make up this loveliness. From those who have seen you, I learn that you are a small, clever, bright and sparkling little girl; sprightly in your conversation, dancing "from grave to gay from lively to severe" with an incredible facility. But as every intelligent girl can judge of her own powers and sketch the prominent features of her own person and character better than any other, I repeat my request for a picture from your own hand.

But you may answer, that it is rulable for *me* to send my picture before I ask *yours,* and hence, not to give you any excuse, you shall have it, drawn for the first time.

I stand 5 feet 9 3/4 inches in shoes—am rather a lean Cassius looking fellow, ranging in weight from 135 to 150 pounds—with a large bony face, brown hair, broad forehead, hazel eyes, roman nose (rather long and sharp)—good sized mouth (with clean teeth), long chin, hollow cheeks, sallow complexion, no whiskers, and altogether having a look that says I am 35 years of age, while in truth I am but 27. Generally, I feel rather younger than I am, but now and then I have an old mummy-like feeling come over me that whispers of an antiquity far beyond three score years and ten. I am frank and cheerful—rather impulsive in my feelings and actions. Never "Blue," and yet never exactly contented—loving the practical rather than the theoretical things of this world—possessing none of the marvelous, and strongly prone to be incredulous and obstinate. Hope, cautiousness, firmness, and combattiveness are prominent features in my character, while no bump rises higher than self esteem, though the craniologists flatly deny me. I am a warm friend, and perhaps what Dr. Johnson would call a "good hater"—very fond of the society of old acquaintances, disliking to make new ones, and at times rather taciturn. Active and energetic, I possess more of the will than the power, and am inclined to skim over the surface of things rather than dive into their hidden depths. I am fond of books, flowers, children, horses and a good dinner, and in fine, have a great many likes and dislikes—many faults and few virtues. There, now, I have given you an honest picture without meaning to fish for compliments on the one hand, or be egotistical on the other. In a word, I am of the *earth, earthy,* but, Kitty, allow your humble servant to say, that great and numerous as his faults truly are, he does not live without the hope of reformation. In other words he expects soon to be married to a young lady who will rub down, soften and polish, if not wholly obliterate many of the rough ugly points that disfigure his character. This lady is Miss C. E. Newton of Albany, with whom I hope you are acquainted.

Heartily ashamed, and begging your pardon for saying so much of myself, I shall hold you responsible for a faithful picture of *yourself,* and will now turn from the above chapter of vanity to more pleasant subjects.

What of your father? Tell me all about him. What of his habits, looks and person? How old is he—is he as erect as ever—is he lean or corpulent etc. etc.? I will remember that 15 years since he was the very soul of fun and good society, a short, straight, white haired and active man, possessed of a large fund of anecdote, humor and practical knowledge. The last time I saw him was one cold winter evening in Charles Dewey's store, sitting between the stove and counter, telling stories, and eating keg raisins, which I remember he said, to my great astonishment, were better than box raisins. Present my best compliments to your father and tell him I remember him with much gratitude as the kind teacher who made clear to my young mind many a hard problem in Algebra and Geometry. Why will he not write to me and give me some good lessons for my riper years?

And where is your dear Mother? Is she among the living or dead? She was so much confined to her room by sickness when I lived with you that I knew but little of her, and only remember that she *was* from the fact that whenever I slammed a door or thundered through the house with my heavy cowhide boots, Netty would call after me, saying "Willy you will disturb Mother." I think I have heard of her death, but it may be all a dream.

Where and how is Antoinette? I heard some years ago that she was married, but to whom or where she resided I have forgotten. Wherever she may be, I ask no greater blessing for her, than that she receive what she *merits*. More than any other member of your family has my heart turned towards her with a fondness akin to that of a brother for a darling sister.

And last though not least, what of Harriet? I know that she is Mrs. Haven of Buffalo, and I have heard all manner of complimentary things of her and her worthy husband. I hear that she is a fine noble woman, a devoted wife and fond mother; and that with a husband in every way deserving of her, leads a very happy life. This certainly is very gratifying news, but it is too *general*, and I ask that you will give me something more detailed. For instance tell me the number of her children, their ages, names, looks etc. etc. Remember me affectionately to Madam Haven and to her good husband though I have not the pleasure of his acquaintance.

This part of the world is much disturbed at present with the great Gold Excitement of California. It exceeds anything you can conceive of. I have several friends who have accumulated large fortunes there within the last few months. Six men, says a private letter from a person of good authority, have gathered $12,000 within the last six weeks.

Another subject of great interest with us is the Trans Pacific Steam Navigation from California or Oregon to China via Honolulu. By the steamers via Panama we shall get letters from the U.S. in 50 days, but we wish to have them in 30. We have a very pleasant and intelligent society of Americans, French & English in our good little city and nothing makes such a feast among us as the arrival of a large mail. I know of no part of the world where letters have such a value as here. No matter what the age or contents of letters be, all are devoured with a gusto.

Among the 600 foreigners that dwell in Honolulu, we have a good deal of heart and intellect, but politics, the conflicting interests of trade and other minor matters have split up the society in every direction. However, we have most of the comforts and luxuries of the world, and take a vast deal of enjoyment in this charming climate. I have conversed with many who have enjoyed the far favored climate of Italy, and they tell me that it will not compare with that of Hawaii. Don't, I beg you don't think we are living in a land of savages and darkness. No, no, the fair blossoms of an enlightened Christian civilization are fast opening in our midst, and you and I, I trust will live to see and taste their fruits. Perhaps it may not be possible to save the Hawaiian race from melting away, before the iron march of the sturdy Saxon, but one thing is certain, no people or power can ever extinguish the pure fire here kindled by the humble Missionary of New England, and these islands will ever be the brightest spot in the broad ocean that laves our coral shores. Hawaii is the sun of the Pacific and long will be.

Healthy and happy, my very dear friend, Mr. Charles Bishop of Sandy Hill, and myself dwell here as contentedly as two single men well can at this distance from home. We expect to remain here a few years longer and then return to our dear native land. I am just now anticipating a great deal of happiness in the prospect of meeting Miss Newton next Spring. Best I do not allow my feelings to run away with me in this matter, lest He whose thoughts are not as man's thoughts, may see fit in his wisdom to scatter the burning ashes of disappointment over the fair flowers that ardent hope has reared. Six months are yet to roll over us ere the vessel that is to bring her will arrive, and I have learned that it will not do to count upon the future. A wide ocean has yet to be traversed before we meet, and who will say that its wild waves may not swallow up that gallant ship and all she bears. I never cast my eye over that six months track, but what I turn away sick with the thought of what *may* be.

If all goes well, I expect we shall be married on or near next May Day, and presenting my best compliments to Miss Scott I beg to request the honor of her attendance on that interesting occasion. Come and be Bridesmaid, and you shall have one of the loveliest groomsman for a companion that lives. I mean my dear friend Bishop. Don't say that it is impossible for you to come, for by taking the steamer in April you can be here in good season. But whether you come or not, I hope you will not forget that I have invited you, or fail to give me due notice of *your* wedding.

What of my old school master Seth E. Gill? Through the public prints I learn that he is a Judge etc., and, notwithstanding the many severe floggings he has given me, I am happy to hear that he is distinguishing himself. What of the Cleaveland family? I have not heard from them in years. What of Mrs. Houghton, my old crony George Cleaveland etc. etc.

By the Ship "Tsar," 200 days from Boston via Rio Janeiro & Tahiti, I have just rec*d* my first letter from brother Cyrus. If you see him please give my love to him and all of his family and say that his letter shall receive immediate attention. This letter and your newspaper are all that I have rec*d* from Buffalo, but I hope for better things from you in times to come. Your newspaper went on a regular voyage of discovery, and if it could speak, might perchance, cast "Omoo & Typee" [Herman Melville novels] all into the shade. From the U.S. it doubled Cape Horn and first landed at Valparaiso. From thence it took passage in a Chilean Vessel for Tahiti. At Tahiti it exchanged the Chilean vessel for a French Man of War, the "Sarcelle", and went to Callao and the city of Lima in Peru, and then by the same vessel came with a large American mail to Honolulu. But the stupid Frenchman, forgetting that he had a mail on Board, sailed without landing it, and carried the newspaper to Christmas Island, where after an absence of a month it returned to Honolulu and made a safe landing, all "tattered and torn" with the multitude of perils and hair breadth escapes that had befallen it both by sea and land. So far, I have never had any letters directed to me at the Sandwich Islands miscarry, but all my Oregon letters and papers are still on their way, or perchance have long since been devoured by some backwoodsman on the Columbia River. To lose letters at this distance from home is provoking beyond all measure.

My dear Miss (not to call you Kitty any longer) I beseech of you not to take offence at the freedom or length of my letter, and filled with a sense of injured dignity resolve never to write me) but sit down like a good girl, as you are, and taking the full benefit of the *lex talionis* [law of retaliation] pay me off with a regular long drubbing letter.

Hoping to receive that picture and a long family letter very soon, I make my best bow, dear Miss, and bid

Adieu
Yours Very Truly
W. L. Lee

Miss Caroline Scott
Buffalo, Erie County
New York

William Little Lee to Caroline Scott from Honolulu, September 28, 1849

Honolulu Sandwich Islands
28 Sept. 1849

My dear Kittie

I had the satisfaction this morning of welcoming your letter of April 15, 1849, and I hasten to answer it before the thrill of delight it gave me has passed away. What a good letter you have given me. So kind, newsy, sisterly and graceful. Without any of the formalities of a stranger, you walk right up to me, take me by the hand, and treat me as a brother. This ease and familiarity is just what I like, and with a most grateful bow, I beg you to accept my thanks for every line of your Eighteen pages.

Really then, the little Kittie of my early days weighs ninety five solid pounds! Very well done! This ranges near the weight I love best, namely, that of the darling Kitty of my older days. My little pet has just looked over my shoulder and swelling with importance, says "My weight is *110* pounds see"! You never saw such an ambitious little creature in reference to weight and height as my good spouse, and she is sure to take it in high dudgeon my comparing her with anything less than an elephant. I have a strong fancy that you and my *cara sposa* [dear wife] are much alike. Perhaps I am confirmed in that fancy by the sight before me, which is no less than my little Kitty Lee sitting in the large rocking chair with her feet curled up under a long white night gown as of yore sat my little Kittie Scott before the stove in the cold winter mornings of Sandy Hill.

Despite your unwillingness to officiate as bridesmaid, I am a married man. My precious darling came to my arms one bright Sabbath morning the 11th of March last, and passing over the scene of meeting, let me usher you into the spacious cabin of the good ship "Leland," where with the Parson [Rev. Samuel C. Damon] and a few friends, was performed the ceremony that made us one. Our courtship and marriage was a perfect romance, but thank God, the finale is that of *real* happiness. My partner (excuse me if I am somewhat foolish in speaking of her) is all a wife should be. Well may you say "Such a girl is worth having," Truly she is, and I hope by a life of tenderness and devotion to repay her for every sacrifice she has made. The trial she underwent was a severe one, but she knew how readily I would have braved wind, waves, fire and death in every shape for her; and casting off all foolish pride launched forth, like a noble little woman, as she is. Kittie, believe me when I tell you that I am not only a *happy* man, but that after being nearly seven months married I can truly say, "The wife is a thousand times dearer than the bride."

How interesting your review of bygones was. I need not tell you. It carried me quite back to the rosy hours of boyhood and brought to mind the scenes of our early days in all the vividness of reality. The image of my playmate Kittie, is as fresh to my mind as ever, and fifteen years of separation have not been able to obliterate a single look or feature. Your delicate form cunning little eyes, rosy cheeks and sweet mouth come up to me with smiles and half tempt—ahem! I had quite forgotten that I was a married man.

The picture of your father is very lifelike and pleasant. A man of sixty and yet how active! I fancy I can see his soldier like form moving with the elastic step that once trod the walks of good old Sandy Hill, and his countenance luminous with all that mirth and cheerfulness that so charmed us little ones. Turned German has he! To see your father buried in Germanic poetry, theology and philosophy in all its transcendental ramifications is too much even for my imagination. Your account of his studies and acquirements during the past six years fills me with equal astonishment and mortification. I blush to say that I have dabbled in three or four languages and know nothing of any. However the labors of so old a man as your father excite my emulation; and if spared to his age, I hope to rival him as a linguist. For the high opinion your father has been fit to express of me I am both proud and grateful; and be pleased to remember me to him with no ordinary affection.

To your dear mother, present my love, and make the best apology for what I said in my last that the case will admit of. My memory has brightened wonderfully since the receipt of your letter, and if I had but little to remember her for last October, I certainly have much now. May she live many years without finding life a burden. What a world of comfort I received in hearing such good news from my dear Netty. I *should* say Mrs. Cobb I suppose, but bygones cling to me with such tenacity that I cannot think or speak of your family otherwise than as I *knew* them. Remember me to Mrs. Cobb with every kind wish for a long and continued life of happiness. I smile whenever I think of that fine boy of hers, 24 years old! and ask myself, can it be that Netty will ever become the mother of my interesting little correspondent. What pretty names Harriet has given her three children. "Little Netty," I select for my pet, and just step in—give her a kiss and say it came from Uncle Will. Don't forget, by the way, to leave my kindest regards for her mother.

You ask for an account of my voyage. It is too monotonous—too much like most voyages around Cape Horn that you read of, to possess the least interest. I kept a full journal, however, which the passengers raised funds to publish, but I was not vain enough to give my consent. Not to trouble you with details, I would say we left home in midwinter under favorable auspices, and were told we should be in the Sandwich Islands in four months and Oregon in six. A few days out, in crossing the Gulf Stream we met a severe storm which swept our decks carrying away our spare spars and every boat but the long boat. As soon as seasickness would permit, we crawled out on deck and faced head winds with cold spray until we neared the Cape de Verd Islands. From there to the Equator we had bearable weather, and then came a succession of calms which putrified our water, maddened with thirst and exhausted our patience. "Calms breed storms," and so with us; for our calms bred storms both within and without. First, we had a mutiny, which ended in throwing our mate more than half overboard—then a storm accompanied with lightning which struck the poor man almost dead, leaving him a cripple, and carried away part of our weather bulwarks. Three months from home we anchored in the bay of St. Catherines on the coast of Brazil, where we ate fruits, shot birds and monkeys, saw sights and enjoyed life as I never did before. The release from our pen on board ship was delightful beyond expression. Every soul of us felt as if Colombus like we could fall down and kiss our mother earth. Here we left our mate, wife and two children, also a Miss Peabody, (a damsel the wrong side of fifty) and in June 1846 put to sea bound round that dreadful Cape Horn. I would have given worlds to have been home, but pride would not let me turn back. From St. Catherines nothing worthy of note occurred until we fell in with storms and ice-bergs off the Cape. For more than a month we were enveloped in snow ice and darkness. Our days were only five hours long at the best and for sixteen of them we drifted about entirely at the mercy of the winds and waves without once being able to catch a glimpse of the sun. Bibles were used then by hands that never opened one before. On the 17th day I caught a peep of the sun, took several observations, and the Captain and I then succeeded in finding our true position, which was far to the south and east. The weather mended—all hands turned to and cleared the vessel of ice—set sail and doubled the Cape. Without fire or warm food our sufferings were very great, and nothing but the kindness of God kept us from a grave in the ocean. You cannot conceive of our joy at the expectation of entering the Pacific where we supposed the winds just ruffled the face of the waters. Imagine our disappointment then, when I tell you that after leaving Cape Horn we had nothing but storms, head winds and rain for a month. Not one fair day did we see until we approached Juan Fernandes, when we took the pleasant Trades and came bounding to Honolulu right merrily. After making the longest passage on record and being abandoned as lost for some months, before we arrived at the Sandwich Islands in safety. We expected to go on to Oregon after obtaining some refreshments, but, upon examination, our vessel was found to be so badly injured as not to be able to make her necessary repairs in three months. We concluded to seek some safer conveyance—stopped—and here we are.

You ask my opinion of the Missionaries. Well you shall have it. I never met their equals. Their line of conduct comes nearer the path marked out by the meek and lowly One than that of any other Christians I ever had the fortune to know. Meek, humble, kind and self-sacrificing, they seem to live for God and their fellow men. All that these Islands are is owing to the good influence of the Missionaries. Mr. Hunt [Timothy Dwight Hunt], the gentleman whose sister you say lives near you, left the Mission some 18 months since and is now in San Francisco doing much good. He is a man of decided talent and one of my cherished correspondents.

This nation will soon pass away and give place to the more sturdy Saxon. The white man with his civilization seems to carry effeminacy and death into every savage nation he visits. Depopulation is at work throughout all Polynesia. The measles have decimated the Hawaiian race within the last year and we fear more epidemics will complete its ruin. Alas! for the poor Hawaiian. My heart bleeds at the thought of his approaching destiny!

My yarn is already too long and I must bid you adieu. Before I go, however, allow me to introduce you to Mrs. Lee, to whom I shall hand this sheet with the request that she give you some particulars respecting our home etc. I will send you and brother Cyrus a few curiosities by the next good opportunity.

Hoping to hear from you often, I close by saying as a friend just said to me—"Happiness, *much* happiness to you! and if this is not enough, *all you wish and all you want forever!*"

I remain, my dear Kittie,
Ever and Truly Yours,
Wm L. Lee

Catherine N. Lee to Caroline Scott, from Honolulu, September 28, 1849

My dear Miss Scott

Trusting you will deem my husband's request as sufficient apology for adding a few—coils to the yarn he has already pronounced too long, I will introduce you to our Pacific home. Honolulu as you may already know, is a town of some twelve thousand inhabitants, eleven twelfths of whom are natives. The remainder is composed of Americans with a sprinkling of English, Spanish, Chinese, and French.

Unlike good old Sandy Hills in days of yore, Honolulu is by no means deficient in "stated preaching," and two large coral churches with a snug little Bethel are weekly filled with attentive, orderly congregations. Our *stationary* society is composed of missionaries, the families of a few merchants, professional gentlemen and foreign representatives, but there is seldom a time when it is not enlivened by the presence of naval officers from different countries. This society is intelligent, social and refined, and could you drop down in the midst of one of our brilliant parties you might easily imagine it a gathering of the elite of our own land. Scarcely a house in Honolulu is destitute of a Piano, and there have been no less than four fine instruments at our boarding place since I have been here. Our house [Washington Place] is a large white coral building surrounded by broad pillared verandas into which open by glass doors the rooms of each story. It is situated in a beautiful grove adorned with every procurable variety of tropical trees, and is certainly one of the most charming residences you can imagine. We board in the family of a widow lady, (Mrs. Dominis) [Mary Dominis, wife of Captain John Dominis who was lost at sea], who runs the estate, and so long as we can enjoy such a delightful home here, I scarcely think we shall burden ourselves with house-keeping cares.

Of our recent disturbances with the French I suppose you have already heard, but I will give you a few particulars concerning it, at the risk of its being a thrice told tale. On the twelfth of last month [August 12, 1849] the French Admiral De Tromelin* arrived here in the ship "Poursuivante," and he in concert with Mr. Dillon [Guillaume Patrice Dillon] the Consul of France, made ten demands of this Government,

* Legoarant De Tromelin, a rear admiral in the French navy, conducted a series of "reprisals" against the Hawaiian Kingdom after presenting 10 demands drawn up by the French consul Dillon.

threatening if they were not complied with to enforce them at the cannon's mouth.

The principal of those demands were—First that the duty on French brandy should be reduced. By the treaty with France the Hawaiian government was allowed to place what duty it saw fit on liquors, provided it did not amount to a total prohibition. So far is this from the case that our town is flooded with the vile stuff.—Second, that the French language should be introduced into all business affairs between the Hawaiian government and French citizens. The law requires that the business of the Departments of State shall be conducted in Hawaiian or English, for the plain reason that those languages are universally spoken on the islands. There are not a dozen French on all Hawaii, and to grant this claim would not only require a host of interpreters, but would afford every other nation a right to make a similar demand. But I will not enter into these claims—suffice it to say that brandy and Catholicism were the foundation of every one of them, and the government determined that neither of those commodities should be forced down its throat, mildly but firmly resisted. After exhausting his catalogue of threat and bravado, the Admiral landed three hundred armed marines who took the Fort, broke up the cannons, emptied a large quantity of powder into the sea, cut down trees, rifled the Governor's house [Kekūanaōʻa], and finally sailed off taking with them a number of ancient relics and the King's beautiful yacht, the "Kamehameha 3rd." The King [Kamehameha III] and cabinet, well aware that peace was the best policy, ordered that no resistance should be made and these gallant Franks perpetrated their outrage without a finger being raised against them. On their own shoulders rests the entire odium of the affair. Every foreign Consul sent in a protest against their proceedings, and they left loaded with the execration of the entire community not excepting their own countrymen here resident. You must not think this untoward affair had annoyed us personally, for not a soul here felt the least alarm, and visiting, business, etc. went on just as usual.

The California fever of which you speak has had its course *here* too, but the crisis has long since passed. Many who left here filled with extravagant anticipations have returned wiser but sadder men, and others have digged themselves graves where they sought only for gold. Many will acquire fortunes in this new Ophir**, but the number of dis-

** Ophir is a region mentioned in the Old Testament as the source of gold.

appointed victims will be fearfully great. My husband is receiving continually the most pressing solicitations to go to San Francisco with the prospect of soon realizing a fortune in his profession, but as yet he remains unmoved. He would not take *me* to such a Pandemonium and he will not go without me. Besides he is laying up two or three thousand a year and with the excellent investment he can make of his funds (legal interest alone is 12 per cent), he thinks he is accumulating fortune rapidly enough.

You mention the possibility of these islands resting under the folds of the stripes and stars. It is a vain possibility, for Great Britain and France would resist such an accession. As an American I should most heartily deprecate that acquisition. I think we have yet to learn whether California will not prove a deadly curse to its new owner.

William has written you such a dismal account of his voyage, that I shall send you a paper giving a slight sketch of *mine* that you may know there is sunshine as well as storm at sea. I claim no credit for "braving the dangers of the deep," for I have had from very childhood a perfect mania for voyaging. The trial of which my husband speaks was merely a struggle between pride and my better self. It was the question—"Shall I go to him, or allow him to give up his business and come home for me?" Thank God I decided as I did! It is with a feeling of bitter self contempt that I now look back upon that same "struggle."

My husband retains so vivid a recollection of you that I can hardly believe thirteen years have passed away since you saw each other. He says he has changed very little since boyhood in person, and I think in character he remains the same. At any rate, as a man he is industrious and energetic, rigidly upright, but generous and warm hearted, and I believe those traits are said to have characterized him in childhood. I can see you laughing over that portrait and saying a wife is no judge, for she will of course speak con amore. You must make us a visit one of these days Miss Kittie and decide for yourself. To your manner of addressing him, I do not at all "object," for you were certainly "dear" to him before I even knew I had such a nice cousin.

Mrs. Gould (the Julia Morgan of my girlish days), I remember perfectly well. I was not much acquainted with her, but she was an intimate friend of one of my cousins, and she used frequently to speak of her with much affection. Please remember us to her very kindly, and tell her that my home for a long time before I left Albany was in the family of Mr. Wm. Newton and that my room-mate was her old friend Mattie.

Well, Miss Kittie, I think I have trespassed long enough upon your patience for an uninvited correspondent, and with the hope you will not only avail yourself of the privilege of which you speak with regard to "a married man," but that you will take the same with a married man's wife.

I remain
Very sincerely yours
C. N. Lee

Catherine Lee to Caroline Scott, no date

My dear Miss Scott

I had intended to fill a sheet to you & say a few words to brother Cyrus in this letter, but William has just told me it must go immediately, as a vessel is about to sail for Panama, so I must dwarf my lines to the compass of a note. My moiety [portion] of William's letter met with a cordial welcome and I hope to be the frequent recipient of such favors.

So you were "the first love" of my fickle spouse! You Miss Kittie, when he had so many times assured me I was the only woman who had ever touched his stony heart! You whom he has deluded me into the belief he admired from a fancied resemblance to my unworthy self! What a whirlwind this "big grownup" rascal has yet to reap from the luckless seed you have sown! By the way would you have any objection to favoring me with your ideas as to the expediency of, agreeability etc. of marrying widowers. The question is of some importance to me under the circumstances, as I have a strong presentiment I shall not survive my liege lord.

On looking over William's letter I see he has given you all the items of interest I could muster; so you will lose nothing but a tedious infliction by my lack of time.

You ask if it is thought that Admiral de Tromelin acted by order of his government in the Honolulu outrages. I believe it is—at all events the French government sanctioned them after they were committed, which was just as dastardly. Have you read Jarves' History of the Sandwich Islands? That will give you a chapter or two respecting the exploits of the "Grand nation" in the Pacific. It has long been a favorite plan of my husband's to spend a year or two in Paris, and he intends doing so on our way to America. Perhaps we shall like the French somewhat better after a domestication in their metropolis. You see I have but an inch of blank space left, and I must say adieu though I would willingly chat with you an hour longer. Very truly yrs. C. N. Lee

William Little Lee to Caroline Scott, from Honolulu, November 23, 1850.

Honolulu
23 Nov. 1850

My dear Kitty

Your interesting letter of Jany 24, 1850 was duly received, and this being one of my leisure Saturday evenings, I have seated myself for one of those tantalizing chats on paper, with one whom I so much wish to talk with face to face. How much I *would* give to spend a few hours with you in recounting the little incidents of our childish days—incidents which you as well as myself seem to have treasured in a choice niche of memory. When shall I have that pleasure? Next year? No, nor the next, but, God willing, sometime. I hold myself in readiness to return home whenever my dear Kate says go, but as she concurs in my opinion that it is advisable to remain here until we can take the overland route, via China, Egypt, the Mediterranean and Europe, perchance we shall not meet until you have become Madam ________ with certain sequences unnecessary to mention. Probably we shall see Father land again in four years.

You say an old Sybil once told you, that you were destined to cross the ocean, and though I do not wish to rob your parents or other friends of your pleasant companionship, yet I trust that oracle may prove a truthful one, if, as you hint, it may waft you to our shores. Sister Mary says, you are a facsimile of my own dear Kate, and if this be true, certainly the fear you express that your arrival will discolor the pleasant pictures I have formed of you, is quite unnecessary. Still, I much doubt your ever getting so far astray as Honolulu, for that "nephew," whom you labor so hard to convince me is too much of a *brother* to be a lover, or some other happy fellow will probably bring you to an anchor before you are fairly out of port.

How blessed your family has been! Your good father has been spared so long to comfort, guide and cheer you—your dear mother sustained as it were by a miracle—Netty well married and happy—and Harriet "fat and fair—gay and cheerful," with a husband all kindness, and children charming and good. Give little Netty Havens another Kiss and remember me to her stately mother with the kindest regards.

What a thriving, busy, important mart Buffalo has become. I wonder if she feels one throb of gratitude in her strong young heart to the meek but gospel-lacking village that has bequeathed her so many of her worthiest citizens. You have the honor of giving us a President, and you may well be proud of him. Filmore [President of the United States Millard Fillmore] I always liked, though I am no whig, and I rejoice in the success which has thus far attended his administration. The admission of California is grateful news to all Americans in the Pacific, and especially do we of the Sandwich Islands rejoice at this approach of our native land.

I am very grateful for your information respecting the scattered Sandy Hillers, for I like to watch the rise and progress of these stray pilgrims. Scott Sherwood, of whom you speak, was my chum for some years, and I know him *au fond.* He was talented, ambitious, and moral, but I hear that, like too many of earth's gifted ones, he has been nearly drowned in the cup.

I have just shipped a box per the Brig "Noble," which sailed this afternoon for New Bedford, addressed to brother Cyrus, and filled with curiosities for you and his children. It is a small box, however, and you must not expect anything wonderful. I have some large or rather long curios, which I found it impossible to send, because I had not enough small articles to fill in a box of the requisite size and length. One of these days, I will make up another box for Buffalo, and then you shall receive them.

There is nothing of general importance in this part of the world worth relating, but we are daily expecting a visit from the cholera which has reached San Francisco, and another from the French who are at Panama. Which of these evils is most to be dreaded is not difficult to determine, for we have more contempt than fear for the chivalrous Gauls. You may think it strange to hear me speak thus of the brethren of Lafayette, but when you know them as well as we of the Pacific, you will agree with us, that they are utterly devoid of all justice, especially when dealing with such a weak nation as this. Our Mission to France has entirely failed and our reliance is upon the justice of our cause and the support of the United States and England.

I have just discovered in looking over your letter that you ask for autographs. I will see that you have some, and will send them either in this or the next letter. I have some fine specimens of the white branch coral, so common at home, but I did not send it, thinking you were supplied with that variety. If there are any shells in the collection I send to the children that you would like, let me know, and in the next box for home, I will forward you some.

You ask if our Mr. Bishop is any relative of Mrs. Dewey's first husband. He is a nephew. He is Collector General of the Kingdom, and was married last summer to a young half-caste chiefess [Princess Bernice Pauahi]. Bishop is a fine looking and noble young fellow, who was my *compagnon du voyage* and has been my bosom friend for years.

A friend of mine has just asked me who Mr. William Treat of Buffalo is. I echo the question, only knowing that he is the compiler of that excellent little book, "Angel Voices."

Remember me to your parents and sisters—brother Cyrus & family—write often, and believe me

Yours Ever Truly
W. L. Lee

Catherine Lee to Caroline Scott, 23 November 1850. Cross writing in the left margin of all four pages of W. L. Lee's letter.

Dear Miss Kittie

Will you please remember me affectionately to brother Cyrus & his family and tell him I fully intended writing him by this opportunity. William wrote a long letter to him in the box, & I sent a note to the children at the same time. Yours etc. C. N. L.

I have just thought of something in the way of a curiosity that I wish had suggested itself before—viz a book of pressed specimens of our flowers & leaves. In our own yard we have over twenty varieties of trees, including the olive, tamarind, pomegranate, guava, india rubber, lime, algeroba, etc. I will arrange a book for you & the children to forward by the next good opportunity. When you see Mrs.Gould please remember me to her affectionately. I hope if cousin Mat does come to Buffalo she will not fulfill her promise of bringing my daguerreotype for my face, which is a very plain one at best, is most distressingly set forth in that same likeness. I would fain spare your compassion my much esteemed but unseen friend.

Kate

You ask if I ever received your first letter—I answer no, and I am sorry for it, as no doubt said missive contained many a rare tid bit and jewel. Please send me another in the place of it.

William Little Lee to Caroline Scott, Honolulu, December 8, 1851

Honolulu Dec. 8, 1851

My dear Kittie

I have been your debtor since last June for a most excellent letter, and should have answered it long ere this, but for a pressure of business and an absence of several months from home. This apology however, I know is an insufficient one, and hereafter I promise to be a more punctual correspondent.

I am gratified to hear the small present I sent you last fall afforded you the least pleasure, and am more than repaid by the simple expression of your thanks. We intended to have sent you and our little nieces another small box this season; but on drumming up our articles, found we had scarcely enough for a sizable box. The first vessel that sails next fall will bear you an addition to your cabinet. Most we have worth sending comes from China, that land of one-toed feet, fans, and fixins, where the people stand still, not having moved one inch since the days of Confucius. Though so obstinately stationary, they are the most wonderful of all the sons of Adam. We see much of these Celestials at the Islands, and they are a never-ceasing mystery.

The news of your illness during that long siege from July to October—the constant care—the unsleeping watchfulness—the tender love of your honored father, and your disappointment in not visiting the dear old home of our childhood, touched me keenly. My memory often travels back to the "Old Scott House," now profaned by a shoe shop on each side of it, and mourns over the departed scenes of other days. I know but little of Sandy Hill of late, for its good people are miserable correspondents, and as for learning any thing from its "Herald," a stray number of which now and then falls in my way, the idea is absurd. Did you ever see such a trashy milk-and-water sheet as our worthy Elisha sends forth. The weak—poverty—stricken fellow never has an idea above "Jabe," "Cy Stevens," and that phantom "quarter" which he has been chasing and cornering for the last ten years.

Our oriental tour is yet, you know, three years in the future, but rest assured that when we make it, I shall bear you in mind, over sea and land—in garden and desert—amid Jew and Gentile, and if possible grant your request.

At present I am tied down to these Islands by business which I cannot well leave; but I am one of those obedient husbands, oftner read of than seen, and shall be on the wing for home at the first intimation of such a desire from my good spouse. We are not as far out of the world as we were a short time since, for by the Steamers, via Panama & San Francisco, we receive our home mail regularly every two weeks. All our friends have to do to communicate with us, is to write their letters—drop them in the P.O. at any country village, and in 50 days they are in our hands at Honolulu. Many thanks to your friend, Postmaster General Hall.

Your items of family news were very interesting. I am glad to hear that your mother is so cheerful a sufferer, and that the hand of time rests so lightly on your dear father. Remember me to both of them, and indeed to all of your family, those happy sisters and their "good husbands" among the rest, with much affection. Certainly that law firm of Fillmore, Hall, and Haven, has been a marvel in the way of success. And Buffalo too is a most remarkable place—yet in its infancy, it exhibits the bone and muscle of manhood, and displays a vigor and enterprise that defies competition. I hear you have had a destructive fire lately, but I trust neither your father or Cyrus have suffered thereby.

Your picture of William Treat was a *Treat* indeed. What a sad fate you predict for the poor unfortunate as a penalty for old-bachelorhood. Fie Kittie! one would think from your severe judgment you were an old maid, which I know you are not, and never will be.

In the line of news I have nothing calculated to interest a lady, and I leave that department to Mrs. Lee. I may remark, however, that our damsels have not yet taken to "Bloomers," [short loose trousers gathered at the knee] though some of our matrons have, probably from the force of *habit*. I'm a strong Bloomerite myself, for I think the proposed reform a sensible one. The talk of annexation grows louder, but I do not imagine we shall become a portion of Uncle Sam's dominions in a day, though we may in time.

Hoping to hear from you very soon & to learn of your health and prosperity

I remain
Yours Very faithfully
W. L. Lee

Catherine Lee to Caroline Scott, Honolulu, December 8, 1851

Honolulu Dec. 8/51

My dear Miss Scott

I wonder if you will allow me to shelter my delinquency in writing behind the broad apology & etc. my husband has made. I deserve no such consideration for I have abundance of leisure, but I thought a communication from me would be of little value in your eyes unless it figured in the rear of one of *his* epistles. I write you know, just to gently remind you that this ardent admirer of yours—this living embodiment of "organic remains" is no longer a bachelor—in short that he has a "little Kittie" of his own who watches his outgoings and incomings with an Argus eye. You do not believe that—do you? The resemblance of which you speak has often been remarked to me and struck William very forcibly when he first saw me in my grown up days. Sister Mary (Mrs. Hunt) who has seen you more recently, also thinks us exceedingly alike. What we are mutually to gain from this resemblance is not clear to me, but is certainly something of a coincidence.

I have been away from Honolulu quite a time visiting our Plantation [Līhu'e Plantation on Kaua'i]. William was obliged to be from home three long months on a "Land Commission" tour of the Islands, and as it was too fatiguing and unpleasant journey for a lady to undertake, I accepted the invitation of the Marshalls (my old ship-mates) [Mr. and Mrs. James F. B. Marshall], and went down with them to Kauai. Our Plantation I believe I have never described to you. It is a tract of twenty five hundred acres of well-wooded, well-watered land with between two and three hundred acres of sugar cane ready for grinding this month. Eighty native laborers are now employed upon it and a large number of coolies or Chinese operatives are expected in a short time. Mr. Marshall, a partner in the Plantation, has built upon it a Chinese house and removed trees, and he has certainly one of the most charming homes on the Islands. His house is a low, but rather extensive building, commanding a fine view of the sea in front, and inland of a magnificent range of mountains. The trees are principally *kukui* or "candle nut" trees, from the nuts of which the natives obtain their oil, bread-fruit, *ohia,* or the native apple, *koa,* the Island mahogany, and a very few orange trees and cocoa-nuts. The under-growth consists of arrow-root, ginger, sandal wood, bamboo, and a variety of shrubs to me unknown. In the way of fruits we have the ohia, guava, pine-apple, papaya, banana, oranges and cocoa-nut. The latter is not considered eatable here in the state you see it home. They are picked before they harden, and the soft, white pulp is eaten with a spoon. My visit I enjoyed as well as a woman *could* in the absence of her husband. Our host had other guests most of the time during my stay, and with the aide of their pleasant society, a fine library and one of Hertz' superb pianos within doors, and pic-nics, sails on the River, horse-back rides, and excursions to the neighboring Plantation to give us a taste of out-doors enjoyment, the dreaded three months passed swiftly and cheerily away. I found Honolulu rather quiet on my return as she had just run the gauntlet of a series of balls, pic-nics, etc. given by and for the Admiral and other officers of two English "men of war," which left our port a while since. There are three "men of war" now in the harbor—two of them American and the third a British vessel [H.B.M. Daedalus], commanded by Captain Wellesley, a nephew of the Duke of Wellington. Last evening we attended a small party given for Capt. Hudson of the "Vincennes." I had intended giving you another leaf but my husband has just come in with an imperative summons "to close directly as the mail is about to leave." Hoping you will excuse such an abrupt leave-taking.

I remain very truly yours. Kate Lee

William Little Lee to Caroline Scott from Shady Nook, Island of Kaua'i, March 15, 1854

Shady Nook, Island of Kauai
15 March 1854

My dear Kittie Scott

You will smile perhaps when I tell you that your pleasant letter of Dec. 8, 1853 came to hand on the 11th of March 1854. The fifth anniversary of my marriage, and just as I was in the midst of a divorce case. Why, what of it? you'll ask. Nothing perhaps, but I simply state the fact without comment, leaving it for you and the Fortune Tellers to claim such inferences as you please.

You will see that my letter is dated at Shady Nook, and naturally inquire where is this. Well, Shady Nook, which I think should be called Sunny Nook, is one of the brightest little spots in the world, situated on the island of Kauai, about a 100 miles from Honolulu, and, is the residence of my dear friend Judge Bond [Edward P. Bond]. To this sunny nook I have fled from the heat of the metropolis to breathe the sweet trades that blow so kind and gently over this Eden Country. In other words, I have come here on the sad errand of seeking health, which I long since squandered.

I am sorry to see by your letter that you are something of an invalid, with "a tendency to colds and a cough," and yet half glad of it too; for if you had never been sick, I should bore you to death with this tale of my complaints. Invalids you know, especially pulmonary ones, are very apt to recount the history of their ills from the first sneeze of a cold down to the present miserable moment, and should never any but invalids for listeners. Poor Kittie, I pity you, but you must submit to my inflictions, so stir the fire a little, in that "cold pitiless winter" you tell about, and make yourself as easy as possible, while I relate my ills to you from the charming Tropics, with the green earth smiling and blossoming around me.

Well, in August last I broke down from excessive labor in-doors, and the care of small pox patients out-doors, and for three months was kept on my back, subjected to all the medicinal & physical evils you can imagine. Was I unhappy? you ask—not for a moment. How could I be with such a dear wife to bend over me, to comfort me, to care for every little want, real or imaginary, and to cheer me up with kind words and kinder nursing? Under her hands I have grown into strength again, & am now permitted to go abroad without her, though I should be much better were she with me. The fact is, I'm a weak child, hardly able to withstand the temptation of pastries, puddings and good living, and need a guardian to watch me constantly.

Are you fond of riding on horseback? If so, you should be here to gallop over this beautiful country with me, and feast on the mingled beauty of ocean, mountain, stream and plain. I am in the saddle every morning before sunrise for a six or eight mile ride, and a thousand times I have wished I had some nice little woman by my side, who could take care of her horse and *keep up.*

"Did you know one Herman Patten?" Yes, and was heartily ashamed of him too. He brought me a letter of introduction from San Francisco —represented himself as a familiar friend and frequent visitor in your family—knew brother Cyrus, etc. etc., and endeavored to impose himself upon the public as my particular friend. But his swell, swagger and disgraceful conduct in Honolulu soon banished him from all decent society, and he left here heartily despised.

"What think of you taking shelter under the wing of our big Eagle?" Very well indeed, if at the same time, we can avoid his *talons.* Perhaps the Giant Douglas [U.S. Senator Stephen A. Douglas from Illinois] will condescend to tack us on to his infamous Nebraska Bill.

Leaving the last page to be filled by my dearest Kittie, and with much love to your dear parents and all the family, I remain as ever

Your sincere friend
W. L. Lee

Catherine N. Lee to Caroline Scott, from Honolulu, April 16, 1854. Letter written on last page of William's letter and "crossways" on the first page.

Honolulu April 16, 1854

My dear Miss Scott

More than a month since Mr. Lee brought up this unfinished letter from Kauai and as the mail is about leaving, I must add my quota to the sheet and send it to the Post Office. I am very glad you received the box at last, though I fear its contents were too much injured to make it an object even to pay Express charges. The vessel in which it was sent sprung a leak and was condemned at Tahiti and I was so confident the box would never reach its destination, that I had concluded not to subject you to the disappointment of knowing it was ever despatched. Did not everything in it bear the marks of having been saturated with salt water?

While I think of it, I must deliver a message to you from my next door neighbor, Mr. Angel [Benjamin Franklin Angel, U.S. Consul to Honolulu]. He sends his kind regards and wishes to know if you remember traveling under his protection from Detroit to Buffalo? Mrs. Angel leaves tomorrow for the U.S. intending to return another year if annexation does not render her husband's recall necessary. By the way, I am very sorry you "deprecate so earnestly" our admission into the Union, and I assure you that though *at first* we might be a little "incongruous," we don't intend to be the least bit "discordant." Don't be afraid of us, for we shall behave most beautifully. My husband has always remained a true American. As he declined taking the oath of allegiance, the King made him a denizen.

After boarding for five years, I am now in the midst of preparations for house-keeping. We are as pleasantly situated as boarders can be, having five rooms and a nice garden all to ourselves, but we begin to feel that it is time for us to contribute our mite to the entertainment of the community as house keepers. Our new home is a large coral house with verandas on each side, extensive tasteful grounds with plenty of trees and shrubbery, and is altogether I think the most charming place in or about Honolulu. Will you not come and make us a visit Miss Kittie if for nothing else than to rid yourself of that "tendency to cold and cough." You must not point to my husband's illness as a bad example of the sanitary effect of this climate for if he had drugged himself with poison he could not have taken more effective means to kill himself. During the prevalence of the pestilence he took the charge of between fifty and sixty of the loathsome small-pox patients, necessarily crowding the labors of the day into unwholesome night hours. *Of course* he caught the variolus [smallpox] fever in the height of which he took a cold (by sleeping in a strong current of air) which settled on his lungs. The moment he could crawl from his room he resumed the care of the miserable sufferers together with his other multifarious duties, paying no attention to his threatening lungs. Only a miracle could have saved him from the sad effects of his recklessness and if he but lays his dearly bought lesson to heart, I shall feel that his sickness has been a blessing in disguise. My husband, though perhaps a wife should not say it, is one of the most generous, unselfish, self-sacrificing persons I ever saw, and he never seems to regard either his own time, comfort or health when the interests of others are concerned. Every one here says that he performs as much labor as half a dozen people ought to *prudently,* and by far the greater part of his work (his arduous duties as President of the Land Commission Board for example), is wholly gratuitous. The poor kanakas in their figurative language call him their "City of Refuge," and it is amusing sometimes to read the address upon his letters such as "To the friend of the poor and those who have no helper"—the "Father of the poor and fatherless," and "Friend of the widow and orphan," etc. I never said so much in my dear husband's praise before, and I must hurry this to the office before he comes home, or it will never see the outside of my room. You, the affectionately remembered friend of his boyish days, will pardon me I know for whispering this much in your own private ear. Crossing letters I abominate and hoping you will excuse me if I have made either William's or my own writing illegible. I remain—

Very truly yr friend
Kate N. Lee

Catherine Lee to Caroline Scott from N.Y., September 8, 1855

New York, Sept. 8, 1855

My dear Miss Kittie

Since my return I have rummaged among my papers to find you the promised autograph of our young King [Kamehameha IV], but can scare up nothing but letters, which might not, for political reasons, to meet a stranger's eye, except the shabby note which I enclose, written to me a day or two before we left Honolulu. He is a fine epistolizer and in justice to him I ought to say that the enclosed is a poor specimen either of his style or chirography [handwriting].

William bore the fatigue of our long journey remarkably well and has now gone on to Boston, leaving me to spend a few days with New York friends. Please remember me very kindly to your father and to your sister & her family, and believe me

Very cordially yours
Kate N. Lee

JOSEPH THEROUX

The Reverend Joseph Dwight Strong

He was an early New England missionary to Hawai'i, a poet, preacher, photographer, editor, translator, traveler (fig. 1). Yet because of his restlessness and his temper, he was never popular, never remained long in any one place. His children would find varying degrees of success: his son and namesake would become King Kalākaua's government artist, while daughter Elizabeth would be called the "American Rosa Bonheur"[1] for her lifelike animal portraits.

The Reverend Joseph Dwight Strong was born June 5, 1823, in Granby, Connecticut, and could trace his family back to the Elder John Strong, a tanner, who had arrived in Massachusetts from England in 1630, nearly 200 years before. Reverend Joseph married 21-year-old Margaret Dewing Bixby of Williamstown, Massachusetts, on September 7, 1852. His older brother, John Cotton Strong, born in 1818, was educated at Williams College, where he excelled at languages, especially Greek and German, and went on to study at the Theological Institute at East Windsor (now Hartford Seminary). Joseph followed him to Williams and East Windsor, where he completed his studies in 1852. John was assigned to convert the Choctaws at Mt. Pleasant, Minnesota, where he eventually settled.[2]

Joseph hoped to serve the foreign missions, to convert the heathen. Instead he was assigned to Westport, where Joe was born, in 1853, and served there for three years. In 1855, a daughter was born,

Joseph Theroux is principal of Keaukaha Elementary School on the Big Island. He has previously contributed to the Journal *and is at present writing a biography of Reverend Strong's son, the artist Joseph Dwight Strong.*

The Hawaiian Journal of History, vol. 38 (2004)

whom they named Elizabeth. About the same time, Reverend Joseph got word that there was an opening in the Sandwich Islands.[3] He could go on his own because, for some reason, the American Board of Commissioners for Foreign Missions would not sponsor him, as they did most New England missionaries.

The early missionaries to the Hawaiian Islands, who first departed in the 1820s, had to travel around the Horn, but by the 1850s many came by way of Panama. The Strong family traveled to New York City in early March and booked passage on the Pacific Mail Steamship Company's SS *George Law,* a three-year-old wooden side-wheel steamer, which departed March 5, 1855. Their voyage to San Fran-

FIG. 1. Although many of the Strong Family were artists and photographers, no likeness of Reverend Strong has turned up. This silhouette is based on a study of composite profiles of several of his sons, as well as his self-description of having "great whiskers." Silhouette by the author.

cisco would be over 5,000 nautical miles. Also aboard the *George Law* were California's first senator, William M. Gwinn, and the founder of the Pacific Mail Lines, William H. Aspinwall. They sailed to the Isthmus of Panama, to the town called Aspinwall (now Colon, on Limon Bay), named for their shipmate. When they disembarked, they were put on a train—then up and running for only two months—which took them across the Isthmus.[4] On the Pacific side, they boarded one of the company's coastal steamers to San Francisco. In San Francisco, they booked passage for Honolulu, departed on the clippership *Spitfire,* on April 18, and arrived in Honolulu on May 1, 1855.[5]

Reverend Joseph was named "interim pastor" at the Fort Street Church, also known as the "foreign church" in Honolulu. The Fort Street Church resembled New England Congregational structures, pale, high-steepled and wide-naved. The street was named for the fort erected in 1816. It was still there in 1855, although it would be torn down two years later when Strong was officially appointed pastor, on January 15, 1857.[6] His first sermon as pastor was "The Right Hand of Fellowship," delivered on February 1.[7] It was generally agreed that pulpit work was his strength, rather than the day-to-day responsibilities associated with the life of a pastor: visiting the sick, consoling the aggrieved, handling administrative tasks, and so forth. His sermons were admired; later some were even published.[8]

The Strongs visited the other islands, taking a mission boat to Maui and the Big Island of Hawai'i. Hawaiian children were fascinated by Reverend Strong's "great whiskers" (fig. 1) and his wife's "long neck."[9] Margaret became pregnant again, and on October 25, 1857, she gave birth to a son whom they called Wallace Kealoha.[10] The children enjoyed the tropics, the weather, and the water. But apparently they only had each other as playmates. Some years later Strong wrote:

> Still those missionary children sometimes got lonesome, and very tired of these beautiful surroundings. There are no other little boys and girls of their own race anywhere in the region round, and the native children are still so uncultivated and unrefined, and have so many bad words on their lips, and such depraved thoughts in their hearts, in spite of all their wonderful improvement, as to make them very unsafe companions for well-trained foreign children. The consequence is that the little missionaries have to play nearly all the time by themselves.[11]

The missionaries became friendly with Kamehameha IV, Alexander Liholiho (1834–1863), and his wife Emma Rooke (1836–1885). Elizabeth Strong's "earliest impression" was sitting in Queen Emma's lap, "while she told my mother about the cruelties of her elderly [sic] husband, crying briefly until she made me cry too. She was so young and handsome we had a little [daguerreotype] of her for years."[12] (Since Liholiho was only in his mid-twenties at the time, he was hardly "elderly"; either Emma was being sarcastic, or Elizabeth's memory was playing her false: after all, her memoir was penned some 60 years later.)

Missionaries were daily confronted with cultural differences, but the Strongs seemed to take them in stride. Elizabeth wrote:

> Another memory was of going to the door with my mother one Sunday morning to find a splendid bronze figure of a Chieftess, there just from her morning swim, dripping wet with her one dress over her arm, so as not to get it wet for Church. All she had on was a wreath of flowers.[13]

Reverend Joseph had a love of horses which he passed on to his children. He took daily rides, sometimes taking tiny daughter Elizabeth in the saddle with him. She recalled that "my father always took me before him on his early morning horse-back ride . . .".[14]

But the congregation had not been happy with their pastor. The missionary paper recounted the complaints that came to authorities in letters, but they did not specify them. A church history does not go into detail, only saying that "some in the congregation were dissatisfied with his ministry . . .".[15] On July 19, 1857, two years after his arrival, he resigned his position, he later wrote, due to "the failure of his health."[16] But the complaints reached the Ecclesiastical Council, and his resignation letter was accepted on October 19. The council met on November 24 to "dissolve the pastoral relations." The council expressed "deep regret" at "any train of circumstance [that led] to his separation."[17]

An unsigned letter to the editor of the *Pacific Commercial Advertiser* chastened him for misleading people about his accomplishments at the Fort Street Church, as well as for having claimed to have increased the congregation. "His observations in regard to doubling of his congregation since he has been here must have been made with a pair of spectacles that saw double," the writer stated, adding a bit of doggerel:

> Of optics sharp it needs I ween
> To see what is not to be seen.[18]

The family lingered in the Islands until December 9, when they departed Honolulu aboard the bark *Yankee.*[19] As the ship pulled away from the harbor, Joe, now aged five, studied the view. He would return in 24 years and paint that same harbor for King Kalākaua's birthday. (His two seven-foot murals of the harbor are now displayed at the Barracks building, next to 'Iolani Palace.)

Joseph and Margaret, with their three children—Joseph Dwight Jr., Elizabeth, and Wallace Kealoha—sailed for California and settled in Oakland. Margaret had been pregnant during the voyage, and, upon their arrival, it fell to her to unpack and set up housekeeping. Joseph served at the First Presbyterian Church. On December 2, 1858, Margaret gave birth to a daughter, Ninole, whose name in Hawaiian means "weak, as an infant." (Ninole is also a village on the east coast of the Big Island.) She may have been a sickly child, but she grew, according to all accounts, into a beautiful girl. Three sons followed in two-year intervals: Nathan Bixby (1860), Mark Hopkins (1862) and Dwight (1864).[20]

Yet he was never able to stay at any one church—or at any one profession—for more than a couple of years. Over the next dozen years, he would be at various times a preacher, an editor, a school superintendent, a writer, and finally set up shop as a photographer. Though talented in many ways, his crusty temperament and his inability to work with others prevented his succeeding in any but solitary enterprises. The longest employment he would have would be some 15 years as a photographer, and even that was not as a portraitist but as a "landscape photographer." He even traveled around Southern California for a time in a "photography car" taking pictures.[21]

His friend and fellow clergyman, Henry Durant (1802–1875), offered him a job teaching Greek at the newly established College of California (which evolved into the University of California at Berkeley, Durant becoming its first president), but Reverend Joseph declined, and instead founded the Presbyterian Church on Larkin

Street in San Francisco, in 1862.[22] With seven children to support, he took to writing poems, articles, and moral stories for publication in *The Hesperian.* Margaret's stories were also published, albeit posthumously.[23]

In August 1862, both took over the job of editing *The Hesperian,* a women's journal produced for the purpose of "inculcating lessons of morality, purity and wisdom" as well as a fashion sense. The Strongs "changed its title to *The Pacific Monthly* and broadened its offerings to appeal to the men."[24]

His work for the *Pacific Monthly* included essays on a variety of topics, such as "The American Flag," "Craters of the Hawaiian Islands," an "Essay on Music," and "Mrs. Amelia B. Welby as a Poet." Having studied German at college, he was able to translate poems by Goethe, Karl Korner, Christian Alexander, and Johann Uhland, as well as contribute original poetry.[25]

In addition to his magazine work and moral stories, Strong published at least two sermons. The first was on the notorious Broderick-Terry Duel, which had occurred September 13, 1859. His "*Plea Against Dueling:* A Discourse Delivered in the First Presbyterian Church at Oakland California Sunday Sept. 25, 1859," was published as a 16-page pamphlet. His "Plea" alone may not have been the cause, but that duel was the last in San Francisco's history. And upon the assassination of President Lincoln, he published "*The Nation's Sorrow:* A Discourse on the Death of Abraham Lincoln, Delivered in the Larkin St. Presbyterian Church, San Francisco, April 16, 1865."

The Strongs edited the *Pacific Monthly* from September 1862 until January 1864. Two years later Margaret died. She was buried at Lone Mountain, San Francisco.

The family continued living at Larkin Street for two more years, until Strong decided he needed a change. In early 1868, he was employed as superintendent of schools at Alameda County, but he either did not find the administrative tasks congenial or he did not get along with the teachers he supervised.

He took an assignment to preach at two parishes on the south side of Cape Cod, Massachusetts, which had had five different pastors in seven years, and had been without any preacher since September 1867.[26] He set out with his seven children in March 1868. It's possible that he parceled his children out to relatives, since church and newspaper records make no reference to his family. Certainly the parishes could not afford a full-time preacher (and could not until as late as 1956), and he would be shared between the Congregational parishes of Hyannis and West Yarmouth.[27] It is known that son Joseph, Jr., spent some of this period with his mother's relatives in Vermont.[28]

Reverend Joseph arrived at Hyannis on March 29, 1868, and served until September 1870.[29]

Baptismal, marriage, funeral, and "admission" records from his tenure are sketchy, though it is known that in the two-and-a-half years he was there he succeeded in "admitting" or enrolling "eight or ten" souls, and officiating at the marriages of several couples. Local papers carried accounts of church activities and the church histories are full of details about their well-loved preachers, yet the same church histories only mention Reverend Joseph.[30]

In 1869, while at Hyannis, Strong struck a deal with the publisher Daniel Lothrop and Co., of Boston, to bring out collections of stories he and wife Margaret had compiled while at the *Pacific Monthly*. The following year, Lothrop brought out a dozen of his collections with titles like *Truthful Jenny* and *Minna's Proud Heart*. They also published at least one of Margaret's titles, *New Year and Other Stories*. Lothrop made a real success with the publication of his own wife's work. Her name was Harriet, but she published under the name Margaret Sidney. Her book was *The Five Little Peppers and How They Grew*. Lothrop encouraged her to produce sequels which were equally popular.[31]

He returned to Oakland with his children. Faced with raising "a large family of small children" and little money, Reverend Joseph home-schooled his children. Yet, despite his strict views, they were often on their own and fending for themselves. Joe's brother, Wallace Kealoha recalled being "thrown upon my own resources much earlier than the average boy." He worked his way through school doing a variety of jobs such as a "coal miner at Mt. Diablo," and a shepherd tending a flock of sheep near Monterey.[32]

Young Joe was out early on his own, like Wallace, and once referred to his "unhappy orphan days"[33]—even though his father would outlive him—because of his estrangement from Reverend Joseph. The father's crustiness in alienating his Honolulu congregation apparently extended to relations with his son. Once, apologizing for a "nasty" drunken episode, Joe wrote, "I am afraid that my father's disposition predominates in my make up after all—what a mean thing to lay to one's father."[34] But, in fact, most people were struck by Joe's genial disposition. He gained a reputation as both a portrait and landscape painter. He went to Hawai'i in 1882 and made a name for himself as the king's court painter and government artist. He also married Robert Louis Stevenson's stepdaughter Belle and lived for several years at Vailima, the novelist's estate in Samoa. He died of heart failure in 1899. Their son, Joseph Austin Strong, became a successful playwright and returned to New England, where he summered on Nantucket and was buried with his wife's people in Rhode Island.[35]

The strain of travel, along with editing, raising seven children, and appeasing a cranky Connecticut preacher had been too much for Mrs. Strong. From her, it is said, the children got their artistic taste. Following her death in 1866,[36] Strong was at loose ends, associated with six different churches and frequently moving around Oakland. He first lived near the waterfront, at the "Bay near Jones," then at Brush Street, San Pablo Avenue, Gilbert Street, and lastly at Montgomery Avenue.[37] His children all lived nearby (after some travel) and pursued professions single-mindedly in photography (Mark), real estate (Ninole), art (Joseph and Elizabeth), and court stenography (Wallace), but son Dwight would take after him the most, being shiftless for many years before finding his niche as a librarian.

In 1904, ill with heart problems, Reverend Joseph was living alone at Gilbert Street.[38] At the beginning of January 1907, he became seriously ill. He was adjudged "senile" and treated for "fatty decomposition of the heart." He died at his home on January 25. He was 83 years old. Dr. Bodle, his brother-in-law, signed his death certificate the same day.[39] His surviving children attended his wake and funeral, and he was cremated two days later. He was buried next to Margaret at Lone Mountain Cemetery in San Francisco.

His obituary, "Rev. Strong is Called to Rest," appeared in the *Oakland Tribune* the day after he died. It recounted his career in Hawai'i and called him "a pioneer resident of Oakland," and, though it would have irritated him no end, listed Wellesley College as his alma mater.[40]

NOTES:

1 Dwight Strong obituary, *San Francisco Chronicle,* Dec. 6, 1938

2 Dwight, Rev. Benjamin W., *The History of the Descendants of Elder John Strong of Northhampton, Mass.,* Vol. 1 of 2 vols., (Albany, New York: Joel Munsell, 1871) 412–413

3 Dwight, *History of the Descendants* 412.

4 *New York Times,* Mar. 6, 1855: "Rev. J. D. Strong, lady and infant" sailed on the *SS George Law* (i.e., Elizabeth, but Joe, though with them, was not recorded in the paper; *The Friend,* however, reported in its June 1855 issue that "Rev. J.D. Strong, lady and two children" arrived on the *Spitfire* on May 1.); see also website: "Passenger Lists—Bound for California," www.pt5dome.com/PassHome.html

5 *F,* June 1855.

6 *F,* Feb. 3, 1855.

7 *F,* Dec. 1857.

8 Strong's sermons were: *The Nation's Sorrow: A Discourse on the Death of Abraham Lincoln, delivered in the Larkin St. Presbyterian Church, San Francisco, Apr. 16, 1865,* (San Francisco: G.L. Kenney & Co., 1865); and *A Plea Against Killing: A Discourse Occasioned by the Terry-Broderick Duel, Delivered in the First Presbyterian Church at Oakland, California, Sunday, Sept. 25, 1859,* (San Francisco: Towne, 1859).

9 Strong, Rev. J. D. *Child Life in Many Lands* (Boston: D. Lothrop and Co., undated, but 1870) 9.

10 Dwight, *History of the Descendants* 412.

11 Strong, *Child Life* 178.

12 Strong, Elizabeth, *Autobiographical Sketch,* (10-page memoir by Joseph Strong's sister, handwritten, unpaginated, and undated, but possibly ca. 1915; BANC Mss. C-H 171, Bancroft Library, U of California at Berkeley), [Page numbers refer to author's annotated typescript] 1

13 Strong, *Sketch* 1

14 Strong, *Sketch* 1

15 Dabagh, Jean L., and Esperett-Case, Suzette, *Central Union Church: A Hundred and One years 1887–1988,* (Honolulu, 1988) 23–24.

16 Dwight, *History of the Descendants* 412.

17 *F,* Dec. 1857.

18 *PCA,* Dec. 10, 1857.

19 *PCA,* Dec. 10, 1857.

20 Dwight, *History of the Descendants* 412.

21 Issler, Anne R., *Happier For His Presence: San Francisco and Robert Louis Stevenson* (Standford, California: Stanford U P, 1949).

22 Strong, *Sketch* 2.

23 Dwight, *History of the Descendants* 412.

[24] Walker, Franklin, *San Francisco's Literary Frontier,* (New York: Knopf, 1939) 258.

[25] California Information File: *Rev. J.D. Strong,* California State Library at Sacramento.

[26] *West Yarmouth Congregational Church History* (bound, handwritten mss. summary of church records, 1840–1940, 271 pp., "Copy from the old Records." (List of pastors, birth, marriage, funeral, and admission records, chronology, index) WYCC archives, West Yarmouth, Mass.) 260.

[27] *Barnstable Patriot,* "The Congregational Church in Hyannis" Apr. 24, 1877 (newspapers, bound volumes, Hyannis Public Library, Hyannis, Mass.); and Vuilleumier, Marion Rawson, *Churches on Cape Cod* (Taunton, Mass.: Wm. S. Sullwold Publishing, 1974) 74, 76.

[28] Strong, Joseph Dwight, Jr., Letters (identified in the Notes as "JDS to CWS," refer to letters from Joseph Dwight Strong and Belle Strong in the Charles Warren Stoddard Collection, reference HM 37959-38165, originals at the Huntington Library, San Marino, Calif.) JDS to CWS, 22 July 1893.

[29] *West Yarmouth Congregational Church History* 260.

[30] *Barnstable Patriot* issues May 12, 1868, June 23, 1868, May 4, 1868, Aug. 4, 1868, Aug. 8, 1868, and Apr. 24, 1877.

[31] "Authors and Books for Children, Margaret Sidney: The Five Little Peppers and Their Creator," at www.elliemik.com/sidney

[32] Strong, Wallace K[ealoha], *Souvenir: Thirtieth Anniversary of the Official Reporter, 1876–1906,* (Eureka, California: Jewett Brothers, 1906) copy at the California History Room, California State Library, Sacramento 2

[33] Letters, JDS to CWS, Dec. 18, 1894.

[34] Letters, JDS to CWS, undated, probably July 1895.

[35] Joseph Theroux, "Stevenson's Pillow: A Sketch of Austin Strong," *Historic Nantucket,* (Winter, 2002) 5–9.

[36] *F,* Sept. 1, 1886; Greene, Charles S., "California Artists: II. Joseph D. Strong Jr.," *Overland Monthly,* 27 (May 1896): 502.

[37] California Information File: *Rev. J.D. Strong.*

[38] California Information File: *Rev. J.D. Strong.*

[39] California Board of Health death certificate #7-000285, filed Jan. 25, 1907.

[40] *Oakland Tribune,* Jan. 26, 1907; another obituary (unidentified source) is attached opposite p. 1 of Strong's *Souvenir.*

DAVID ZMIJEWSKI

Mark Twain's Dual Visions of Hawai'i: Censoring the Creative Self

ON MARCH 7, 1866, Samuel Langhorne Clemens, who came to be known to the world as Mark Twain, shipped aboard the steamer *Ajax* for Honolulu, the capital of the Sandwich Islands. Already known as a humorist on the West Coast, Twain had accepted an assignment to write a series of travel letters for the Sacramento *Daily Union*. This was Twain's first trip off the North American continent, and the four-month sojourn to the island kingdom influenced the writer throughout his career.[1] As a traveling correspondent for a major newspaper, Twain had an agenda to follow. Richard Pressman describes Twain as a "capitalist hero," a role that would require attention to details other than the humor for which he was becoming famous.[2] Of course, Twain entertained his readers with the Hawaiian letters, but he often juxtaposed such anecdotes with detailed reports concerning the Islands and their importance for America.

The humorist was on a serious mission, and he realized that unsubstantiated remarks could damage his career. Although he had earned a reputation for being controversial in San Francisco, Twain tempered his reports and avoided certain contentious topics while in Hawai'i. The *Union* was Twain's only public platform where he published opin-

David Zmijewski has previously written on Mark Twain for the Journal. *He is completing a book that traces the Hawaiian influence on Mark Twain in* Adventures of Huckleberry Finn. *Dr. Zmijewski holds a Ph.D. in American Studies from the University of Hawai'i at Mānoa and is an associate professor of American Studies at Baika Women's University in Osaka, Japan.*

The Hawaiian Journal of History, vol. 38 (2004)

ions on the state of Island affairs, that is, until he returned to San Francisco and took the Hawaiian adventures on the lecture circuit. Twain's first public performance, which was held on October 2, 1866, was a resounding success; so much so, that Twain toured California and Nevada all through the autumn of that year talking up Hawai'i in town after town. Since each venue was different, Twain soon learned that the demands of individual audiences had to be considered if he wanted to continue to draw crowds. Not only were his lectures regularly adapted, but his own views as well were undergoing a transformation. The differences between his private opinions (basically those found in the journals of the trip) and the ones he made public verify that Mark Twain was holding back. His role as a "capitalist hero" required Twain to yield to the greater causes of regional and national interest, and this often prevented him from speaking his mind. In this paper, I will examine Twain's public and private writings on Hawai'i in an attempt to analyze how the reporter's opinions on economic cooperation, the monarchy, and the American Protestant missionaries in the Islands, differed depending on whom he was writing for or speaking to.

I

In the 25 letters published in the *Union,* Twain used humor as a buffer between more serious topics. Edgar Marquess Branch writes of the three objectives of the mission to Hawai'i. Twain reported on

> Hawaiian industry and trade, with particular reference to American commercial enterprise. He wanted to explain the islands and their populations: the natives' surroundings and traditions, and their social and political life. Finally, he wanted to amuse his readers with the personal, sensational, and fictitious.[3]

On this assignment, Twain found respectability, and it was a new outfit for him to don in public. The hoaxster who had befuddled readers with tales of massacres and petrified men, as well as the "criminal" who skipped out of Virginia City rather than face death in a duel suddenly commanded a reputable voice.[4] Henry Nash Smith interprets the change and what it meant for Twain. Smith explains, "This assignment tended to detach him from his irresponsible Bohemianism and make him into a spokesman for respectable opinion."[5] In other words, Twain's assignment for the *Union* changed not only the substance of the message, but also the messenger himself. By accepting the post, the humorist had expanded his audience, yet because of the nature of the appointment, he had also voluntarily consented to being reined in.

Twain wastes no time making the transition to respectability. His earliest letters written en route tell of the need for more American residents, capital, and a dependable means of commercial transport between the Islands and the mainland. In his "Second Letter to the *Union*," Twain is decidedly in favor of establishing the California-Hawai'i steamer line:

> But the main argument in favor of a line of fast steamers is this: They would soon populate these islands with Americans, and loosen that French and English grip which is gradually closing around them, and which will result in a contest before many years as to which of the two shall seize and hold them. I leave America out of this contest, for her influence and her share in it have fallen gradually away until she is out in the cold now, and does not even play third fiddle to this European element.
>
> But if California can send capitalists down here in seven or eight days time and take them back in nine or ten, she can fill these islands full of Americans and regain her lost foothold.[6]

Twain regards the *Ajax* and ships like her essential if America hoped to increase its clout in Hawai'i. Dependable steamship connections would lead to more economic interdependence. However, to help precipitate this eventuality other measures were needed. In the "Third Letter to the *Union*," Twain discusses the advantages of trade between the United States and Hawai'i before proffering an opinion on how to secure those mutual benefits. Twain writes, "Let Congress moderate the high duties somewhat; secondly—let the Islands be populated with Americans."[7] Twain surmised that investment in the islands would boom once the U.S. government took a committed stance. Political decisiveness would encourage capitalists who required some guarantee that their investments would be backed by tangible support.

In 1866, Twain believed in America and the extension of its influence; the anti-imperialist character of his later years had not yet formed. The ideas quoted above are the public expressions of a man following an agenda; however, there was a private side to the writer which often clashed with the public one.

At the time of Twain's trip there was renewed interest in a trade reciprocity treaty between the United States and Hawai'i. With a great deal of support from the sugar planters, most of whom were American residents in Hawai'i, the proposed legislation aimed to stabilize the economy by eliminating tariffs on island sugar exported to the United States. Numerous other items would also pass duty free between the two nations once this treaty became law, but sugar stood out as the most important item for Hawai'i.[8] It was supposed that such a treaty would revitalize the ailing industry and also encourage more investment from the mainland. In light of the decline in whaling, Twain thought that a flourishing sugar industry represented the best way of rescuing the island economy. The entire "Twenty-Third Letter to the *Union*" is an exposé on the sugar industry. Twain calls Hawai'i "the king of the sugar world, as far as astonishing productiveness is concerned."[9] This letter contains detailed statistics showing the dollar value of the sugar industry to the United States, and discusses the means to obtain cheap labor from China to replace the declining Native Hawaiian population. Twain also argues for the importation of Chinese laborers to California, then ends the letter with a jingoistic prediction of how rich California will become once the Pacific trade is secured.

In these letters, Twain fulfills the first purpose of his mission as documented by Branch. Yet, what did Twain really think about American economic intervention at this time? Although his personal papers contain a few brief mentions of the sugar industry and the discussion between annexation and reciprocity, Twain himself seems unconvinced of the best course. Despite his assertion that the elimination of the tariffs might save the sugar plantations, in his *Notebooks & Journals* Twain considers a more sobering reason for the difficulties: "*All* planters on the islands have begun too late . . . most of the plantations are in debt—to see their extravagance, it is a wonder they survive at all."[10]

Twain was not above pandering to audiences when there were

advantages to be had; however, his equivocation sometimes makes it hard for scholars to understand just where Twain stood. Privately, he juxtaposes a local opinion on annexation with his own on reciprocity. Concerning the former, Twain explains that "Americans want annexation, of course, to get rid of duties," before advancing his own cautious view on the latter, "It would be fair to have reciprocity anyway—then—no duties at either end, Cal would have entire S. I [*sic*] trade."[11]

Twain visited sugar plantations on O'ahu, Hawai'i, and Maui, and occasionally stayed as an overnight guest. He collected statistics and compiled an extensive report on the industry in the "Twenty-Third Letter to the *Union*." As a paid reporter, Twain had to accommodate his employer, but when he stepped onto the lecture platform Twain became his own boss. Since the responsibility for success rested solely on Twain's own shoulders, the lecturer had to be cognizant of the prejudices and opinions of his audience. California-Hawai'i trade was a topic of much discussion on the West Coast, and although Twain's lectures were billed as humor, he still managed to spotlight serious issues, some of which he had already introduced in the *Union* letters. In the copies and fragments of the lectures that survive, Twain waxes patriotic. He heralds the richness of the sugar industry and its potential contributions to America's coffers. In an incomplete manuscript of the lecture, Twain declares that the duties are crushing the planters and destroying the industry. He writes, "the planters always <u>will</u> be burdened with that exasperating duty until the Islands belong to America. . . ." He then continues, "I have dwelt upon this subject to show you that these islands have a genuine importance to America—an importance which is not generally appreciated by our citizens."[12]

Twain did express ideas intended to influence the public at a time when reciprocity and annexation were newsworthy subjects. Yet, what was best for the Islands does not seem to have been the main concern for him at this time; he suggested that America should pass mutually beneficial trade legislation to put some distance between Hawai'i and the Europeans jockeying for control. Twain did shift his public stance about American intervention six years later following the death of King Kamehameha V in December of 1872. Twain wrote two letters for the New York *Daily Tribune*, and in the second of those letters, dated January 9, 1873, Twain ends with a section entitled "Why We

Should Annex." In this sarcastic diatribe, Twain trumpets the benefits that the mighty American civilization would bring to its new citizens. He closes:

> We *must* annex those people. . . . We can make that little bunch of sleepy islands the hottest corner on earth, and array it in the moral splendor of our high and holy civilization. Annexation is what the poor islanders need. 'Shall we to men benighted, the lamp of life deny?'[13]

By 1873, Twain had two successful books under his belt and another popular lecture based on his 1867 trip to the Holy Land, but in 1866 he had been a novice lecturer and regional reporter with no committed following. The younger man had yielded to caution.

In the same lecture quoted above (P & S Draft No. 5), Twain deleted two passages that more strongly advocated the annexationist alternative. In both of these sections, he suggests that independence is not a viable option for Hawai'i. Twain first wrote, then crossed out, "The property has got to fall to some heir— + why not to the U. States?"[14] Since the second of these excised quotes is very hard to decipher, Twain obviously felt strongly about withdrawing this opinion from the script. In that passage, Twain explains: "The Kanakas will all die out some day + then the Sand. Is. are going to be gobbled up by France or England or America. I don't know which, by America may be if such be the will of Providence."[15]

In 1866, Twain made a case that a Hawai'i-U.S. trade treaty would rescue the Islands' plantations and benefit America. He claimed that the high duties were hurting the planters and would ultimately destroy the sugar industry unless Congress removed the tariffs. He did not openly tout annexation, yet as the omitted passages show, he had originally intended to. The annexationist idea was gaining support in political circles, and soon even the possibility of a military takeover was to become a real concern.[16] However, there may be another reason Twain deleted those passages. Although both passages can be interpreted as supporting annexation, in them Twain speculates about the demise of the Hawaiian people. With American residents and capital in place and few if any Native Hawaiians to interfere, inheritance of the Islands rather than annexation was possible. A smooth transition in power, yes, but rather a tactless position to publish.

II

At the time of Twain's visit, Hawai'i was a constitutional monarchy. King Kamehameha V ruled the nation, and the legislature composed of local representatives was watched over by ministers, some of whom were emigrants from the U.S. and Europe. Differences of opinions concerning the welfare of the nation led to argumentative legislative sessions which the 30-year-old, patriotically inclined Twain wrote about. He championed America, but what he saw in Hawai'i caused him to question the spread of democracy. Twain actually favored the 1864 decision to revoke universal male suffrage. Amy Kaplan verifies this when she writes that Twain "supported the decision of the Hawaiian government to rescind universal suffrage and reestablish property holding as a requirement for voting. . . ."[17] So where did Twain stand on monarchical rule and democratic reforms taking place in Hawai'i? Well, it really depended on whom he was addressing. As a reporter, Twain could not afford to alienate the monarchy, since according to him, Americans were already operating at a disadvantage. Twain describes the prejudice against Americans in both his published and private writings. In the *Union,* he has this to say:

> One of our lady passengers from San Francisco, who brings high recommendations, has purchased a half interest in the hotel, and she shows such a determination to earn success that I heartily wish she may achieve it—and the more so because she is an American, and if common remark can be depended upon the foreign element here will not allow an American to succeed if a good strong struggle can prevent it.[18]

Here, Twain erects the framework of a conflict. Curiously, he refers to a "foreign element." But what were he and the Americans? As the previous discussion confirms, Twain argued that America should increase its demographic presence as well as its business in Hawai'i. In effect, an influx of people and investment would lead to American domination. But to take control from whom? The Hawaiians? No,

Twain perceives the threat to be the British and the French. Somehow, they had inveigled themselves into the king's good graces, and because of this, Americans were suffering. The main foreign influences on the king were: the Anglican Bishop of Honolulu, Thomas Nettleship Staley; the minister of foreign affairs, a Frenchman Charles De Varigny; and an American expatriate who served as the minister of finance, Charles Coffin Harris. Given this international representation, one would think the interests of all countries were being considered equally, but to Twain this was not the reality.

Twain regarded Americans as bearers of civilization, religion, and prosperity, and in private he railed against the king's prejudice toward Americans. Blaming the king's disdain of Americans on a racial incident that occurred long ago, Twain expostulates that the king:

> remembers to this day, & grieves over a trifling unintentional offense offered in the US. years ago to his *private* individuality—*not* to his official <great> rank—& who hates America and Americans for it yet—but who is so guiltless of genuine, <true,> manly & kingly pride as to forget that his fathers, his whole people & his whole country have on noted occasions <not far in the past,> to wh I have referred, been humiliated, insulted, wronged, abused—<yea, at least figuratively speaking,> spit upon & trampled under foot—by <the> two great *nations* (not insignificant, unofficial <& irresponsible> nobodies in a steamboat), by two nations, England and France—<but,><yet> and who to-day, purchased by the gimcrack & tinsel adulation those peoples have conferred upon his house, <he> with a spirit proper to a soul that is capable of remembering a trivial <woul> wound inflicted upon its poor personal vanity & forgetting a great national affront, licks the hands of the foreign princes who kicked & cuffed Hawaii-nei through her representatives his fathers.
>
> The King gets his <cherished compliments> <cheap but> loved and cherished compliments from the English <Court> & his revenues from the Americans—his gew-gaws & cheap adulation from the one & whatever of real worth & greatness his country <is possessed of> possesses from the other—& with characteristic consistency he worships the men who have degraded his country & hates the strong & steadfast <American> hands that have lifted <it> her up.
>
> Dam! [*sic*]
>
> Royalty!—I don't think much of Hawaiian Royalty![19]

In private, Twain accused the king of prejudicial treatment of Americans and of damaging the interests of the nation; in public, though, he had to be careful about disparaging the monarch. Twain was not a representative of the government and therefore possessed no official voice. Inflammatory remarks could have proved an embarrassment for the United States, and might even have derailed him from the career track along which he was hurrying. Perhaps it was fortunate that he stumbled on Harris and Staley, for they proved suitable targets for his anger over what he deemed an official policy of prejudice against Americans.[20]

The king was a genuine source of news, and one he had to write up, but as just seen some of his opinions were not suitable for publication. Twain had to devise a way of bringing the king and other nobility into his reports. He did this initially through humor. In the "Fourth Letter to the *Union,*" Twain describes the landing at Honolulu and his first glimpse of Hawaiian "royalty." On having the king pointed out to him, Twain explains how I "took out my notebook and put him down: 'Tall, slender, dark; full-bearded; green frock coat, with lappels [*sic*] and collar bordered with gold band an inch wide; plug hat-broad gold band around it; royal costume looks too much like a livery; . . .'"[21] Disappointment soon follows. The man he has depicted is not really the king, but a carriage driver for some dignitary. The hapless Twain had missed the monarch by a day, for "the comfortable, easy going King Kamehameha . . . had been sitting on a barrel on the wharf, the day before, fishing; . . ."[22]

Here, Twain introduces a "king" to his readers. This seemingly innocent humor masks his sarcastic intent. Royalty should exude a recognizable regalia. Twain takes the nobility of Hawai'i down a notch by confusing the king with a carriage driver. The sarcasm finds expression in the image of the monarch perched on a barrel, fishing, which is an all-too-democratic pose for a king. To evade censure, Twain was not openly derogatory about the king, his appearance, or his policies in public, but in his artful manner he depicted Kamehameha V as being indistinguishable from the rest of humanity.

So was the king such a vindictive, unforgiving man as Twain wrote privately? Or a source of levity as shown above? Twain's private comments go so far as to cast racial slurs on the king. In one virulent notebook entry, he refers to the monarch as a "heathen blackamoor."[23]

Yet, even in private Twain is not always so deprecatory; some personal comments are laudable. Notebook entries on both Kamehameha IV and V verify this. He writes:

> IV was remarkable man—ambitious—proud, accomplished, profound in thought & wisdom—a deep thinker—ashamed of his family & did not like old K I & Cooks murder recalled—did not like to be reminded that he came of race of savages.—thought he was worthy of nobler origin.[24]

On Kamehameha V, Twain has this to say: "Present King is penetrating—sound judgment—dignity—accomplished—has good sense & courage & decision—& became acquainted with business by long apprenticeship as Minister of Interior."[25]

Even though the above comments praise the present and former kings, Twain cannot refrain from bringing up the past. His opinion that Kamehameha IV was chagrined by his heritage has some credence, for it was he who requested an English Bishop be dispatched to Honolulu and who named his son after Queen Victoria's husband. The *Union* letters are filled with pages of historical references documenting the savagery of the nobles and commoners. This non-Christian history seems to have obsessed Twain. He warns that the pull of the past could be overpowering even to the enlightened. Privately, he concedes that the

> King is a heathen—an old sorceress has him under her thumb—picks out the fish he may eat—tells him <where> in what house he may sleep, &c. Accompanies him in all his excursions. He was educated in a Christian school but has never submitted himself to Christianity—discovered his predilections for heathenism in his youth.[26]

If the monarch himself could fall prey to the cultural pitfalls of the past and reject the "enlightenment" that Americans had bestowed on the country, would not others have difficulties assimilating to the new cultural norms? Perhaps, yet once again Twain's public persona espouses opinions different than the private man.

Twain maintains that a complete transformation from a heathen to an educated Christian was possible. Here too, though, Twain makes much of the wild past. In the first of two letters dealing with the legislature, Twain describes the president of the assembly, M. Kekuanaoa, the king's father. Twain paints a portrait of a handsome man with a noble bearing. As usual, though, he cannot avoid placing this man in the cultural framework of heathenism popularized by 19th-century chroniclers of Hawai'i. Twain takes the reader on a speculative journey into the world that Kekuanaoa may have once inhabited. He soliloquizes:

> I could not help saying to myself, 'This man, as naked as the day he was born, and war-club and spear in hand, has charged at the head of a horde of savages against other hordes of savages far back in the past, and reveled in slaughter and carnage; has worshipped wooden images on his bended knees; has seen hundreds of his race offered up in heathen temples as sacrifices to hideous idols. . .'[27]

After more examples of such sensationalist press, Twain continues:

> Look at him, sitting there presiding over the deliberations of a legislative body, among whom are white men—a grave, dignified, statesmanlike personage, and as seemingly natural and fitted to the place as if he had been born in it and had never been out of it in his lifetime.[28]

Even though the man overseeing the workings of the government is educated and refined, Twain still reminds the readers of the distant past of the Hawaiian people. And, one must consider, why?

Twain implies that regression was a real possibility; therefore, reporting on the progress made after the arrival of the Americans was integral to his mission. If Hawai'i hoped to enter the modern world, the past must be discarded once and for all. There was another source of lingering danger which Twain did not approve of, yet here, too, his pen was stilled—immodesty was not a suitable topic for newspapers. He wrote at length on the demise of Princess Victoria Ka'ahumanu Kamamalu which took place while he was in Hawai'i. Three of his letters provide minute details of the month-long mourning ceremony and royal funeral. However, nowhere in those reports does Twain publish the cause of Princess Victoria's death. He notes the reason only in his journals. Why would he withhold this information from his reading public? Surely, Americans would be curious as to why a young, healthy, benevolent, Christian woman of the nobility passed away so suddenly. He obviously was aware that the truth would have raised embarrassing questions about the moral integrity of Hawaiian nobility, and perhaps about the nation as a whole. Twain uses historical references to supplement his interpretations of the funeral rituals, which he describes as "heathen orgies."[29] He blames Bishop Staley for this recidivistic behavior that negated four decades of progress under the auspices of the American missionaries. The reason for the princess's death might not have jeopardized relations between the two nations, yet Twain prudently chooses not to headline events that might impede the formation of a stronger alliance. This is how Twain describes the cause of death in his private writings, "Pr. V. died in forcing abortion—kept half a dozen bucks to do her washing, & has suffered 7 abortions."[30]

Twain was obliged to write reports that reinforced the need for American investment and encouraged closer economic ties between the two nations, so it is probable that he understood any attacks on Hawaiian royalty could have led to a straining of relations. Mind you, the monarchy might not have concerned itself with the reports of an insignificant writer like Twain, but if American public opinion shifted after reading his reports, the results would have been counterproductive.

Of course, royalty would have been a topic of interest to Americans, and Twain realized that his American audience wanted news of the monarchy. Yet, as many of the contradictory comments thus far have shown, Twain's ideas varied greatly. Still, kings were something of an enigma to the American experience, and the existence of monarchy could be detrimental to American democratic interests.

Twain must have believed that a favorable representation of the king was vital if his countrymen were to be persuaded of the benefits of better trade relations. The legislature was divided into representatives of the people and nobles, the latter of which Twain explains served as the "mouthpieces" of the king.[31] Democracy at this time was primarily an American offshoot, although, waves of change had incorporated the concepts in various forms around the world. According to Twain, Hawai'i had adopted a democratic form of government which placed limits on the power of the people, but none on the monarch. Twain explains that "even if the Representatives were to assert their strength and override the Nobles and pass a law which did not suit the King, his Majesty would veto the measure and that would be the end of it, for there is no passing a bill over *his* veto."[32] This uncontested veto power is a fundamental difference between the Hawaiian constitutional monarchy and American democracy. America has a system of checks and balances which prevent any president from usurping too much power. If Hawai'i was, in fact, ruled by a tyrannical monarch, this disclosure might negatively impact America's future there. Twain dismisses this fear by adapting his private assessment of the king's acumen for the *Union.* He writes that the monarch is not capricious or dangerous in the least:

> The King is invested with very great power. But he is a man of good sense and excellent education, and has an extended knowledge of business, which he acquired through long and arduous training as Minister of the Interior under the late King, and therefore he uses his vast authority wisely and well.[33]

Just in case his message was missed, Twain published "A Correction" in his "Thirteenth Letter to the *Union.*" Again, he makes it clear to Californians that the king is trustworthy. If indeed, Kamehameha had lapsed in his youth, he had repented and earned forgiveness. Twain writes:

> Some people in California have an idea that the King of the Sandwich Islands is a man who spends his time idling about the town of Honolulu with individuals of questionable respectability, and drinking habitually and to excess. This impression is wrong. Before he ascended the throne he was 'faster' than was well for him or for his good name, but, like the hero of Agincourt, he renounced his bad habits and discarded his Falstaffs when he became King, and since that time has conducted himself as becomes his high position.[34]

Twain was irate that the monarch favored the British, yet a well-educated, business-savvy king would make a good ally. Since the cause of the king's prejudice against Americans was long past, would not a wise leader, who hoped to do the best for his country, forget such a trifling insult? Twain used his discourse to promote better relations between the two countries, and his diplomatic treatment of the monarch reveals that he knew certain subjects were sacrosanct. A "heathen," superstitious king could prove unreliable, or at least, unpredictable, and thereby an embarrassment, if not a real danger, to America. No matter what Twain's real opinions on the monarchy were, he only published those that promoted his mission without detracting from, or causing harm to, his own growing reputation.

III

Twain is very clear in his opinion that the people of Hawai'i were better off after the arrival of the American missionaries than they had been before. He credits the missionaries for transforming Hawai'i into one of the most educated nations in the world. But if they were so educated, why does he constantly refer to what he seems to regard as an atrocious past? The main reason may have been to show that no matter how far Hawaiians had come, there was much further to go. In an unpublished draft of his Sandwich Island Lecture, Twain details the impact the missionaries had on the people of Hawai'i. He writes:

> They were a rusty set all round—those Kanakas—in those days. But the missionaries came and knocked off the shackles from the whole race—broke the power of the King + the chiefs + set the common man free + elevated his wife to an equality with him— + got a patch of land set apart + secured to each to hold forever. And the missionaries set up schools + churches + printing presses and taught the people the Christian religion after a fashion + taught the whole nation to read + write with facility in the native tongue— + now I suppose there is not an uneducated Kanaka in the Kingdom. <The K's are as nearly civilized too, as they can ever be—+ that is not saying a very great deal.>[35]

Surely, from the viewpoint of Twain and the missionary-historians, Hawaiians had made great progress, but the attitudes of these 19th-century observers were not, as we now know, accurate interpretations of Hawaiian society. By pointing out the foibles of the local people, such writers may have actually encouraged mainlanders to step up efforts in acculturating the natives. For Twain, though, the missionaries were more malleable as a source of humor than the monarchy. Although their mission to convert and civilize was considered a worthy one, humor at their expense was not forbidden. And since the missionaries could be perceived as being both, accommodating and overbearing, Twain could write from either perspective without compromising his objectives. Even with all of Twain's waffling in his treatment of the missionaries one thing remains true, his sympathies lay with the Americans rather than the British ecclesiastics. In his "Fourteenth Letter to the *Union*," Twain satirizes the American missionaries, but he rails more bitterly against Bishop Staley for his meddling. Twain writes:

> Mr. Staley, my Lord Bishop of Honolulu—who was built into a Lord by the English Bishop of Oxford and shipped over here with a fully equipped 'Established Church' in his pocket—has frequently said that the natives of these islands are morally and religiously in a worse condition to-day than they were before the American missionaries ever came here. Now that is not true . . . Our missionaries are our missionaries—and even if they were our devils I would not want any English prelate to slander them.[36]

Twain had to take sides. His assignment required him to support the American intervention from the past to the present, and also to show how improved relations would be better for the future of both countries. The American missionaries may have had their faults, which Twain sometimes exploited for humor, but the good they had done the nation was a fact he truly defended.

What had the American missionaries given the people of Hawai'i? In his "Sixth Letter to the *Union*," Twain juxtaposes their accomplishments with comments about what conditions had been like for the common people in the pre-missionary days. He explains, "The missionaries have clothed them [the Hawaiians], educated them, broken up the tyrannous authority of their chiefs, and given them freedom and the right to enjoy whatever the labor of their hand and brains produces, with equal laws for all and punishment for all alike who transgress them."[37] Here, Twain promulgates definite democratic progress with which Americans would certainly approve. The humorist, however, could not help analyzing the cost at which such achievements were obtained. Earlier in the same letter, Twain writes of the courageous missionaries who

> braved a thousand privations to come and make them [the Hawaiians] permanently miserable by telling them how beautiful and how blissful a place heaven is, and how nearly impossible it is to get there; and showed the poor native how dreary a place perdition is and what unnecessarily liberal facilities there are for going to it; showed him how, in his ignorance, he had gone and fooled away all his kinfolks to no purpose [he is referring to human sacrifices]; showed him what rapture it is to work all day long for fifty cents to buy food for next day with, as compared with fishing for pastime and lolling in the shade through eternal Summer, and eating of the bounty that nobody labored to provide but Nature. How sad it is to think of the multitudes who have gone to their graves in this beautiful island and never knew there was a hell![38]

Twain could poke fun at the missionaries, yet at the same time, he could admire their contributions. The missionaries did not approve of his humor, as an entry in his notebooks confirms. He confesses that "The mish's are outraged by the levity of my letters, & have so expressed themselves—but in sorrow, not in anger."[39]

There was, however, a more cynical side to his interpretation of missionary influence. Twain perceived the missionaries as being interested in securing private gain here on earth, while opening heaven to the benighted Hawaiians. Historical documents, such as this June 21, 1852, letter by Reverend W. P. Alexander, confirm this trend. Alexander confessed that not only did he survey land on Saturdays for profit (in direct violation with the decrees of the church), but he also possessed 32 cattle. Alexander defended his right to work for the benefit of his family's comfort, as well as that of his flock; "I did desire to retain as close and intimate a relation with the mission as possible and was glad to be reckoned a corresponding member; yet if this involves a subjection to the arbitrary rule of the Prud. Com I do not desire to continue in the relation."[40] What did Twain think about missionaries who profited from the privileged positions they held in the community? An answer might be seen in his "Nineteenth

Letter to the *Union*," where he relates a story about one clergyman who turned a substantial profit by speculating in land. Twain explains that the unnamed missionary acted to prevent the native-owned land bordering his own from falling into the hands of some foreigners of whom he knew nothing. The missionary paid $1,500 and with no further investment soon sold the land to another foreigner for $10,000 in gold. Twain's none-too-subtle irony becomes clear when he writes, "We naturally swell with admiration when we contemplate a sacrifice like this."[41]

There were opportunities to make money in Hawai'i and, it is true, that some missionaries were involved in land transactions, sugar plantations, and politics. Twain's private writings document how some families expanded their interests from the ecclesiastical to the secular. One entry explains how votes in the nation's legislature could be controlled: "House of Nobles appointed by King, & Lower House elective. Under Universal suffrage, Missionaries used vote their flocks for certain man, & then sit at home & control him. One member (missionary's son) said out loud in open <ne> house, he controlled eleven votes (a majority) in the House."[42] As always with Twain, there are contradictions. On the same page in his notebooks, he applauds the honesty of a very influential missionary of an earlier era, Gerrit P. Judd. Twain writes: "Judd always kept country out of debt & cleaned up his tracks—since been out country gone badly in debt. He went out poor as a rat. To prove his honesty, he *was the government* & might have cabbaged the whole country."[43]

Twain often commented on the missionaries in his letters and private writings. Interestingly, it is his private writings that are more often tolerant than the public writings. This is because the missionaries were a rich resource for innocent, good fun. Twain could ridicule them without damaging the Church, because his reading audience would not have taken seriously his attacks on those who forsook the comforts of home to convert a nation to Christ. The following list of missionary accomplishments reveals what Twain truly thought of the 46-year-old American mission in Hawai'i:

> Missionaries have made honest men out of nation of thieves.
> Instituted marriage.
> Created homes.

Lifted woman to same rights & privileges enjoyed elsewhere.
Abolished infanticide.
" intemperance.
Diminished licentiousness (the hula, where copulation in public).
Given equal laws.
" common Native homesteads.
" whereby chief's power of life & death over his subject is taken away.
In a great measure abolished idolatry and (until this King & his Bishop Church) destroyed power of Kahunas (now however, King licenses them).
Have *well* educated the people.[44]

A modern-day scholar could not only prove that Twain's comments are inaccurate, but may also argue that the missionaries aimed to destroy the culture of the Hawaiian people. However, Twain saw these as positive goals that not only showed the humanitarian, democratic spirit of the American mission, but which also paved the way for more investment. His own ideas on the achievements of the missionaries he recorded in his notebooks, but the public persona portrayed the missionaries differently. Twain begins his assessment of the missionaries with a disclaimer:

> I judge the missionary, but, with a modesty which is entitled to some credit, I freely confess that my judgment may err. Now, therefore, when I say that the Sandwich Islands missionaries are pious; hard-working; hard-praying; self-sacrificing; hospitable; devoted to the well-being of this people and the interests of Protestantism; bigoted; puritanical; slow; ignorant of all white human nature and natural ways of men, except the remnant of these things that are left in their own class or profession; old fogy—fifty years behind the age; uncharitable toward the weaknesses of the flesh; considering all shortcomings, faults and failures in the light of crimes, and having no mercy and no forgiveness for such—when I say this about the missionaries, I do it with the explicit understanding that it is only *my* estimate of them—not that of a Higher Intelligence—not that of even other sinners like myself. It is only *my* estimate, and it may fall far short of being a just one.[45]

Twain makes fun of the missionaries without slandering them. Perhaps, he just wanted them to lighten up. Even though the object of the following notebook entry is not specifically mentioned, it very possibly refers to the missionaries because of the context. Twain writes, "I'll tell you what's the matter with you—you have no conception of a joke—of anything but awful Puritan long-facedness & petrified facts."[46] Twain may have felt that the missionaries were too dogmatic and therefore incapable of appreciating his humor, yet this did not prevent him from teasing them. Although he made fun of their ideas and their inflexible attitudes, he also believed in their cause and sided with them against the Anglican Church. Except for the Natives—their exotic customs and culture—the missionaries were the major source of humor for Twain in his writings and lectures on Hawai'i.

Conclusion

Hawai'i was a landmark in Mark Twain's life. It provided him with unique subject matter that contributed to the advancement of his writing career. Equipped with these Hawaiian experiences, Twain embarked on the lecture circuit, and thereby reached new audiences and augmented his earning capacity. No matter how liberating the posting to Hawai'i proved, it also restrained Twain and taught him to moderate his reports when either employer or audience demanded discretion. And, it seems that Twain learned this lesson well. The reporter who wrote up the Islands in his letters for the *Union* came to understand that his personal opinions on economic cooperation, the monarchy, and the missionaries had to be censored if they did not comply with the objectives of the assignment. He could neither afford to hinder the purpose of his mission, nor get sidetracked from the career path on which he was travelling. Twain's "Letters to the *Union*" provide insight into how a budding writer could conform and still retain his creative expression.

Notes

1 For a detailed study of the Hawaiian influence on the fiction of Mark Twain, see David Zmijewski, *Huck Finn and Hawaii: A Study of Hawaiian Influence on the "Adventures of Huckleberry Finn"* (Ph.D. diss., U of Hawai'i at Mānoa, 1998).

2 Richard Pressman, "A Connecticut Yankee in Merlin's Cave: The Role of Contradiction in Mark Twain's Novel," *American Literary Realism: 1870–1910* XVI (Autumn 1983) 58–72, rpt. in *Mark Twain Critical Assessments,* Vol. III. Ed.

Stuart Hutchinson. (The Banks Mountfield, East Sussex: Helms Information Ltd., 1993) 476.

3 Edgar Marquess Branch, *The Literary Apprenticeship of Mark Twain* (Urbana; U of Illinois P, 1950) 161.

4 Some of Twain's hoaxes can be found in *Early Tales & Sketches Volume I 1851–1864,* Edgar Marquess Branch and Robert H. Hirst, eds. (Berkeley: U of California P, 1979). "Petrified Man" 155–9, and "A Bloody Massacre near Carson" 320–6. For an account of the duel, see *Mark Twain's Letters, Vol. 1,* Edgar Marquess Branch, Michael B. Frank, and Kenneth M. Sanderson, eds. (Berkeley: U of California P, 1988) 287–301.

5 Henry Nash Smith, *Mark Twain: The Development of a Writer* (Cambridge, Mass: The Belknap Press of Harvard U P, 1962) 13.

6 Mark Twain, "Second Letter to the Sacramento Daily *Union,*" Mar. 19, 1866, rpt. in Walter Francis Frear. *Mark Twain and Hawaii* (Chicago: Lakeside P, 1947) 266. All of Twain's "Letters to the *Union*" quoted hereafter are reprinted in Frear.

7 Twain, "Third Letter to the *Union,*" Mar. 1866, 271.

8 "The Sandwich Islands Treaty," *PCA,* Oct. 17, 1867:4. Some of the other products on which the tariffs would be eliminated were, coffee, raw cotton, fruits, vegetables, furs, and hides.

9 Twain, "Twenty-Third Letter to the *Union,*" Sept. 10, 1866, 398.

10 Mark Twain, *Notebooks & Journals,* Vol. I *(1855–1873),* Frederick Anderson, Michael B. Frank, and Kenneth M. Sanderson, eds. (Berkeley: U of California P, 1975) 126.

11 Twain, *Notebooks & Journals* 124.

12 Twain, "Sandwich-Island Lecture," No. 5 P & S Draft, 10. Mark Twain Project, Bancroft Library, U of California, Berkeley.

13 Twain, "The Sandwich Islands," Jan. 9, 1873, rpt. in Frear 500.

14 Twain, "Sandwich-Island Lecture," No. 5 P & S Draft, 2.

15 Twain, "Sandwich-Island Lecture," No. 5 P & S Draft, 12.

16 For an investigation of the threat of a takeover, see David Zmijewski, "The Conspiracy That Never Existed: How Hawai'i Evaded Annexation in 1868," *HJH,* vol. 37 (2003) 119–138.

17 Amy Kaplan, "Imperial Triangles: Mark Twain's Foreign Affairs," *Modern Fiction Studies* vol. 43, no. 1 (Spring 1997) 245.

18 Twain, "Fifth Letter to the *Union,*" Mar. 1866: 279.

19 Twain, *Notebooks & Journals Vol. I (1855–1873),* 150. < > indicates deletions in the text made by Twain.

20 For details on how Twain used Harris and Staley as targets in his letters and lectures, see, David Zmijewski, "Mark Twain and Hawaiian Politics: The Attack on Harris and Staley," *Mark Twain Journal* vol. 31, no. 2 (Fall 1993) 11–27.

21 Twain, "Fourth Letter to the *Union,*" Mar. 1866: 275.

22 Twain, "Fourth Letter to the *Union,*" 275.

23 Twain, *Notebooks & Journals* Vol. I *(1855–1873)* 149.

24 Twain, *Notebooks & Journals* 206.
25 Twain, *Notebooks & Journals* 206–207.
26 Twain, *Notebooks & Journals* 141.
27 Twain, "Twelfth Letter to the *Union*," May 23, 1866: 319.
28 Twain, "Twelfth Letter to the *Union*," 320.
29 Twain, "Sixteenth Letter to the *Union*," June 30, 1866: 352.
30 Twain, *Notebooks & Journals* Vol. I *(1855–1873)* 129.
31 Twain, "Twelfth Letter to the *Union*," May 23, 1866: 318.
32 Twain, "Twelfth Letter to the *Union*," 318.
33 Twain, "Twelfth Letter to the *Union*," 318.
34 Twain, "Thirteenth Letter to the *Union*," May 23, 1866: 326–327.
35 Mark Twain, "Sandwich Islands Lecture," No. 6 Bancroft, Crosshatch, Paris Paper: 38. Mark Twain Project, Bancroft Library, U of California, Berkeley. Bracketed passages have been deleted from the manuscript by Twain.
36 Twain, "Fourteenth Letter to the *Union*," June 22, 1866: 331.
37 Twain, "Sixth Letter to the *Union*," Mar. 1866: 289.
38 Twain, "Sixth Letter to the *Union*," 288.
39 Twain, *Notebooks & Journals* Vol. I *(1855–1873)* 153.
40 W. P. Alexander, Lahainaluna, to [Rev. Rufus Anderson, Honolulu], June 21, 1852, Alexander & Baldwin Papers, 1824–1911, HMCS, Honolulu, Hawai'i.
41 Twain, "Nineteenth Letter to the *Union*," Jul. 1866: 373.
42 Twain, *Notebooks & Journals* Vol. I *(1855–1873)* 115.
43 Twain, *Notebooks & Journals* 115.
44 Twain, *Notebooks & Journals* 154.
45 Twain, "Fourteenth Letter to the *Union*," June 22, 1866: 331.
46 Twain, *Notebooks & Journals* Vol. I *(1855–1873)* 154.

NORA CONATY

The Old *Shibai:* Japanese Theater in Hawai'i

The *Issei,* or first generation of Japanese in Hawai'i, traveled thousands of miles to a few isolated islands in the middle of the Pacific Ocean in search of wealth. Though far from home, they were not far from their theatrical roots. The *Issei* brought all kinds of Japanese performances with them. Theatrical presentations varied, ranging from professional to educational, from pure entertainment to political propaganda. Different types of theater could be experienced in the urban center of Honolulu or in rural plantation towns. Sometimes groups would come in from Japan. In all cases, the performances were an exciting even widely patronized by the Japanese community in Hawai'i.

Surprisingly, scholars have paid very little attention to this fascinating period in Hawai'i's theatrical history. For those who do not read or speak Japanese, most of the information about Japanese theater in Hawai'i is found in photographs, oral histories, newspaper clippings, and so forth. Piecing these bits of information into a comprehensive picture of the Japanese theater scene in turn of the century Hawai'i will be a challenge for interested academics, but I hope that this paper may be a small start. By identifying the performer, the audience, the venue, and the content of different performances they may be broken down into different types: professional, community, educational, and political. A brief overview of the types of Japanese theater in Hawai'i

Nara Conaty is currently pursuing her M.F.A. in costume design at the University of Hawai'i at Mānoa. She is a former member of the board of directors of Kumu Kahua Theatre and has great interest in local theater and theater history. She is a graduate of Yale University.

The Hawaiian Journal of History, vol. 38 (2004)

as compared to types of theater of the same era in Japan shows that, with the exception of state-supported professional companies, the range of performances available to Japanese in Hawai'i and Japanese of comparable socioeconomic standing in Japan were similar. The social and political functions of performances in Japan and in Hawai'i were also alike, although immigrants sometimes adapted old traditions to suit their new surroundings. Japanese theater in Hawai'i at the turn of the century was an important social activity whose primary role was to reaffirm the cultural identity and values of Japanese immigrants to Hawai'i.

Background

Japanese immigrants to Hawai'i came at a turbulent time. In the late 1800s, both Japan and Hawai'i were experiencing social and political upheaval. In the 1880s, the Native Hawaiian population was shrinking due to disease and low birth rates. The Hawaiian government, under pressure from American business leaders, looked abroad for laborers to support a growing sugar industry. Hawaiian government recruiters toured Japan, giving public speeches to promote plantation labor in Hawai'i. Japanese farmers in the provinces were struggling in the unstable socioeconomic circumstances of the time, and so they were a receptive audience.

Japanese immigrants who arrived in Hawai'i as early as 1868 but increased in number between 1885 to 1908 had been mostly tenant farmers in Japan. Peasants in the provinces at this time suffered: the price of rice fell, soil conditions were bad, the number of farmers who had to lease land increased, and wages dropped. Different provinces handled these economic problems in different ways. Historically, some provinces preferred to concentrate on internal development, while others sent workers out to more urban areas to make money. Provinces that had a history of sending workers to the city in times of economic stress had higher rates of emigration.[1] Dr. Allan Moriyama of Yokohama National University summarizes:

> from international events to local soil conditions, [factors] worked together to create a reasonable, logical option for these farmers, fishermen, and laborers. For perhaps the first time in their lives they saw

before them a chance to earn some money and better their lives, and many chose to do so.[2]

Professional Theater

The professional theater of Japan in the Meiji Era, in the late 19th century, was in a time of tremendous change. The opening of the country in 1854 introduced Western influence to all aspects of Japanese culture, and the theater was greatly affected. Several societies for the reform of the theater were organized. *Kabuki,* which had always been the theater of the common people, rose to be appreciated by the upper class and soon replaced *Noh* as the national theater. Current events became the basis for *kabuki* scripts, and women appeared in female roles on the professional stage.

It was customary for actors to tour provinces from time to time, often for financial reasons. According to Japanese scholar Toita Koji, a well-known *kabuki* actor of the Meiji Era toured "the provinces to pay off his debts."[3] Conflicts within theater companies also prompted tours. In September 1879, Morita Kan-ya, a daring actor fond of new experiments with Western theater, sent two actors "off touring the northern provinces, largely, it is said, because of Kan-ya's desire to keep those conservative actors at a distance."[4] It is conceivable that a tour to Hawai'i would be consistent with touring shows in the provinces—hard times with home audiences may have prompted a few companies to try to make a profit in Hawai'i. Franklin Odo and Kazuko Sinoto assert that "there was considerable social and cultural interchange between Hawaii and Japan. Theater troupes, athletic teams, and entertainers routinely traveled from Japan to Hawaii."[5]

Be that as it may, there are very few written records of professional companies touring to Hawai'i. The *Hawaiian Star,* a popular English language newspaper of the time, records the first professional Japanese theatrical company to perform in Honolulu in 1893. The paper lists the name of the company as "Japanese Theater Company" and refers to the production as "the Japanese play" rather than by title. There were 20 in the company—seven women and 13 men. They returned to Hawai'i in July of 1894. On February 4, 1919, the English section of the *Nippu Jiji,* a widely circulated Japanese language newspaper, contains an article titled, "Noted Theatrical Persons To Visit

Here Next Month." The theatrical persons named are K. Okamoto and his stage manager B. Isaka, and S. Uyeyama and U. Yamaura of the association of modern plays. They were all en route to the United States and Europe to "make a careful study of the arrangements of the stage and other theatrical managements" and obtain "theatrical informations." Unfortunately, there is no mention of any performances by these venerable visitors.

More can be ascertained from oral histories given by immigrant plantation workers. There are quite a few collections of oral histories focusing on Hawaiian plantations. These usually include histories of laborers from various cultural backgrounds. Information recorded in the oral histories of three Japanese plantation residents on different islands show that their theater-going experiences were comparable. Professional companies coming through Honolulu also toured plantation towns. Residents looked forward to these events, and the whole community would turn out to watch the *shibai*.

Mrs. Kiku Yoshida came to Hawai'i in 1916. She worked with her family on the plantation in Waipahu on the island of O'ahu. Mrs. Yoshida describes a "social club" that patronized the theater. Families paid a monthly fee to see movies and the occasional Japanese touring group. Tanji is the interviewer:

> YOSHIDA: There was an outdoor theatre behind the Hongwanji. There was a small stage which also housed the screen. Twice a month there was a movie. Sometimes there were entertainers from Japan. Actually it was called a social club.
>
> TANJI: Did you pay any dues?
>
> YOSHIDA: The dues was 25c a month for a family. I used to collect that from the families in the neighborhood. On the day there was a picture, people would lay their mats on the ground early in the morning. . . . it was an event everybody looked forward to.[6]

Mrs. Kishi Mukaisu worked on the plantation in Pu'ukoli'i, on the island of Maui. Here she recalls the effort it took to attend a performance. Hara is the interviewer, and Tsubaki is a friend of Kishi's who assisted the interview:

> HARA: Did you go to the theater in town?

KISHI: Yea, we walked down and we walked back (laughing) carrying our children. A play would come from Japan and where was it?

TSUBAKI: Wasn't it behind the Shingon Mission?

KISHI: Where was it?

TSUBAKI: The Japanese theater [was behind the Shingon Mission].

KISHI: The Japanese theater? Well, we would all walk and *oppa* (carry).

TSUBAKI: It was behind the Shingon Mission.

KISHI: Huh? That was the *mon picture.* The play?

TSUBAKI: The *mon picture* and the play.

(pause)

KISHI: To go down we would hurry and take the store car, but coming back was hard. (laughing) we would go down to the Daijingu Shrine. We'd all go down together but coming home, we'd have to walk all the way back.[7]

The Big Island of Hawai'i supported the largest Japanese population at the turn of the century. In Kona, a town where many residents were Japanese plantation runaways, Mr. Minoru Inaba describes his experience:

INABA: Every so often, the Japanese *shibai* used to come around. They had a stage there in Holualoa. Where the audience sat was on a grassy lot. We used to go about, oh, 4 o'clock in the afternoon and stake out the family's portion. During the show, we used to have chicken *hekka.* The elderly people, the adults, used to drink *sake.* And we used to have a grand old time. I still remember, when I was a youngster, the day after the *shibai* or show, I used to go there early in the morning to look around for money. You know, hoping that somebody dropped some money. By golly, we used to find, every so often, used to find money there.

INTERVIEWER: Who else went with you to do that?

INABA: Oh, all the youngsters in the neighborhood. We used to go there early in the morning. The guy that went there first was the lucky one, of course.

INTERVIEWER: How often did they come around?

INABA: *Shibais,* I would say, not too often. They used to come from Honolulu. I would say, maybe four or five times a year. Used to be the old, what we call, the *kabuki shibai.*

INTERVIEWER: Do you know about how much it cost?

INABA: Oh, gee, I don't recall. Was very minimal.

INTERVIEWER: How did they travel around?

INABA: Well, those days, we had cars there, 1910.

INTERVIEWER: Was it only Holualoa?

INABA: No. Used to be Holualoa, Kealakekua, Honaunau. Honaunau used to be a thriving community There were a lot of Japanese people in Honaunau. Those were the three places that usually they performed. Honaunau, Kealakekua, and in Holualoa.[8]

Plantation residents' descriptions of their theater-going experiences sound very much like the "shrine plays" described by Koji:

> [. . . prior to 1868] there had been in addition to the three theatres prescribed by law small troupes playing in the busy parts of the city and in shrine precincts. They were known as 'shrine plays,' and, particularly when they were presented on the grounds of shrines and temples, they were considered beyond the control of the town office and left quite unregulated. They were somewhat vulgar, but they were cheap and very popular."[9]

As described in the oral histories, the cost of the *shibai* is minimal enough that a plantation worker could afford to bring the whole family a few times a year. The entertainments are popular, involving the whole community. Finally, the performances are held on or near religious grounds. In Waipahu, the theater is near a religious building, and in Pu'ukoli'i the performance is at the Daijingu shrine.

Descriptions of performance venues are also in keeping with descriptions of rural stages in Japan. Folk performances were often associated with religious celebrations, and stages were commonly built on the grounds of local shrines. In one example, a far-village stage, or *noson butai,* "is built on a slope within the grounds of a local shrine. Plays are given at shrine festivals, with the audience sitting on mats laid on the ground under the open sky."[10] The oral histories describe just such an arrangement in Hawai'i.

Professional tours did not maintain a steady presence in Hawai'i, and so local Japanese theater groups also provided entertainment. By the 1900s in Japan, Ibsen became a widespread source of inspiration, and Shakespeare was translated, studied, and performed. In 1912 in Honolulu, the Honolulu Japanese Dramatic Society performed a Japanese translation of *Othello.* It seems that this group was a community organization rather than a professional theater, although "the actors were said to have been 'accomplished professionals of the local stage.'"[11] Apparently the production was quite successful, as it prompted the society to consider producing more plays, including Japanese classical plays. At least one other Japanese theater group was formed: Edwin G. Burrows writes of "the Japanese actor Zenjiro Hosokawa (stage name Shusui Hisamatsu) [who] came to Honolulu in 1918. In 1920 he organized "the *Shinsei Gekidan* or New Voice theatrical troupe, which played not only in Hawaii but also along the American Pacific Coast from Canada to Mexico. This one man . . . was the leading influence in the continuance of Japanese drama in the islands at that time."[12]

Community Theater

Laborers coming to Hawai'i at the turn of the century had little education. However, they would have been exposed to some form of folk theater in Japan. *Kabuki,* the theater of the people, was and is still performed by communities in Japan's rural areas. Japanese in the country incorporated various types of performance into their social and cultural practices over centuries. "Performing arts, many of them done by professionals, were brought into communities from political and cultural capitals—mainly, Nara, Kyoto, Osaka, and Edo. Local residents subsequently developed them into 'folk performing arts'."[13] Folk performing arts vary from prefecture to prefecture, but performances pervade the fabric of every community's life. Plays and dances are associated with shrine festivals and the agricultural cycle—there are even planting and field dances. There are large-scale performances such as the *bon* dance and huge parades where floats become stages for plays and puppet performances. There are also many folk versions of *no, kyogen* puppet plays, and *kabuki.* In fact, most Japanese immigrated to Hawai'i near the end of "the heyday of folk *kabuki* and puppet plays in the mid- to late-nineteenth century."[14] It makes sense, then, that there would be a demand for such community performances in Hawai'i.

Indeed, Japanese in rural plantation communities put on performances of their own. Plays were put on for various reasons. One was simply entertainment.

> INABA: You know, those days, whatever entertainment had to be provided by the local people, because there were very few of these people coming from outside. Transportation was a problem. Whenever they had a celebration, the local people would get together. They put on *shibais* like that.[15]

Performances also generated money. *Shibai* in Waimea were "the most successful fundraisers for the Honoka'a Hongwanji Mission, the Kamuela [Young Buddhist Association], or the Waimea Japanese Language School in the Japanese community where most farmers were not prosperous."[16] The English section of the *Nippu Jiji* often advertised fundraisers featuring entertainment given by community members: "The 'Kabuki' play entertainments will be given for two nights, Monday and Tuesday nights, at Asahi Theater on Maunakea Street by the members of the Nichiren Mission. The net profit, which may be realized by the entertainments, will be used for religious expansion of the Buddhist mission."[17] These events were often quite successful, and the funds raised were boasted about after the fact: "Three hundred fifty-nine dollars and twenty-five cents was the sum realized by the Palama Japanese school from the 'Naniwabushi' [recitation] entertainment recently given."[18]

Japanese performances provided opportunities for individuals to make money in the greater Hawaiian market, as there was some demand for them outside of the Japanese community:

> INABA: I remember every time a ship came when I was a youngster that I would go down and dance for 3 years I went to classes, and I even go a stage name. I must have been pretty good because every time they'd have celebrations like the Emporer's birthday or when naval ships came

> in they'd ask me to go and dance. And when I dance and the audience they threw half dollar silver on the stage. And I used to make about twenty dollars a dance. That was quite a bit of money you know in those days. So I never hesitated going. In fact, some of them I volunteered.[19]

Old photographs taken at Japanese social events give some idea of what a plantation community production looked like. In *A Pictorial History of the Japanese in Hawaii,* there is a photo of a group of men posing for a cast picture on a stage. (fig. 1). The Japanese immigrants from Fukuoka prefecture performed the play *Pistol Goto* (Robber with Pistol), Sadakichi Shimizu.[20] The cast is assembled on an outdoor stage maybe three feet high. The width of the stage is not shown in the picture. Banners hung at the foot, sides, and top framing of the stage creating a proscenium. The banner overhead displays a half sun, rising or setting, rays unfurled, at the very center. There is a banner behind this one with writing on it, but the writing is obscured. The banner at sidestage also has writing on it, as does the banner at the foot of the stage. The scenery behind the cast resembles a series of

FIG. 1. Japanese play, "Pistol Godo [or Goto] Shimizu Sadakichi," by Kiyoshhi Tsubaki, performed by the Fukuoka Ken people, Kekaha, Kaua'i, Hawai'i, November 3, 1908. B. Takaoka, Bishop Museum.

shoji doors. A makeshift awning covers the acting area; the awning appears to consist of some cloth draped over a few two-by-fours and laid on top of the boxy frame of the stage, as light can be seen coming through the spaces between this ceiling and the hanging fabric making up the side and back walls. Also in front of the stage are three wooden posts, looking like trees that once grew in the spot but were chopped off at just above stage height and fitted with what appear to be metal cans at the top. Perhaps these functioned as lanterns in the evening, or perhaps they were an actual part of the show. A small block or crate stands on the ground stage right, likely used as a step up to the stage. There is a small table next to the step, with no apparent purpose.

The Kekaha stage seems similar in many respects to the description of a stage used for *Kowaka Mai* (a folk art from Fukuoka prefecture) narrative and dance presentations in Japan. As described, "The players perform in front of a dark-blue cloth backdrop that bears three large crests in white. . . . The wooden stage is approximately twenty-feet square and stands three feet above the ground. Thatched-roofed and enclosed on three sides, it is dark even at midday."[21] Though the roof on the Kekaha stage is not thatched, a similar effect is obtained with the awning overhead. There are cloth drops used for the side walls, which cause most of the stage to appear dark. The stage height is about the same.

Pistol Goto required a large cast: those shown in the picture include 27 men and three children. Their costume is mixed—some wear *kimono* and *geta* while others wear suits, overalls, and uniforms of various kinds. A few have very pronounced mustaches and fake-looking beards. Some carry swords, others sticks. One man carries a fan. Most of them are wearing or carrying Western-style hats. The costuming suggests that the performance was of *shimpa* or *shingeki*—it is quite Western for *kabuki.*

Simple observation of this picture shows that the play was of some importance. Effort was made to erect and dress a stage, a large number of people were cast and would have committed time to rehearsals and performance, some thought was given to costumes, and a formal picture documented the event. The stage and bit of grassy lot visible in the picture liken it to the shrine plays and folk performances discussed earlier.

There is also an account of a community *shibai* in Waimea, Hawai'i. The pictures of this *shibai* are dated c. 1938. This *shibai* was written and directed by amateurs who wrote their material based on scenes from traditional *kabuki* as well as contemporary Japanese drama. As in traditional *kabuki,* men performed in all roles, both male and female. The costumes were made by the wife of a Parker Ranch worker, and from pictures in the text they were quite beautiful. The set in the picture is a painted backdrop, and the actors sit around a low table set with props. Eleven actors are named as participants in the *shibai,* all *Nisei* (second-generation Japanese) ranch workers with no previous theater experience.[22]

The performing arts foster a sense of cultural identity and community. In modern Japan, the folk performing arts are protected by the law. Designating a type of performing art as *bunkazai* "signifies official recognition of cultural importance . . . *bunkazai* are the focus of official efforts to protect and conserve Japan's cultural heritage."[23] The emphasis on protecting *bunkazai,* or cultural property, is rooted in scholarly interest in Japanese folklore that developed in the 1910s. The strong ties Japanese immigrants maintained to Japan in the early part of the 20th century may have encouraged a similar interest in Japanese folk performances in Hawai'i. Further evidence of the importance of performing arts to the Japanese community in Hawai'i can be found in appeals made to members of the community to participate in such events as a part of civic duty: "American citizens of Japanese parentage can serve Hawaii by participating in the political affairs of the community in which they reside. This contribution consists in playing a part with interest in the game of community life involving consideration of such problems as: public health, good roads, adequate hospital accommodations, proper school supervision, law observance, *public celebrations,* and protection of individual right and properties."[24]

Educational Theater

The Japanese in Hawai'i were very concerned with the education of their children, and Japanese schools were very popular in the Islands. The curriculum in Japanese schools included Japanese language, culture, and values. "The schools became centers of activities for the

Japanese community, including the celebration of Japanese holidays such as *tenchosetsu,* classes and exhibitions in the martial arts, and lessons in music and dance."[25] Theater was a part of the Japanese schools in two ways: as a part of the curriculum and as a valuable fundraiser.

In Meiji-era Japan the theater was rising in importance and became an educational vehicle in itself:

> Some men became particularly concerned with the possibilities of using Kabuki as a means of indoctrinating the people. As early as March 1872 a Department of Instruction *(Kyobusho)* was established. ... It was organized along the lines of a central temple with branch temples, and it had as its task the instruction of the common people. The instructors appointed for the most part were Shinto priests, Buddhist priests, and scholars of the Japanese classics, but in the provinces *Kagura* masters were also made instructors. . . . It was at the same time a task of the Department of Instruction to supervise the drama.[26]

Educational theater in Hawai'i was not taken to this extreme. It is clear, however, that theater was a part of the cultural instruction In Japanese schools. The performance skills taught at Japanese schools seem to have varied according to the expertise of members of the community who could serve as teachers. In Pu'ukoli'i, children were taught plays by a man who "used to work for the Maui Trading Company taking orders through the camp. Later . . . he started his own business peddling food to the camps."[27] In this excerpt from an oral history, Tsubaki is assisting the interviewee Kishi. Hara is the interviewer.

> HARA: [. . .] could you tell me about any fond memories and reminiscences about camp life?
>
> KISHI: I don't have any great memories.
>
> TSUBAKI: There were plays in the camp by Mr. Hasuike.
>
> KISHI: Who?
>
> TSUBAKI: Mr. Hasuike put on plays.
>
> HARA: Were the plays put on for some celebration?

> KISHI: No, no, it wasn't for any special occasion but there was a Mr. Hasuike, who came and taught my younger sister and others every night, and we all [watched them perform] . . .[28]

Drama was not always included in the curricula of Japanese schools. Students in some schools learned traditional dancing, sword dancing, and other performing arts.

It appears that some productions of *kabuki* at Japanese schools were quite artistic. Odo and Sinoto include in their *Pictorial History* an undated black and white picture of a "Children's *kabuki* theater group, Ha'ikū, Maui."[29] The backdrop in the picture is elaborately painted in perspective to achieve the effect of a long hallway. There are 17 people in the picture, with no discernable instructor. The pupils vary in age and gender. They are in full makeup with hair done in various styles, and they are wearing boldly patterned *kimono.* All are barefoot.

Entertainments were often given as fundraisers for schools as well. In January and February of 1919, the English section of the *Nippu Jiji* contains a few articles promoting two programs to benefit Japanese schools. "The first program, consisting of 'Naniwabushi' recitation by famous Hototogisu, Japanese flute solo, sword dance, music and other entertainments" . . . was given by the Palama Japanese language school, in January of 1919. It was highly successful.[30]

POLITICAL THEATER

The *soshi shibai,* or political drama also known as *shimpa,* was "created by adapting the realism of the *Kabuki* to social themes." *Shimpa* were staged political propaganda, and its proponents viewed theater as "the ideal vehicle for spreading enlightenment."[31] *Shingeki,* another new form, started with the introduction of Ibsen's work in 1907. A whole new genre of "Ibsenesque social dramas" sprang up, containing "social and intellectual messages quite unprecendented in the Japanese drama."[32]

At least one example of a Japanese drama used specifically for a political purpose in Hawai'i has been documented. *A Play to Be Given in Formosa Fifty Years Hence,* by Motoyuki Negoro, was produced on January 15, 1909. The production, said to be at the Honolulu Theater, was meant to kick-start the higher wage movement among the Japanese plantation workers in Hawai'i. It opened with a depiction of the wage disparity between Japanese and Caucasian (mostly Portuguese) laborers working on the plantation, and the extreme financial difficulties many Japanese laborers faced. It then showed a group of laborers meeting to discuss relief measures, and proposed a movement for higher wages as the only solution. The play continued with direct references to the management of the Japanese newspapers of the day and an open criticism of one editor's opposition to the higher wage movement. This editor then suffered a nightmarish scene in which the ghosts of all Japanese laborers who died in poverty because of his opposition to the higher wage movement swarmed around him. The play concluded with the Higher Wage Association singing as they waved banners proclaiming their success—monthly wages of $22.50.

The play was based on fact. In 1908, "about 14 persons met at the Asahi Theater to discuss means of translating the growing sentiment for higher wages into action."[33] Those supportive of the higher wage movement agreed that to ensure success all the Japanese newspapers should present a united front. However, Sometaro Sheba, editor of the *Hawaii Shimpo,* was receiving monetary support from the Hawaii Sugar Planters Association (HSPA), and would not cooperate.

Despite the schism among the editors of the Japanese newspapers, interest in the movement for higher wages grew, and on December 1, 1908, the Higher Wage Association was formed. Representations were made to the planters, but the planters "peremptorily denied the requests."[34] The Higher Wage Association finally called for a strike. The HSPA looked for any act of violence among strikers that might give them justification for arresting the leaders of the movement; eventually ". . . the authorities tried to shut down *Nippu Jiji* and break the strike by arresting the leaders on charge after charge.

Negoro's play was considered significant enough to be used in arguments to prosecute and jail the four leaders of the movement. "Terada, manager of the *Shimpo,* [a Japanese newspaper] testified that the play presented at the Honolulu Theater on January 15th had been written by Negoro—. . . that he, Terada, had heard Negoro drilling the actors, that the play had greatly excited the audience, which had cried, 'Sheba, Sheba! Kill him! Fix him!'"[36] The planters' aim was to show that the play had incited violence. In fact, as the trial was underway and the Japanese defendants were successfully countering the prosecution, a young Japanese man attempted to murder Sheba.

The use of the play in encouraging the higher wage movement and the importance given to the play in the trial of the movement's leaders speaks to the power of political theater. The establishment of the theater as an institution within the Japanese community could only have helped the theater's political function.

Venues and Stages

Japanese communities in Hawai'i had designated areas where performances took place, such as the Japanese theater behind the mission in Pu'ukoli'i and the outdoor theater in Waipahu. In Waimea, the platform-like store porch served as a movie theater and stage. "When the I. Oda Store platform was occupied, a *shibai* was sometimes held at the Japanese language school hall."[37] *A Pictorial History of the Japanese in Hawaii* contains two pictures of theaters, the *Asahi-za* in Honolulu and the *Eirakuza* theater in Hale'iwa. The strong presence of theaters in Japanese communities in rural as well as urban areas underlines the significance of the theater to the people.

The Eirakuza Theater in Hale'iwa, O'ahu, "was built in 1911 with modern facilities, including generated electricity and piped water (fig. 2). Tomitaro Aino from Yamaguchi prefecture was the owner." The theater rises three tall stories off the ground. There is a full balcony visible on the front facing side of the second floor, and three smaller awnings above the balcony protect what appears to be a large window. A few smaller banners hang above and near the entrance. Part of the roof of an adjacent building can be seen in the photograph, but there is no mention of its name or what type of building it is—another low building can be seen down the slope of the hill to the left of the theater. An open car is parked next to the theater.

The *Asahzi-za* or Asahi Theater in Honolulu (fig. 3) may be meant to emulate the state-sponsored theater in Edo, Japan, of the same name. The picture of the *Asahi-za* in 1915 is impressive. It is a neat two-story structure with a formal entrance adorned with an American flag, a Japanese flag, and several tall banners exceeding the height of the building. Japanese banners hang from the eaves of the building. The caption identifies the *Asahi-za* as the first Japanese theater in Honolulu. The theater opened in 1899, was destroyed by the Chinatown fire in 1900, and rebuilt in 1908.[38] The *Asahi-za* was not only a center for entertainment. Like the theaters of Japan, the *Asahi-za* served multiple social and political functions. It became the sometime meeting place of Japanese leaders organizing for political causes. In one case, "Frederick Makino of the *Hawaii Hochi* . . . held a mass protest meeting at the Asahi Theater on March 12, 1919 and sent the pronouncements made at the meeting to some of the more powerful members in the Hawaii legislature."[39]

In her discussion of the stage in the Japanese folk performing arts, Barbara Thornbury says:

> Although the stages of professional *no, kyogen, kabuki* and *bunraku* are, for the most part, fixed, the folk performing arts are far less wedded to certain locations or to particular types of structures. . . . the kind of presentation, the occasion, and the requirements and desires of a community . . . determine where and what a stage may be.[40]

FIG. 2. Eirakuza Theater, Hale'iwa, O'ahu, 1912. Bishop Museum.

This does not mean, however, that structures are not built specifically for performance purposes. In Japan today, "community support for the folk performing arts [. . .] includes constructing local folk performing arts centers." The presence of designated performance venues in shrines, plantations, and towns with large Japanese populations in early 20th century Hawai'i might also reflect the importance attached to presentations given in these areas. The construction of Japanese theaters with modern conveniences in locations around the Islands further supports the value of the Japanese performing arts to the Hawaiian Japanese community.

Publicity and Funding

I found very little information on publicity for any of the types of entertainments discussed. Newspapers were commonly read among members of the Japanese community in Hawai'i, and it makes sense

Fig. 3. Asahi Theater, Honolulu, O'ahu, ca. 1915. Bishop Museum.

that some publicity was achieved through advertisement in the Japanese language newspapers of the day. The *Nippu Jiji* in particular had wide circulation.

> By 1927, the paper held three local branches on Oahu (Waialua, Waiau, Waianae), eight on Maui (Kahului, Hamakua Poko, Lahaina, Keahua, Kaanapali, Hana, Kihei), six on Hawaii (two on Hilo, Kealakekua, two on Holualoa, Hawi), two on Kauai (Kapaa, Kilauea), and one on Lanai (Lanai City). News from Japan was gathered from the *Nippu Jiji* branches in Tokyo and Osaka. In 1920 the *Nippu Jiji* became a member of the Associated Press (English section only) to receive direct news from the mainland U.S."[41]

The articles on Japanese entertainments, the theater scene in Japan, and notable Japanese theater people contained in the English section of the *Nippu Jiji* indicate that it was a popular vehicle for theater publicity. It is also likely that events were publicized by word-of-mouth, as workers on the plantations would have common knowledge of community events and less access to news resources far from the plantation.

Information on funding for Japanese performances was also scarce. It is possible that local businesses helped to produce theatrical endeavors; "the *Nippu Jij* . . . sponsored various events including drama."[42] *A Play to Be Given in Formosa Fifty Years Hence* was produced by an individual named Tsukasa Saito. It is even possible that the plantations themselves subsidized plays in some form; plantations were known to support Japanese language schools financially. A deeper investigation into the financial history of Japanese theater in Hawai'i may reveal some interesting connections between performance and the community at large. It will also help to more clearly define the theater's social and political significance.

Audiences

In general, Japanese immigrants made up most of the audience at a Japanese performance. It appears that in some cases the theater was patronized mostly by men, and that in most rural plantation towns a play was a family event. Audiences were not solely Japanese, however. In Waimea, "the *shibai* was always a big success, and no empty seat was seen in the hall. Often it attracted many Hawaiians as well as Japanese as though the entire population in the community had gathered there."[43] Japanese performances were sometimes advertised in the English newspapers as well as the Japanese newspapers, indicating that Caucasians also patronized Japanese theaters.

Japanese Theater Since Immigration

In Japan, World War II "greatly affected the folk performing arts themselves—mainly by causing presentations to be suspended. After the war was over there seemed to be little interest in reviving local performances."[44] Japanese performance in Hawai'i suffered a similar fate. During World War II, people of Japanese descent living in Hawai'i were not allowed to gather in public, and had to remain indoors from dark to dawn with their lights off. Prominent leaders in the Japanese community were put in internment camps, and these prisoners included principals and instructors or the Japanese schools and journalists from the Japanese language newspapers.

Today one can still find Japanese performing arts in Hawai'i. There are annual festivals celebrating the cultural exchange between Japan and Hawai'i. Bon dances are popular summer events. The Japanese Cultural Center in Mō'ili'ili provides an anchor for the Japanese community in Hawai'i, offering classes in various cultural activities. Students taught by master teachers from Japan perform in productions at the University of Hawai'i, and occasionally *kabuki* will be included in the seasons of other theatrical groups.

Conclusion

"By 1927, the divergent strains comprising the world of the Japanese immigrant had at last solidified into a permanent way of life. The spirit of community had been internally strengthened through religious and cultural institutions; the family and home had been established; values, beliefs, and customs had been largely transposed."[45] Japanese theater in Hawai'i was an integral part of the Japanese community's development, and served the cultural, political, and social interests of the Japanese community. Both professional and grass roots theaters had places in the theatrical world of the time, and followed trends of theater in Japan on a smaller scale. The unique circumstances of immigration probably caused differences in the evolution of the folk performing arts in Hawai'i and in Japan; the presence of an established field of study in Japan will greatly aid future study of the folk performing arts in Hawai'i by providing a theoretical framework wherein Hawaiian-Japanese performances can be examined and compared with their Japanese predecessors. Further research will illuminate more about the immense cultural exchange of this period and the significance of the Japanese performing arts to the people of Hawai'i today.

Notes

1 Alan Moriyama, "Causation in Emigration History," in *Proceedings of the Japanese Kan'Yaku Imin Centennial Lectures,* ed. The Japanese Educational Fund of Hawaii (Honolulu: np. Lecture Jul. 25, 1985) 87.

2 Moriyama 88.

3 Toita Koji, "The Kabuki, the *Shimpa,* the *Shingeki,*" in *Japanese Music and Drama in the Meiji Era,* Ed. Komiya Toyotaka, Trans. Edward G. Seidensticker and Donald Keene (Tokyo, Japan: O Bunsha, 1956) 187.

4 Koji 193.

5 Franklin Odo and Kazuko Sinoto, *A Pictorial History of the Japanese in Hawaii 1885–1924,* (Honolulu: BPBM, 1985) 215.

6 Misao Tanji, interview and trans. by Charlotte Tanji, *Eight Life Stories Japanese Senior Citizens of Waipahu* (np: Feb. 4, 1984) 38.

7 Kishi Mukaisu, assisted by Sue Tsubaki, interview by Maya M. Hara, *An Oral History on Issei in Lahaina* (Lahaina: West Maui Cultural Council, Aug. 21, 1991) 39.

8 Minoru Inaba, interview, Kealakekua, Kona, Kona Historical Society, Nov. 24, 1980.

9 Koji 180.

10 Barbara E. Thornbury, *The Folk Performing Arts, Traditional Culture in Contemporary Japan.* (Albany: State U of New York P, 1997) 24.

11 Rosalie Du Val Roberts, "A History of the Professional Legitimate Theatre and Opera in Honolulu 1910–1920" (M.A. thesis, U of Hawaii, 1958) 12.

12 Burrows 185

13 Thornbury 36.

14 Thornbury 24.

15 Inaba 1980.

16 Jiro Nakano, *Parker Ranch Paniolo,* (Honolulu: United Japanese Society of Hawaii, 1992) 71.

17 *Nippu Jiji* Feb. 16, 1919.

18 *Nippu Jiji* Jan. 30, 1919.

19 Minoru Inaba, interview, Kalukalu, South Kona: Kona Historical Society, Jul. 10, 1995.

20 Odo and Sinoto 121.

21 Thornbury 24.

22 Nakano 72–73.

23 Thornbury 55.

24 Kensuke Kawachi, "How 'New Americans' May Serve Hawaii," in Dennis M. Ogawa, *Kodomo no tame ni,* (Honolulu: U P of Hawaii, 1978) 220, emphasis mine.

25 Odo and Sinoto 128.

26 Toyotaka 28.

27 Mukaisu 34.

28 Mukaisu 34.

29 Odo and Sinoto 124.

30 *Nipu Jiji,* Jan. 24, 1919.

31 Koji 264.

32 Koji 287.

33 Take and Allan Beekman, "Hawaii's Great Japanese Strike," in Dennis M. Ogawa, *Kodomo no tame ni,* (Honolulu: U P of Hawaii, 1978) 156.

34 Beekman 159.

35 Beekman 166–167.

36 Beekman 167.

37 Nakano 71.

38 Odo and Sinoto 123.

39 Chiyo Yanagida, The Nippu Jiji and the Japanese Language School Issue in Hawaii, 1919–1927, (M.A. thesis, U of Hawai'i, 1996) 63.

40 Thornbury 23–24.

41 Yanagida 33.

42 Yanagida 34.

43 Nakano 73.

44 Thornbury 45.

45 Ogawa 148.

ROBERT C. SCHMITT

Centenarians and Supercentenarians in Hawai'i, 1896–2000

THE DECENNIAL CENSUS taken in the year 2000 was notable for being the first in U.S. Census history to show age and sex for persons more than 100 years old. Such persons 110 and over are called supercentenarians.

Supercentenarians in 2000 were tabulated by age, sex, race, and geographical area. For Hawai'i, females outnumbered males 194 to 81, and persons aged 100 to 104 accounted for 249 of the 275 persons reporting age.[1]

Centenarians—persons 100 and above—have fluctuated widely in past years. First shown separately for 1890, they ranged from 8 in 1910 and 1950, to 175 in 2000. Further information on Hawai'i's centenarians and supercentenarians is reported in the accompanying tables.[2]

Table 4 presents data on the oldest deaths and centenarian deaths for the last 19 years.

NOTES

1 Ira Rosenwaike and Leslie F. Stone, "Verification of the Ages of Supercentenarians in the United States: Results of a Matching Study," *Demography*, vol. 40, no. 4 (Nov. 2003) 727–739.

2 Robert C. Schmitt, "Extreme Old Age in Hawaii, *Population Report*, 14 (Nov. 1982) 1–10.

Robert C. Schmitt is retired statistician for the Hawai'i Department of Business, Economic Development, and Tourism. He is a frequent contributor to the Journal.

The Hawaiian Journal of History, vol. 38 (2004)

Table 1. Population, Total and 100 Years Old and Over: 1890 to 2000

		100 YEARS OLD AND OVER			
	Total	Both Sexes			
Year	all ages	Number	Percent	Males	Females
1890	89,990	(NA)	(NA)	(NA)	(NA)
1896	109,020	19	0.017	9	10
1900	154,001	24	0.016	14	10
1910[1]	191,909	8	0.004	2	6
1920[1]	255,912	28	0.011	18	10
1930[1]	368,336	(NA)	(NA)	(NA)	(NA)
1940[1]	423,300	(NA)	(NA)	(NA)	(NA)
1950	499,794	8	0.002	5	3
1960	632,772	30	0.005	8	22
1970[2]	768,561	213	0.028	98	115
1980	964,691	113	0.012	51	62
1990	1,108,229	132	0.012	40	92
2000	1,211,537	275	0.023	81	194

NA Not available

[1] Data include Midway (and, in 1940, other outlying minor islands), not part of the Territory of Hawaii.

[2] The revised state total, not distributed by age, was 769,913.

Source: Official reports of censuses conducted by the Hawaiian government, 1890 and 1896, and the U.S. Census Bureau, 1900 to 2000.

Table 2. Age and Sex of Centenarians, by Counties: 2000

Age and sex	State total	Honolulu	Hawaii	Kauai	Maui & Kalawao
All Centenarians	275	211	23	17	24
Sex:					
Male	81	57	7	9	8
Female	194	154	16	8	16
Age:					
100 to 104	249	190	20	15	24
105 to 109	22	17	3	2	–
110 and over	4	4	–	–	–

Source: U.S. Census Bureau

Table 3. Race of Persons 100 Years Old and Over, by Age: 2000

Race or ethnic group	100 or over	100 to 104	105 to 109	110 and over
All races	277	251	22	4
Specified race alone:				
White	46	42	3	1
Black or African American	1	–	1	–
American Indian or Alaska Native	1	1	–	–
Asian	203	183	17	3
Native Hawaiian or Other Pacific Islander	6	6	–	–
Specified race alone or in combination with one or more other races:				
White	56	50	5	1
Black or African American	1	1	–	–
American Indian or Alaska Native	1	1	–	–
Asian	216	194	19	3
Native Hawaiian or Other Pacific Islander	18	13	1	–

Source: U.S. Census Bureau

Table 4. Centenarians Deaths: 1982 to 2000
(Excludes deaths of Hawaii residents out of the state)

		Age 100 and over		Highest age (years)	
Year	All ages	Male	Female	Male	Female
1982	5,123	5	18	102	105
1983	5,409	4	19	106	113
1984	5,571	7	13	110	105
1985	5,751	10	23	114	109
1986	5,788	10	19	106	106
1987	6,147	14	21	107	103
1988	5,970	14	24	102	107
1989	6,380	13	27	104	106
1990	6,687	14	36	105	104
1991	6,696	23	37	109	107
1992	6,846	9	34	104	111
1993	7,226	14	38	106	110
1994	7,206	5	30	104	111
1995	7,488	13	47	108	106
1996	7,803	11	52	106	110
1997	7,710	14	42	105	110
1998	7,969	11	51	105	108
1999	8,125	16	57	112	110
2000	8,163	20	52	106	110

Source: Hawaii State Department of Health, as reported in the *State of Hawaii Data Book,* 1985 to 1999.

RIÁNNA M. WILLIAMS

Hawaiian *Ali'i* Women in New York Society: the Ena-Coney-Vos-Gould Connection

I FIRST HEARD of Kaikilani Coney Vos in 1991, when I saw a painting of her in the small Kaua'i Historical Society museum on the grounds of the Coco Palms Hotel. My casual inquiry as to who she was was greeted with an equally casual reply of her name, and that she was from an old Kaua'i family. The painting, which fortunately survived the 1992 Hurricane 'Iniki that devastated most of Kaua'i, was moved to the present Kaua'i Historical Society office in downtown Līhue in 1995.

The memory of Kaikilani's beautiful, serene, and aristocratic face soon had me researching her and her family, which turned out to be a story of "old Hawai'i," ties to Hawaiian *ali'i* (chiefs or nobility) and to East Coast "high society," plus an artistic connection to the last Empress of China. I wrote Kaikilani's story in 1993, donating it to the Kaua'i Historical Society to help fill out what information they had about her. This is an updated version of that story, with additional and current information included, published with permission from Mary A. Requilman, executive director of the museum.

"Belles of the court of King Kalākaua." Such was a newspaper description of sisters Eleanor Kaikilani Coney and Elizabeth Likelike Coney.[1] Kaikilani, sometimes referred to as Eleanor or Ellen (fig. 1), was born in Nāwiliwili, Kaua'i, on December 27, 1867, one of six children of High Chiefess Laura (or Lala) Amoy (also spelled Ami, Amoe,

Previously published in the Journal, *Riánna M. Williams is a researcher and writer of Hawaiian history.*

The Hawaiian Journal of History, vol. 38 (2004)

FIG. 1. Eleanor Kaikilani Coney Graham Vos, painted by Hubert Vos. Kaua'i Historical Society.

or Amoi) Kekukapuokekuaokalani Ena Coney and American John Harvey Coney.[2]

Kaikilani Coney was named after her maternal great-grandmother, High Chiefess Kaikilanialiiwahineopuna, a descendent of the Kamehameha line and the last high chiefess of the Puna district of the island of Hawai'i.[3] Her maternal grandmother had the same name and was married to John Ena.[4] These two Kaikilanis were descended on the male side of the Kamehameha line through Lonoiakamakahiki of Kealakekua, son of Keawenuia 'Ume, chief of Ka'u and Puna, and from High Chief Kalaniopu'u of Maui and his wife Manoua of Ka'u.[5]

The Enas had three children: Amoe Ululani Kapukalakala, born in 1842 (later married to High Chief Levi Ha'alelea); John Ena Jr., born in 1843; and Laura Amoy Kekukapuokekuaokalani, born in 1844 or 1845 (later, Laura Coney, Kaikilani's mother).[6]

John Harvey Coney, Eleanor Kaikilani's father, was born in New York City and came to Hawai'i after participating in the 1848 Mexican war against the United States over the independence of Texas.[7]

Laura Ena (fig. 2) and John Harvey Coney married in 1860, when Laura was 17 years old. John, supposedly through his wife's family's court connections with King Kamehameha IV, was soon appointed sheriff of Hilo, where Laura's ancestral lands were located. He held this job for 18 years.[8]

Laura and John Coney's six children were Mary Ululani (who was married four times, and became, in order, Mrs. Stewart, Mrs. Samuel J. Levy, Mrs. Ashton, and Mrs. R. A. Monroe); Clara (or Clarissa) Piilani Amoy (Mrs. Julian Monsarrat); John Ha'alelea Coney (married to Mary Ellen Kelly); and Elizabeth Likelike Kekaeikapuokalani (Mrs. Heinrich H. Renjes); and William Hulilauakea Hawks Coney.[9]

Eleanor Kaikilanialiiwahineopuna, generally known as Kaikilani and the main link in the family story, was the Amoy-Coney couple's fifth child. She first married John L. Graham, and after they divorced she married artist Hubert Vos.

A reference to the year 1865, when Laura was only 22 years old and she and John were living in Hilo, described Laura as

> an exceptionally fine woman of high character, gracious manner, generous instincts and kind disposition. . . . The Coneys lived in a long grass

> thatched house on the *mauka* (toward the mountain) side of the courthouse lot, and later built a pretentious residence which is now [1922] the County Building. . . . [10]

It's not known when they moved to Honolulu, but most likely it was in 1878 or 1879, after John's 18 years as sheriff of Hilo. Another reference stated that family life centered around Laura, a small woman with the carriage of an aristocrat, the dignified ease of a Victorian lady, and the graciousness of Hawaiian manners and culture of the day.[11]

She taught her children not to speak of their *ali'i* blood, to forget about high chiefs and chiefesses, and to make their own way in the world because the days of chiefs and chiefesses were gone. Daughter-in-law Mary Ellen Coney was quoted many years later: "I remember a time when the king [Kalākaua] was calling on Mother Coney. He was busy at the time collecting the genealogies of the nobility and the

FIG. 2. Laura Amoy Ena Coney (Mrs. John Harvey Coney). Alexis Kekuakapuokulani Hutton Talpash collection.

mele (songs, chants) of the Hawaiians. He said to Mother Coney, 'Tell me, Mrs. Coney, who were your ancestors, I know that you belong to the Kamehameha line.' 'Adam and Eve were my ancestors,' she replied."[12]

Laura reportedly raised her family in the strict traditions of the missionaries in which she herself had been raised, yet the family were staunch royalists. Outside of her family, her time was devoted to Kawaiaha'o Church.[13]

In 1898, after the overthrow of the monarchy, the *Chicago Herald* sent a female reporter to Honolulu to interview the old nobility, to learn their reactions and feelings to the situation.[14] According to Kaikilani, Laura Coney greeted the woman most graciously, serving afternoon tea. Laura promptly monopolized the conversation with all kinds of small talk, parrying with innocuous questions about Chicago whenever the reporter was able to get in a question about the old families and the political situation. The reporter, treated to typical Island courtesies of food and conversation, left the visit no wiser about the old nobility than before she arrived.[15]

Laura and John Coney's home in Honolulu, "Halelelea" (which they translated as "Pleasant House") was near 'Iolani Palace, on the corner of Hotel Street and Richards Street, and was often the setting for many of the city's "brilliant entertainments" during the Kalākaua monarchy.[16] At least up until April 1902, Rapid Transit conductors called out "Stone wall on the right" when passing the house on Hotel Street, as the coral wall was apparently a kind of landmark.[17]

The land was apparently an 1848 *Māhele* grant to High Chiefess Kekau'ōnohi, a granddaughter of Kamehameha I and a wife of Kamehameha II. Upon her death in 1851, she left her lands to her second husband, High Chief Levi Ha'alelea.[18] Levi's second wife was Amoe Ululani Ena Ha'alelea, sister of Laura Ena Coney and aunt of Kaikilani.[19] John Harvey Coney also owned land in Honouliuli, O'ahu, where James Campbell bought 41,000 acres from him for $95,000 in 1877. Campbell soon started the Honouliuli Ranch, and in 1879 the first artesian well in Hawai'i was drilled on this land.[20]

John Harvey Coney died in Honolulu on October 9, 1880, at the age of 60.[21] Laura Ena Coney died in Honolulu on February 24, 1929, at the age of 85.[22] In a funeral recitation for Laura given by the Reverend Akaiko Akana, pastor of Kawaiaha'o Church, on February 24,

1929, Laura was referred to as "one of the old and prominent kamaainas who has helped to build Hawaii, not only by her personal effort, but through her influence on her husband, children and influencial [sic] associates and acquaintances throughout these islands."[23] There are two marble plaques in Kawaiaha'o Church commemorating members of the Coney family, both above the *mauka* royal pew. Donated by her daughters Kaikilani and Elizabeth, one reads: "In Memory of Laura Kekuakapuokalani Coney 1844–1929 Always a devoted member of Kawaiaha'o Church, she often said, *"Ka wahi e nele ai, e haawai* Where need is, there give." The other plaque reads: "In Memory of Levi Haalelea 1828–1864 His wife Ululani A. A. Haalelea 1824–1904 and Richard Haalilio 1808–1844."

Kaikilani and Elizabeth Coney are included in a list of "fashionable young ladies of refinement" who could be observed on Sundays at Queen Emma Square, acknowledging attention from stylish young men. They attended balls at 'Iolani Palace, dancing to Gilbert and Sullivan waltzes, wearing gowns often made in Paris, their hair decorated with jasmine blossoms, and attended afternoon tea dances aboard visiting warships, always accompanied by a chaperon. They filled their days with picnics, teas, and musicales. Witty conversation was as much a requirement as the playing and singing of Hawaiian songs, often written by members of the royal family or Royal Hawaiian Bandmaster Henry Berger. They performed in pageants and plays to raise money for church work, and played tennis and attended horse races and later polo games in Kapi'olani park.[24] In 1896, as married ladies, Kaikilani and Elizabeth were included in the formation of Honolulu's first golf club, along with Republic of Hawai'i President Sanford B. Dole and soon-to-be prominent businessman Walter Dillingham.[25] Marion Durant, whose aunt was married to Kaikilani's nephew, remembers Kaikilani in her later years as being regal and very much the grande dame, and Elizabeth as being prim and proper.[26]

Historian Albert P. Taylor wrote that Kaikilani's sister, Miss Lizzy (Elizabeth) Coney, was a lady-in-waiting to Princess Likelike during the coronation of King Kalākaua in 1883.[27] Another source states that Clarissa (Clara) Coney, another sister, was a lady-in-waiting to the household of Queen Kapi'olani.[28]

Kaikilani was described by Queen Lili'uokalani as "a pleasant companion" and "of great service."[29] In December 1896, the former queen was traveling by train across the United States from San Francisco to Boston. Kaikilani Graham and her two children, John and Anne, were on the same train, heading for New York City. Lili'uokalani wrote that people crowded into the railway stations eager to get a glimpse of the Queen of Hawai'i, and at times were so troublesome that train officials were obliged to lock the car doors in order to prevent physical intrusion. Kaikilani, described by Lili'uokalani as "tall, handsome, very commanding in her presence, and very ladylike and polite in her manner," would converse with the onlookers, courteously giving them information regarding Lili'uokalani and her journey, essentially keeping them at bay.

Two reports of Kaikilani's brother John Ha'alelea "Dad" Coney's 75th birthday *lu'au* at his home in Niumalu, Kaua'i, appeared in the June 5 and June 15, 1939, issues of the *Honolulu Star-Bulletin.* This was a gala event attended by over 350 guests, which included family, friends, co-workers, and employees. Family members at his birthday were his wife, his five children and their children, and his two living sisters, Kaikilani Vos and Elizabeth Renjes, both widows. The sisters had spent the winter on Kaua'i, having decided to settle in the Islands.[30]

John Ha'alelea "Dad" Coney was born in Hilo, Hawai'i, in 1864. He finished his education at The Ohio State University, worked for awhile in Columbus, Ohio, and returned to Honolulu in 1890 to work for the Hawaiian Hardware Company. He moved to Kaua'i in 1893 where he became deputy sheriff and then served as sheriff from 1894 to 1906. He was also a contractor, his firm named Coney & Hansen. He constructed the Wilcox Library and a number of Kaua'i school buildings. He also enjoyed the dual distinction of being the oldest member of the Masonic Lodge and the oldest Scottish Rite Mason from Kaua'i. Mary Ellen Coney said her husband had an endless repertoire of stories and the ability to sing and play the *'ukulele,* which made him a *Beau Brummell* in his youth

Facing "Dad" across the head table in the *lu'au* party pavilion was the family Hawaiian flag, under which he was born. It had been made by members of the Coney family in the days of King Kamehameha III. Although showing its age, it had been carefully patched and preserved by the family. This birthday celebration was its first unfurling since the day Hawaiian flags were supplanted by American flags 41 years earlier. The flag sat among ti leaves, coconut fronds, maiden hair fern, and palm blossoms, all of which graced a Hawaiian feast that had been in preparation for weeks, and of which every article of food had been produced on the honoree's property.

Several toasts were given in Hawaiian. One, by County Attorney Abraham G. Kaulukou, praised "Dad's" mother, Laura Ena Coney. He said Laura had "taught her children the highest principles of Hawaiian morality which are: regard your parents, regard your family name, regard your race, and play the game of life straight." Judge Carrick H. Buck said, "To a prince of friends, a prince of hospitality and a prince of Hawaii nei, John Haalelea Coney!"

During the *lu'au,* "Dad" recounted a story of Princess Ruth's often and generally unexpected calls at the Coney family home in Honolulu. When Princess Ruth's carriage drew up, the Coney children knew they would not have any mashed potatoes for dinner, because Ruth had a passion for mashed potatoes and would eat the entire amount prepared for the whole family. He went on to say that Princess Likelike actively encouraged the re-establishment of hula. He described Queen Kapi'olani as a loveable lady with a sweet disposition who never raised her voice or quarreled with anyone, and who regularly rose by 6 A.M. to take a walk around the palace square, often calling on friends such as the Coneys for morning coffee. He added that although Queen Lili'uokalani was somewhat of a puritan, she smoked a big, black cigar in private. She rose even earlier than Queen Kapi'olani and continued the custom of early morning coffee at the Coneys.

It's not known how or where Kaikilani met her first husband, John Graham. According to the January 6, 1886, issue of *The Friend,* Kaikilani and John Graham of New York City were married in Honolulu at the Fort Street Church on December 17, 1885. Her obituary of September 11, 1943, in the *Honolulu Star-Bulletin,* states that she married Graham, a "well known San Franciscan," in 1890. They lived in San Francisco after their marriage. They had two children, John and Anne.[31] Nothing seems to be known about John Graham the elder, and little is known about John the younger, except that he lived in New York, married, and had five children.[32] Anne married Jay Gould II, lived for years in New York, and had three children.[33] More on Anne Graham Gould shortly.

How Kaikilani met and married Hubert Vos is also unclear, although Kaikilani was divorced from Graham at the time of her marriage to Vos.[34] Her 1943 obituaries in the *Honolulu Advertiser* and *Honolulu Star-Bulletin* state she married Vos in New York City in 1895, and that the couple embarked on a world tour during which they celebrated the coronation of Queen Wilhelmina of the Netherlands while visiting in the Dutch East Indies in 1896. However, according to the *Columbia Encyclopedia,* Wilhelmina did not become Queen of the Netherlands until 1898, her mother being regent until then.[36] According to the biography of Hubert Vos in David W. Forbes' *Encounters with Paradise,* Vos met Kaikilani when she was traveling east as a companion to the former Queen Lili'uokalani [1896], and they were married in St. Paul, Minnesota, on November 5, 1897.[37] Vos's biography in the 1936 *The National Encyclopedia of American Biography* states he married Kaikilani on November 4, 1897.[38]

The marriage of Kaikilani and Hubert Vos was also a second marriage for Vos. His obituary mentions a daughter in Ostend, Belgium, and a son in Paris, France, along with his stepdaughter, Anne Graham Gould of New York City.[38] Hubert was born in the ancient holy city of Maastricht, Netherlands, on February 17, 1855, and apparently showed an early talent for drawing and painting. As a young man he studied and traveled in Europe, returning to Holland where he participated in art exhibits, winning many honors. He moved to London in 1887, establishing a painting studio specializing in portraits, and gave lessons. In 1893, the Dutch government sent him to the Chicago World's Fair as art commissioner for the Netherlands. He soon embarked on a world tour, painting hundreds of portraits of the known and unknown.[39]

Of particular interest to us in Hawai'i are Vos's paintings done here. Three of them, painted in 1898 and 1899, were on display in the 1992 "Encounters with Paradise Views of Hawai'i and Its People, 1778–1941" exhibit at the Honolulu Academy of Arts. The following descriptions of the three paintings are from David W. Forbes' book about the exhibit: "Ekekela: Hawaiian Flower Girl," an oil on canvas, portrays a flower seller, according to Vos's notation on the frame. She is a well-dressed Hawaiian woman of dignity and strength, looking rather grave. She wears a lei of *maile* leaves, and *'ilima* entwined with *maile* encircles her hair. "Kolomona: Hawaiian Troubadour," oil on canvas, portrays a pleasant looking Hawaiian man, possibly a *po'olā,* or stevedore, because of the red shirt he is wearing. He is strumming an *'ukelele,* his pleasant face framed in a large hat. (An earlier description of this painting describes Kolomana—the name regarded as a musical version in Hawaiian of Solomon—as a minstrel and a cab driver, leader of sports and merriment, one of the "characters" of Honolulu. He was also described as looking like a Venetian gondolier.)[40] The painting was reproduced in brown and sepia tones for the cover of *The Hawaiian Journal of History,* volume 37 (2003).

The third, entitled "Study of Hawaiian Fish," also oil on canvas, is just that, various Hawaiian fish depicted on a marble slab. It's thought it was probably painted from sketches of fish Vos saw at local fish markets. This painting is done in the manner of a Dutch or Flemish still life. An incongruous corner addition to the fish scene is a *kou* calabash. Having nothing to do with the preparation of fish, one wonders if Vos added it as a sort of homage to his wife's ancestry. The first two paintings are in private collections, and the "Study of Hawaiian Fish" is owned by the Honolulu Academy of Arts.

Vos's greatest honor was undoubtedly painting the portrait of the Dowager Empress Tz'u-hsi of China in 1905. For a Westerner to be given such a commission in that era was unheard of and says a great deal about his ability and reputation. His letters to Kaikilani are full of the etiquette and intricacies of the Chinese court and the diplomacy needed in painting the empress, Vos being both an outsider and a Westerner. He was required to begin work in a special room in the Peking Winter Palace at 5 A.M. (having risen at 4 A.M.). He painted continuously, in a hot room he said must have reached 500 degrees, until late afternoon. The empress allowed only five sittings, each time arriving carried in a gilt chair born by eight eunuchs. Although 70 years old at the time, the empress ordered that she be painted at about age 25 or 30: no shadows, no lines, no wrinkles.[41] Possibly unknown to her, Vos also painted a realistic portrait of her, which he brought back to the United States. Left to the Fogg Art Museum at Harvard University in 1943, it is presently hanging in a university administration building (fig. 3).[42]

The artist and empress apparently got on well. She was pleased with the painting, and made Vos a Commander of the Double Dragon, the Chinese dragon representing strength and goodness.[43]

Fig. 3. H.I.M., The Empress Dowager of China, Tz'u-hsi (1835–1908), painted by Hubert Vos, 1905–1906. Courtesy of Fogg Art Museum, Harvard University Art Museums, bequest of Grenville L. Winthrop.

(An undocumented account from the Kaua'i Historical Society files states that after many difficult attempts to paint the empress's hands he finally substituted the hands of his wife, Kaikilani. There is no mention of this in his detailed letters from China nor anywhere else. However, according to family member Marion Durant, Kaikilani told her family that Vos painted her hands on the portraits of wealthy women in Newport, Rhode Island, where he had a studio.)[44]

The touched up painting of the empress resides in the Hall of Relics in the Summer Palace in Beijing, although it is not on display. Vos' grandson of California, also named Hubert Vos, has been working with the Getty Museum to have the painting restored at the Getty Restoration Institute. Mr. Vos went so far as to offer a painting by his grandfather of Yuan Shi Kai, the first president of the Chinese Republic, to China as a gift and inducement for them to allow the painting to come to Los Angeles for restoration. Vos's and Getty's negotiations with China have been ongoing for several years, but periodic problems at the Beijing end have prevented any action.[45]

The book jacket of Bob Dye's *Merchant Prince of the Sandalwood Mountains* shows a photograph of a painting of the book's subject, Chun Afong. According to Mr. Dye, the original painting was done by Vos in China when Afong was visiting there, about the time Vos painted Empress Tz'u-hsi. The painting presently resides with an Afong descendent in San Francisco.[46]

Hubert Vos died in New York City on January 8, 1935, at the age of 80. His last painting was a portrait of Hugh D. Auchincloss, who was soon to become the stepfather of Jacqueline Bouvier (later Kennedy, then Onassis).[47] Five years earlier, Kaikilani sent out charming invitations to his 75th birthday, inviting guests to his W. 67th Street studio at 8 P.M., "to celebrate Hubert's 3/4 of a century with a little to eat, a little to drink, some music and frolic."[48] Kaikilani returned to Kaua'i not long after Vos's death, living there until her death in 1943, at the age of 75.[49] It's not known where she is buried. She left seven grandchildren and two great-grandchildren.[50]

The Kaua'i Historical Society owns two oil portraits of Kaikilani painted by her husband. One is a bust and is undocumented. The Society account says it was purchased in New York for $125 and "brought back" to Hawai'i. There is no additional information and nothing as to how it was acquired by the Society.

A second oil painting of Kaikilani by Vos, this one life-size, was donated to the Society in 1997 by Richard Penhallow of Kamuela, Hawai'i. His late wife, Olive McKeever, received the painting from her mother, who had received it as a gift from Kaikilani. Painted in 1900, it shows a stately Kaikilani standing in the gardens of her Nāwiliwili home.[51]

Kaikilani's sister, Elizabeth Likelike Coney Renjes, another "belle of the Kalākaua court," married Heinrich Renjes. He lived in Honolulu for a quarter of a century, having been a partner in the F. A. Schaeffer & Co. firm. The Renjes moved to Germany in 1900 or 1909, after Heinrich retired.[52] He died in Wiesbaden, Germany, in 1911, at the age of 56.[53] Elizabeth Coney Renjes moved into the Halekulani Hotel in Honolulu probably in the 1930s (fig. 4). She lived there until her death on December 31, 1952, at the age of 86, and is buried at Honolulu's O'ahu Cemetery.[54]

Kaikilani and Elizabeth's brother, William Hulilauakea Hawks Coney, died at the Coney family home in Honolulu in April 1904.

FIG. 4. *(left to right)* Elizabeth Coney Renjes; Mary Ellen Coney, Mrs. John Ha'alalea Coney; John Ha'alalea Coney; and Eleanor Kaikilani Coney Graham Vos, on the occasion of John Ha'a1alea Coney's 75th birthday, 1939. Alexis Kekuakapuokulani Hutton Talpash collection.

Educated at The Ohio State University, he returned to Honolulu in 1895 where be became a reporter on the *Pacific Commercial Advertiser*. Three years later he became city editor of the *Evening Bulletin* until his death. He was at one time secretary of the Territorial Republican Central Committee.[55]

Kaikilani's daughter, Anne Douglas Graham, married Jay Gould II at St. Thomas's Episcopal Church on Fifth Avenue in New York City on April 29, 1911. Nearly two full columns of the *New York Times* on April 30 were devoted to the marriage under a headline reading, "Jay Gould Weds Miss Annie Graham." Jay II was the second son of Mrs. and Mrs. George Jay Gould and grandson of "the" Jay Gould, tycoon, robber baron, and financial scoundrel.[56] It was a typical large society wedding of the time, with a huge crowd of onlookers which necessitated use of the New York City mounted police. However, the reception was small and held at the studio of Hubert Vos, Anne's stepfather.

A paragraph was devoted to the guest "who attracted the most attention at both the church and the reception:

> Princess Kawananakoa of Hawaii, formerly Miss Abigail Campbell, a daughter of James Campbell, a sugar merchant of the Hawaiian Islands. The Princess wore a trailing gown of black lace and chiffon over white, with panels and sash of a brilliant orange-tinted red satin, topped by a very large black plumed hat, and also some wonderful jewels. She arrived in town Wednesday, and is sailing on the George Washington to attend the coronation ceremonies in London.[57]

Mrs. Vos, the bride's mother, wore a gown of black chiffon over white, topped by a black hat.

Gifts to the bride were reported to be "rare and numerous," including quantities of diamond, emerald, and pearl jewelry and a town house on 5th Avenue. The newspaper went on to report:

> Relatives of Mrs. Vos, who are natives of the Hawaiian Islands, sent many presents. One was a large table of koa wood, which resembles mahogany, the table being inlaid with various kinds of Hawaiian woods. Mr. Vos, who is a portrait painter, gave his step-daughter and Mr. Gould his portraits of them. The koa table is thought to have been a wedding gift from the bride's grandmother, Laura Ena Coney.[58]

Four paragraphs were given to the church seating arrangements, the beginning one reading:

> The seating arrangements at the church were as follows: Mr. and Mrs. Hubert Vos, the Princess Kawananakoa, and Mr. Spreckles (Claus Spreckles, California and Hawai'i sugar magnate) sat in Pew 37; Mr. and Mrs. George Jay Gould, the parents of the bridegroom, Mrs. Anthony J. Drexel, Jr., George J. Gould, Jr., and the Misses Edith and Gloria Gould occupied a pew near by.

A lengthy article in the *Honolulu Star-Bulletin* on July 4, 1917, concerns the young Goulds vacationing in Honolulu, the first visit for Jay. They were accompanied by their daughters, ages four and three (they later had a son). Although Anne and Jay spent their two-month visit staying at the "more-than-80-year-old Coney family home on Richards St.," the children, their governess, and maid stayed at the Moana Hotel. The Goulds stayed in a small annex of the main house. It was called the studio, since Hubert Vos painted pottery there when he visited Hawai'i. It was surrounded by mango, banana, and poinciana trees. The earlier mentioned landmark wall surrounding the house was, according to a *Honolulu Star-Bulletin* article on July 4, 1916, "the only one of its kind still standing in Honolulu," and quotes Laura as saying that the Outdoor Circle wanted the wall torn down, that it was ugly and out of place in attractive Honolulu, but the Coneys refused. The wall was constructed of coral block, with extensive gardens, trees, shrubs, grass, and shaded walks. The house's first and second floors were surrounded by shaded verandas.[59]

The July 4, 1917, article continues:

> Back of that century-old Hawaiian wall, the only one of its kind still standing in Honolulu, is a history which the Coneys, nolulu [sic] is a history which is not often told. That the home in which they live, however, was primarily Chiefess Kekanonohi's [sic], said to have been a grand-daughter of Kamehameha I, is the pretty story. There is even a hint that the Coneys are related to the chiefess.

When Kaikilani's sister, Elizabeth Renjes, died in 1953, her January 4 *Honolulu Advertiser* obituary stated that the family home was opposite the Hawaiian Hotel, placing it on the *makai* (toward the ocean) side of Hotel Street. An article in the April 26, 1902, *Pacific Commercial Advertiser* states the house was at the corner of Richards and Hotel Streets.

Jay Gould II died in Margaretville, New York, on January 26, 1935, at the age of 46, from a variety of illnesses.[60] A Coney family relative thinks that Anne Graham Gould also died in New York, in the late 1930s or early 1940s, at least before her mother Kaikilani died in 1943.[61] With their desires to remain private, ending this story here would undoubtedly please descendants of both Coney and Gould families.

Notes

1 Clarice B. Taylor, "J. H. Coney, Kauai Kamaaina, 75 June 10; 360 Are Invited To Attend Birthday Luau," *HSB,* June 5, 1939:9.

2 Taylor 9.

3 Taylor 9.

4 Peggy Kai, "Chinese Settlers in the Village of Hilo before 1852," *HJH,* vol 8 (1974) 64. Ena's original surname was In but was adapted to the Hawaiian language, alternately pronounced Enner, Enna, and Ina before settling on Ena. He was one of a group of Chinese men who started a sugar plantation and mill in Hilo, Hawai'i, about 1845. Ena Road in Waikīkī is named after his son, John Ena II, a prominent Honolulu businessman and member of the House of Nobles.

5 Taylor 9; Samuel M. Kamakau, *Ruling Chiefs of Hawaii* (Honolulu: The Kamehameha Schools 1961) 47.

6 Kai *HJH;* A. Grove Day *History Makers of Hawaii* (Honolulu: Mutual Publishing Co. 1984: 40 states that John Ena Jr. was a businessman, eventually becoming president of the Inter-Island Navigation Co. He was a member of the House of Nobles, decorated by King Kalākaua in 1888, served on the Board of Health under the Provisional Government, and was a member of the constitutional convention for the Republic of Hawai'i.

7 "Life History of Late Mrs. Hubert Vos Told," *HA* Sept. 18, 1943.

8 Taylor, *HSB,* June 5, 1939:9.

9 Taylor 9.

10 Kai, *HJH* 1974:68.

11 Taylor 9.

12 Taylor 9.

13 Taylor 9.

14 Taylor 9. This was most likely Mary H. Krout, author of *Hawaii and a Revolution* (New York: Dodd, Mead and Co., 1898). She states in her book that she was a newspaperwoman in Chicago, and that she was a cousin to Rear Admi-

ral George Brown, commander of the *U.S.S. Charleston,* the ship which took King Kalākaua to San Francisco in 1890 and brought his body back to Hawai'i in 1891. Brown was held in high esteem by the royal family, which would explain Krout having been given access to many people and places in Hawai'i, including personal interviews with the widowed Queen Kapi'olani and former Queen Lili'uokalani, and many Provisional Government members during her 1893 visit. Krout also visited Hawai'i in 1914, again apparently working for the Chicago newspaper. The book *Seven Authors of Crawfordsville, Indiana* (Indianapolis: Indiana Historical Society, 1952:16), by Dorothy Ritter Russo and Thelma Lois Sullivan, states that Krout worked for *The* (Chicago) *Inter Ocean* newspaper between 1887 and 1897, and lived in Hawai'i for awhile.

15 Taylor 9.

16 "Mrs. L. Coney Succumbs to Long Illness," *HA,* Feb. 24, 1929.

17 *PCA,* Apr. 26, 1902.

18 Lilikala Kame'elehiwa, *Native Land and Foreign Desires* (Honolulu: BPBM Press, 1992) 307.

19 Kai, *HJH,* 1974:69.

20 *James Campbell Esq.,* (Honolulu: The Estate of James Campbell, no publisher, Fourth Printing 1992) 14.

21 *F,* Nov. 1, 1880:85.

22 *HA,* Feb. 24, 1929.

23 Copy from Kaua'i Historical Society to author, Mar. 5, 1993.

24 Taylor, *HSB,* June 5 1939:9.

25 Robert C. Schmitt, "Some Firsts in Island Leisure," *HJH* Vol X11 (1978) 99.

26 Marion Durant, interview by author, Nov 27, 1993. Durant's aunt Mattie was married to Mike Coney, son of John Ha'alelea Coney (Kaikilani's brother), and Durant knew most of the family.

27 A. P. Taylor, *Under Hawaiian Skies* (Honolulu: Advertiser Publishing Co., 1922) 322.

28 Taylor, *HSB,* June 5 1939:9.

29 Lili'uokalani, *Hawaii's Story By Hawaii's Queen* (Boston: Lothrop, Lee & Shepard Co., 1898) 310.

30 "Life History of Mrs. Hubert Vos," *HA,* Sept. 18, 1943.

31 *HA* Sept. 18, 1943.

32 Letter from Marion Durant to author, June 11, 1993.

33 "Jay Gould Weds Miss Annie Graham," *New York Times* Apr. 30, 1911: 13; "Jay Gould Dies; Was Champion At Court Tennis," *New York Herald Tribune* Jan. 27, 1935.

34 Durant to author, letter June 11, 1993.

35 *Columbia Encyclopedia,* Ninth Printing 1968, 2326.

36 David W. Forbes, *Encounters With Paradise Views of Hawaii and Its People, 1778–1941* (Honolulu: Honolulu Academy of Arts, 1992).

37 *National Encyclopedia of American Biography* Vol XXV (New York: James T. White & Co., 1936) 52.

38 "Hubert Vos Dead; Portrait Painter," *The New York Times,* January 9, 1935:19.

39 Charles De Kay, "Painting Racial Types," *Century Magazine,* Vol. LX, No. 2 (June 1900) 163.

40 David W. Forbes, "Encounters With Paradise Views of Hawai'i and Its People, 1778–1941" (Honolulu: Honolulu Academy of Arts, 1992).

41 Hubert D. Vos, grandson, letters to author, 1993. The original Vos letters, now lost, were handwritten. Kaikilani had them, along with a summary, typed for the possible use by a magazine. Mr. Vos sent the author xeroxed copies of the typed letters.

42 Sara Jablon, e-mails to author, June 11, 2003, and June 20, 2003. Jablon is curatorial assistant, modern, contemporary, and American art, Fogg Museum. Grenville L. Winthrop (1864–1943), the donator, was a Harvard alumnus who left a large and important art collection to the Harvard art museums. He purchased the Empress painting in 1940 from the Kende Galleries in New York. A color photo of the painting is on the jacket cover of *Dragon Lady The Life and Legend of the Last Empress of China,* by Sterling Seagrove (New York: Knopf, 1992).

43 *National Encyclopedia,* Vol XXV; C. A. S. Williams, *Outlines of Chinese Symbolism and Art Motives* (New York: Dover Publications, 1976) 132.

44 Marion Durant letter to author, Aug. 13, 1993; *National Encyclopedia,* Vol XXV: 52.

45 Hubert D. Vos letters to author Sept. 5, 1997, and June 18, 2003.

46 Bob Dye, *Merchant Prince of the Sandalwood Mountains* (Honolulu: U of Hawai'i P, 1997); Bob Dye fax to author Nov. 18, 1997.

47 *The New York Times* Jan. 9 1935, 19.

48 Copy from the Kaua'i Museum to author 5 Mar. 1993.

49 "Mrs. Hubert Vos Dies at 75 at Her Home on Garden Isle," *HSB* Sept. 11, 1943.

50 "Life History of Late Mrs. Hubert Vos Told," *HA,* Sept. 18, 1943.

51 *Kaua'i Historical Society Quarterly,* vol 7, no. 2 (Dec. 1997).

52 "Former Honoluluan Dies In Germany," *HG,* Aug. 15 1911, 8.

53 *HG* Aug. 15, 1911.

54 *HA* Jan. 4, 1953.

55 *PP* Apr. 1904, 9.

56 Maury Klein, *The Life and Legend of Jay Gould* (Baltimore: Johns Hopkins U, 1986).

57 Coronation of King George V, grandfather of the present Queen Elizabeth II.

58 Durant, interview with author, Nov 27, 1993.

59 Edward B. Scott, *Saga of the Sandwich Islands* (Lake Tahoe, Nevada: Sierra-Tahoe Publishing Co. 1968) 160.

60 *New York Herald Tribune,* Jan 27, 1935: 1.

61 *HSB,* Sept 11, 1943.

ALFRED L. CASTLE

President Roosevelt and General MacArthur at the Honolulu Conference of 1944

HAWAI'I EMERGED from its relative obscurity in 20th century world events to play a prominent role in World War II. The war suddenly began for Hawaii and the United States when an expansionist, imperial Japan, on December 7, 1941, gambled that a surprise, disabling attack on Pearl Harbor would guarantee permanent access to needed strategic resources in the British and Dutch colonies of Southeast Asia. The first six months of the war were a time of unbroken Japanese military victories, while after May of 1942, Japan saw its thrusts into the south and central Pacific blunted by the carrier battles of the Coral Sea (May 1942) and Midway (June 1942). U.S. naval forces commenced the offensive against Japan in late 1942 in the Solomons and the Papuan areas of eastern New Guinea. These tentative steps toward victory were quickened by the successful amphibious offensives in the central Pacific from the Gilbert Islands to Okinawa joined by the advances across the northern coast of New Guinea into the Philippines. Ultimately a full scale invasion of Japan was rendered unnecessary through the deployment of the atomic bombs at Hiroshima and Nagasaki in August of 1945. The war in the Pacific officially ended September 2, 1945.

Alfred L. Castle is executive director of the Samuel N. & Mary Castle Foundation and the author of Diplomatic Realism: William R. Castle, Jr., and American Foreign Policy, 1919–1953 (1998); *"Herbert Hoover and the Elusive Quest for Peace" in* Uncommon Americans: The Lives of Herbert and Lou Henry Hoover *(Praeger, 2003); and* A Century of Philanthropy: A History of the Samuel N. & Mary Castle Foundation *(rev. ed., 2004).*

The Hawaiian Journal of History, vol. 38 (2004)

As epochal as the attack on Pearl Harbor was, the often overlooked Honolulu Conference of 1944 played a critical role in determining the outcome of the successful completion of the Pacific war against Japan, and provided political cover for one of America's greatest presidents. Moreover, it played a significant role in convincing nervous American voters that a secretly dying President could complete an unprecedented fourth term in office. In addition, the conference, carried out in semi-secrecy, signified Honolulu's strategic role in America's post-war plans for the Pacific. Though no original transcripts were kept of the meeting, various participants recorded their memory of the events in subsequent memoirs.

In July of 1944, Franklin Delano Roosevelt was nominated for an unprecedented fourth term as president of the United States. His campaign opponent, Thomas E. Dewey, a popular former governor of New York and moderate Republican, had openly questioned FDR's health and ability to conduct the government through the dangerous and uncertain final months of World War II. Other than also questioning FDR's concessions to the Soviet Union and the ongoing Republican criticisms of purportedly wasteful deficit of New Deal spending, Dewey lacked a compelling case for his campaign. Yet with the national emergency not yet over in Europe or the Pacific, Dewey argued that Roosevelt's health was a liability that could not be ignored.

Today, we know that FDR's doctors, closest friends and advisors, and attending physicians did in fact hide from the public that he was, by 1944, dying of protracted cardiovascular disease. As the former Indiana University historian Robert Ferrell discovered in medical files only released in the late 20th century, FDR had lost vigor, suffered from constant weariness, and had trouble with his handwriting. His severe related hypertension and hypertensive heart disease, combined with dangerously high blood pressure, led doctors to conclude he would never finish a fourth term in office.

Partly in order to conceal his alarming condition, FDR decided to astound those who doubted his vigor by calling suddenly for a conference with General Douglas MacArthur, supreme commander of the South-West Pacific area, and Admiral Chester W. Nimitz, commander in chief of the U.S. Pacific Fleet, in Honolulu in July of 1944. In addition, it allowed him to have decisive conferences with Nimitz and MacArthur over differences that had arisen over the final strategy for defeating Japan. MacArthur was of particular concern to FDR, as he had acquired powerful friends among civilian congressional leaders, former state department officials, and Herbert Hoover, the Republican president from 1929 to 1933. MacArthur, a stern critic of the New Deal and a popular figure among many Republicans, represented potential political problems for the president. FDR felt that a face-to-face meeting with this potential political adversary might dissuade him from causing trouble during the critical 1944 election. Finally, FDR hoped that the five-day ocean voyage to Hawai'i from San Diego would give him needed time to rest away from the glare of media.

The deuteragonist at the Honolulu Conference was the imperial Douglas MacArthur. One of America's most political generals, he had been America's most decorated soldier in World War I. Raised by ambitious parents to be a great military commander, MacArthur had worked assiduously to make alliances among powerful Republicans, the men who made up much of the government from 1921 until FDR's ascendancy in 1933. Although his career languished in the 1930s, he found his opportunity for greatness restored with the outbreak of World War II.

Yet, in 1942, MacArthur had presided over the biggest defeat in army history when he was forced to surrender 70,000 American and Filipino troops on the Bataan peninsula guarding Manila Bay, and the attendant fortress of Corregidor. Moreover, Japanese planes had destroyed much of his air force on the ground, despite warnings that a Japanese attack was imminent, in December of 1941. Forced by military orders to flee the Philippines for Australia in the spring of 1942, he felt that his redemption lay in crossing New Guinea and rescuing the men he had left behind. Specifically, his honor could be restored if he could advance across the jungles of New Guinea faster than the Navy could advance toward Japan through the central Pacific.

MacArthur also disagreed with the navy's general strategy for defeating Japan. He favored moving up on Japan through the Solomons and Bismarcks by what he called the New Guinea-Mindanao Axis. He wanted to have the entire fleet and amphibious forces under his command to liberate the Philippines before advancing on Japan itself. Admiral Chester W. Nimitz, in charge of navy general strategy, however, was for a quicker advance in the Pacific, taking key points in the Gilbert, Marshall, and Caroline Islands on the way through the Marianas, to Taiwan, and finally to China's coast to establish a base to attack Japan. The plan that was adopted in May 1943 was a combination of these two positions, allowing a dual advance with China as the ultimate strategic launching pad for the final invasion of Japan. Under this compromise, and by the end of February 1944, the Gilbert and Marshall Islands had been secured and the Bismarcks Barrier had been broken. From then on, MacArthur's forces advanced steadily, taking the Admiralties at the same time that Nimitz' forces drove into the Marianas, Tinian, and Guam. During the months that followed, MacArthur continued to lobby for liberating all of the Philippines and using Luzon as the springboard to Japan.

But by the spring of 1944, Chief of Naval Operations Admiral Ernest J. King wanted a faster, more direct route to Japan. The navy had developed newer, faster carriers that could reach Japan through the Marianas and Formosa. There they would establish strategic bombing sights for the B-29 bombers, and the will of Japan to continue fighting could be challenged through massive bombing missions. MacArthur was crushed to learn that many in the navy wanted his famous New Guinea campaign to end in the Southern Philippines. The recapture of Luzon and the freeing of his captured soldiers would have to wait until the real war was won through taking the fight directly to Japan. An indignant MacArthur had long distrusted the motives of his political enemies in Washington, D.C., and demanded an audience with FDR to argue his case. The Pentagon, alarmed at his constant complaints, ordered MacArthur to meet Roosevelt on July 26, 1944, in Honolulu. MacArthur hurriedly packed his bags and headed for Honolulu knowing that he had political cards to play with Roosevelt, a man he personally detested for his character and his policies.

Roosevelt departed for Honolulu from San Diego on the heavy cruiser *Baltimore* on July 21. Surrounded by family, he spoke to reporters of the need for his re-election in order to conclude the war and to make a strong peace. He also promised to lay the groundwork for additional government programs to provide economic and social stability in post-war America. Privately, Roosevelt seethed that MacArthur's political dislike for him had become public. Using his political connections with leaders in Congress, MacArthur had implied that he would allow himself to be drafted by the Republicans to run for president in 1944. He had, for example, correspondence with Hoover's former undersecretary of state, William R. Castle, scion of a prominent New England and Hawai'i family, in which he sharply criticized Roosevelt's friendliness with the Soviet Union and his expensive New Deal programs. When his dalliance with party operatives and congressional Republicans came to light, Roosevelt was shocked with the disloyalty in the midst of war. Although he did not comment publicly, the political intrigues of MacArthur ratified Roosevelt's long dislike and distrust of a general who would use a political club to leverage supplies, attention, and strategic priorities.

Departing San Diego amidst unconfirmed reports of Japanese naval activity 200 miles north of Honolulu, FDR's cruiser took a zigzag route for much of the five-day trip to Honolulu. As the report of Japanese activity proved incorrect, FDR took advantage of the calm of the Pacific voyage to lie on deck with officers and sailors. His dog Fala by his side, he spun stories, snoozed, read through coded mail, and chatted with the few advisors he had brought along for this quickly called and unofficial conference.

The *Baltimore* docked at Pearl Harbor at 3:00 P.M. on July 26. Only an hour before, MacArthur had arrived after a 26-hour flight from Brisbane, Australia. Hardly settled at Fort Shafter, home of the Pacific Command, he was summoned by Roosevelt to his cabin room. Always one for a symbolic gesture, MacArthur kept FDR and the top Pacific command waiting on ship as he rounded up a grand open touring car procured from a well-known Honolulu brothel madam. As FDR, Nimitz, and other high officials prepared to go below deck, MacArthur arrived to the cheers of the crowd, waved regally, and strutted to the top of the gangplank in an open shirt and leather jacket. After a brief meeting, the two giants had their pictures taken for release during the campaign season. Agreement was reached on the meeting times the next day as well as a carefully orchestrated set of photo opportunities of the two inspecting Hawaii's troops. Then, FDR was transported, in a humble closed car, to spend the night in Waikīkī at the beach estate of the prominent businessman Chris R. Holmes, a three-story home with an outside elevator.

Back in his officer's quarters at Fort Shafter, MacArthur raged to aides that FDR knew nothing of military matters, was "a fake," and had come to Honolulu on a junket to fool the American people about his health. Moreover, he raged that Roosevelt was only intending to use him for photo opportunities to win votes. He also told aides that the president was clearly dying and that he ought to admit his real condition to the American people and drop out of the race. Moreover, he fumed to devoted aides about how his entire career had been a battle with incompetent bureaucrats for proper resources to do his job.

The next day, Roosevelt chose Honolulu's only other long open touring car, owned by the Honolulu fire chief, to inspect all of the nearby military bases with MacArthur (fig. 1). Teams of photographers caught their every move much to the pleasure of the president. Such photos would be published widely and would give every impression of a healthy president who was an active commander in chief. Interestingly, a few staff officers advised Roosevelt to exclude *Nisei* soldiers: that is, soldiers who were sons of Japanese immigrants born in the U.S., from camera range on the distant possibility that a fanatic

FIG. 1. The Presidential motorcade sweeping up the driveway of St. Louis College in Kaimukī, as part of the President's tour of military bases. The school was serving as the army's 147th General Hospital in 1944. DeSoto Brown collection/National Archives, U.S. Navy.

might attempt to assassinate him. Roosevelt quickly dismissed such fears and asked that any *Nisei* be photographed with him along with other soldiers.The conference itself did not begin until after dinner at the Holmes estate. Admiral Nimitz spoke first and argued cogently for the navy's position of speeding an attack on Japan through Formosa. Doing so, he argued, would place the U.S. squarely between Japan and the Philippines, with the coast of China within range of fast moving carrier forces. Japan, with American submarines blockading her shipping and facing daily bombing raids, would need to move its forces off of Honshu and Hokkaido and take the battle to Formosa.

With barely controlled intensity, MacArthur stood to take his turn in front of the maps laid out in front of the President. He reviewed his humiliation at Bataan, his promise to return and its importance to the morale of the American people, and his frustration in having to fight the joint chiefs of staff over making the Philippines a high priority. His plan, which he identified with "American honor," was to retake Manila.

FIG. 2. Tokyo is the target of Admiral Chester Nimitz's pointer as General Douglas MacArthur, President Franklin Roosevelt, and Admiral William Leahy look on during their Waikīkī conference. DeSoto Brown collection/National Archives, U.S. Navy.

Apparently at a strategic stalemate, FDR adjourned the planning group and spoke to MacArthur alone. Seizing the initiative, MacArthur used his political trump card. Reminding the president that this was a reelection year, he argued that abandoning 7,000 starving POWs and 17 million Filipino Christians would turn public opinion against him. According to what MacArthur would later tell former President Hoover, in 1946, Roosevelt was shocked with the general's blunt threat and abrasive manner. Nonetheless, when the others rejoined the discussion, Roosevelt announced that he would make no decision about strategy until the next day and praised both Nimitz and MacArthur for their grasp of grand strategy.

The next morning, at 10:30 A.M., the group reassembled for further discussion. The mood was friendlier, and those present agreed to work closely together on behalf of the common goal of defeating the Japanese. MacArthur also firmly restated his position and promised to hand the Philippines over to Roosevelt within six to nine months with minimal loses. He repeated his claim that if only the navy had been prepared for Japan's attack in 1941, he could have reinforced and properly defended his position in the Philippines. Now he had an opportunity to make up for the country's embarrassment by retaking the Philippines.

At about noon, on this final day of the conference, FDR said he had heard enough, waved his hands, and said he had accepted MacArthur's proposal and would expect Nimitz to assist MacArthur in the recapture of Luzon. With no further comment, he dismissed the group for lunch. Overjoyed at this successful resolution of a nagging strategic stalemate, MacArthur rushed to catch a waiting plane at Hickam Field. Before leaving, however, he made one more speech praising FDR for his sound strategic mind. With that he sped off to catch his plane while privately telling an aide that FDR would be dead within a year.

As Roosevelt prepared to leave Honolulu for military inspections in the Aleutians, he gave a brief press conference in which he praised MacArthur for his progress in the war with Japan, extolled the state of training and readiness on Hawai'i's bases, and noted with pleasure how many changes had come to Honolulu since his vacation in the city 10 years before. He compared Honolulu to the major sophisticated cities in the U.S. and predicted a flourishing of its economy after the war.

Although no official transcripts of this conference exist, MacArthur would later tell several people that he had used Roosevelt's need to show progress in the war and an image of good health to strike his own bargain. Clearly no official decisions were made in Honolulu, and the debate continued in the Pentagon. The final decision to provide MacArthur his support came officially in mid-September after naval intelligence had revealed real Japanese vulnerability at Leyte in the central Philippines.

For historians, the short Honolulu conference is of interest more for what it tells us about Roosevelt in his final year of life and of MacArthur than of the strategic decisions adumbrated in its unofficial proceedings. Roosevelt, the supreme politician, was able to neutralize possible opposition for Republicans and the conservative press by placating the politically well-connected general. On the other hand, MacArthur's unusual political influence and powerful connections in Washington led him to test, at least indirectly, the constitutional divide between civilian and military authority. He would later test the commander in chief's authority in a more alarming and direct way when he challenged President Harry S. Truman's strategy in the Korean War in 1951. His success in negotiating his strategic preferences at the Honolulu conference would be an important precedent for this later infamous action.

NOTES

Good secondary accounts include Clayton D. James, *A Time for Giants: The Politics of the American High Command in World War II* (New York: Franklin Watts, Inc., 1987); Michael Schaller, *Douglas MacArthur: The Far Eastern General* (London: Oxford U P, 1989); James A. Bishop, *FDR's Last Year, April 1944–April 1945* (Pocket Books, 1975); Robert Ferrel, *The Dying President: Franklin D. Roosevelt 1944–1945* (Columbia, MO: U of Missouri P, 1998) and William D. Hassett, *Off The Record With FDR* (New Brunswick, NJ: Rutgers U P, 1958).

Notes & Queries

The Journal *welcomes responses to previously published articles, statements on Hawaiian and Pacific history, and queries for information that will assist research. Opinions expressed here and elsewhere in the pages of the* Journal *are those of the authors and do not necessarily reflect those of the Editorial Board or the Hawaiian Historical Society.*

More on Honolulu's Red Light District

Ted Chernin has requested that the following corrections be made to his article, "My Experiences in the Honolulu Red-Light District" (*HJH* 34, 2000: 203–217.

On page 204, second paragraph, last line: The name "Leon" should be corrected to "Leong."

On page 205, top paragraph, these two sentences:
"Muller, who worked in the Radio Section, stayed behind. I wanted to, also, but our boss, W. W. McIlhenny, would allow only one of us to stay, and I lost the toss of the coin."

should be replaced by:

"Muller, who worked in the Radio Section with me, wanted to leave also, but our boss W. W. McIlhenny would allow only one of us to leave. He tossed a coin for it, and I won."

On page 213, third paragraph, last two lines: The following phrase should be eliminated: ". . . so that I would be her first customer in the bull pen."

The Editors

More About Harry Maitey, from Polynesia to Prussia

In 1976, when I researched the life of the Hawaiian Harry Maitey in Berlin, the Cold War was going on and that city was divided by the infamous wall (*HJH* 11, 2000: 125–161). Many parts of Berlin where Maitey, from 1824 until 1872, could roam freely were inaccessible to me, as were significant archives and libraries. All this changed when the wall fell on November 9, 1989, when the Brandenburg Gate (fig. 1) was opened, and the reunification of Germany, with Berlin as its capital, began.

The Brandenburg Gate, built more than 200 years ago, is emblematic for Berlin—especially the quadriga, the monumental chariot on top of the gate, which is closely connected with Berlin's history. The creator of the quadriga was Johann Gottfried Schadow (1764–1850), in his time Berlin's foremost sculptor. He was also an assured graphic artist, a keen and methodical observer of nature and of cultural life, a diarist, teacher, and the director of the Prussian Academy of Arts.

In 1824, when the teenager Harry Maitey arrived in Berlin, Schadow took the measurements of the young Hawaiian's head, drew his

Fig. 1. Berlin: Brandenburg Gate
Landesarchiv Berlin/Barbara Esch-Marowski

portrait in black chalk and graphite, and identified it "Harry, Sandwich Islands, October 26, 1824." (Fig. 2)

Schadow had always been interested in the proportions of the human body—not only as a sculptor but also as an intellectual—and in his time various theories developed concerning the forms of the cranium and their relations to the human mind. Throughout his professional life, he collected data by carefully measuring and exactly drawing. Only in 1835 did he publish the results of these studies as *Physiognomies.*[2] They consisted of a text on the "differences in facial features and cranial forms of the peoples from all over the world" and of 29 plates of illustrations. Harry Maitey was grouped with "savage peoples from very different locations" and commented on twice in the text: "Between Mexico and China are the Sandwich Islands. From there the ship *Mentor* brought an inhabitant by the name of Harry whose portrait—front and profile—is shown on plate VII."[3]

Most of the persons depicted on the plates were short-term visitors to Berlin. Harry, however, stayed in the city or nearby. He always remained under the supervision of royal officials with whom Schadow had constant contact. Thus he was able to follow the young Hawai-

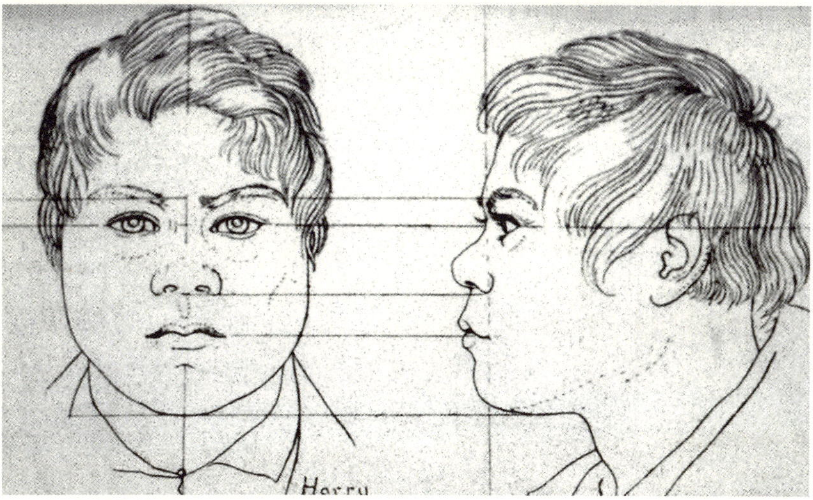

Fig. 2. Gottfried Schadow
Harry of the Sandwich Islands, October 26, 1824
Akademie der Künste Berlin

ian's development from his arrival in 1824 until the publication of his treatise in 1835.

> Since he remained here, everybody can observe that his facial traits do not differ from ours. The broad cheek bones can also be found here. His skull is a bit narrower—which is concealed by his heavy growth of hair. The only difference is a somewhat darker skin. He does not have the aptitude for a finer cultivation of the mind.[4]

It would be interesting to know how much the last sentence of Schadow's assessment is based on his own observation, on some of the prevailing phrenological theories, or on the reports by the royal Prussian bureaucrats.

Schadow's portraits of Harry Maitey are known in three versions:

1. The original black chalk and graphite drawings of October 26, 1824. Those are located in the archives of the Art Academy in Berlin.[5]
2. A second version was ordered by Schadow according to entries in his unpublished diary/calendar of 1825: "on January 27 I went to the Academy where Mr. Rolling lithographed the Sandwich Islander drawings" and "on January 28 Mr. Rolling lithographed the Sandwich Islands man."[6]
3. Finally, for the publication of the "Physiognomies" in 1835, zinc plates were produced.[7]

While the sketch of Harry Maitey in my original article of 1977 is without date and by an unknown artist, the portraits in this addendum are well documented.

In Berlin, Maitey's memory is kept very much alive around Peacock Island and Nikolskoe's Saints Peter and Paul Church. In the city, the area where he lived from 1825 to 1830 now glows again in dignified elegance.

Submitted by Anneliese Moore

NOTES

[1] Anneliese Moore, "Harry Maitey; From Polynesia to Prussia," *HJH,* Vol. 11 (1977), 125–161.

[2] Gottfried Schadow, *National Physionomieen* oder Beobachtungen ueber den Unterschied der Gesichtszuege und die aeussere Gestaltung des menschli-

chen Kopfes, in *Umrissen bildlich dargestellt auf neun und zwanzig Tafeln, als Fortsetzung des Polyclet,* Berlin 1835.

3 *Ibid.* 26.

4 *Ibid.* 26–27.

5 Akademie der Kuenste Berlin, Archiv. Nr. 974.

6 Schreibkalender 1825. Zentral-Archiv der Staatlichen Museen Berlin.

7 Schadow, *National Physionomieen* 1835, Plate VII.

"Aloha 'Āina" Revisited

A previously published article by Amy Ku'uleialoha Stillman (*HJH,* 33, 1999: 83–99) explored the authorship of the Hawaiian nationalist song, "Aloha 'Āina," now commonly referred to as "Kaulana Nā Pua."[1] To recall, Stillman tendered the possibility that Jose or J. S. Libornio, director of the short-lived Hawaiian National Band, was composer of the tune once attributed to the song's lyricist, Ellen Kekoaohiwaikalani Wright Prendergast. In late 2001, while looking through the Lili'uokalani Collection at the Bishop Museum, I discovered another unpublished manuscript of "Aloha Aina."[2] That a copy of this *mele* was found among Lili'uokalani's possessions should come as little surprise: The poetic text, which protests her overthrow and pledges allegiance to her sovereignty, would no doubt have been very special to her. And as Stillman points out, J. S. Libornio was a loyal associate of the queen and Mrs. Prendergast her close friend. What is significant about the Bishop Museum manuscript, handwritten in the elaborate script of the Victorian era, is that it credits arrangement of the song to I. Libornio, further complicating the matter of musical attribution.

Who were the Libornios? We know little beyond the information already provided by Stillman. An initial search of the Hawai'i State Archives and Bishop Museum yielded no biographical data on I. Libornio and raised only intrigue concerning Jose.[3] In the absence of detailed personal records for either individual, we may still surmise something about the Libornios' relationship from their music. The back cover of the 1895 "Aloha Aina" sheet music copyrighted by J. S. Libornio also identifies him as the composer of "Maui Girl Waltz," a song for which I. Libornio held an arrangement copyright.[4] This confirms the distinction between composition and arrangement upheld by U.S. copyright law, and indicates the latter musician's familiarity with the work of the band director.[5] The Bishop Museum manuscript is also clearly marked as an arrangement. Why, then, would it raise any questions about musical authorship? It would do so because a comparison of Jose's 1895 published composition with I. Libornio's undated and unpublished arrangement reveals so few discrepancies. Both are in the same key (D major), but greater significance lies in the arrangement of parts. I. provides harmonized voice parts as an alternative to the single melody line offered by the sheet music. I.'s harmonizations, however, are almost identical to the right-hand piano accompaniment of J. S.'s composition. Likewise, brief broken chord figures in the right hand of both piano accompaniments happen in most of the same places, with same or similar voicings. There is even a match between certain text treatments (e.g., "aina" capitalized in the fourth verse, but not in the last). The complete lack of information on I. Libornio and the marked correspondence between the published and unpublished versions offer the possibility that Jose wrote under more than one name (though we might reasonably ask why) and adjusted his own composition either before or after publication. The simpler left-hand accompaniment pattern of I.'s arrangement may, for example, have been written to accommodate the desires of a particular pianist. And the vocal harmonizations written immediately above the text in the same arrangement could have facilitated part-singing by members of the Royal Hawaiian Military Band[6] or the Hawaiian National Band.

If we presume that I. and J. S. Libornio are *not* the same person, the musical equivalencies may be explained as the product of a mutually creative relationship, though we might also imagine something less reciprocal. Certainly their contributions to the realm of publication were not equal: I. Libornio appears to have published less and to have arranged material composed by J. S. Libornio, but not the other way around. To the extent that I. Libornio was known to be an arranger of another J. S. Libornio composition, the manuscript adds credence to Stillman's thesis.

It is also important to note that if Mrs. Prendergast was the composer of the melody of "Aloha 'Āina," she is not acknowledged as such on the Bishop Museum manuscript. However, neither is J. S. Libornio. The absence of the lyricist's name is in keeping with the American practice of privileging music over text. Given the importance of oral tradition, however, the identity of the composer(s) of both text and music may have been common knowledge to local audiences or to the manuscript's recipient. Hence, the arranger or copyist may have deemed formal recognition unnecessary. It is also worth noting that as an unpublished document, the arrangement was not subject to legal scrutiny. Indeed, the manuscript pushes us to ponder some finer points of U.S. copyright law. Despite the extraordinarily slight differences between the two Libornio creations, one was clearly considered an arrangement. It is not clear whether I. Libornio would have been able to secure a copyright for something that so closely resembled the originally published sheet music, if indeed that was ever the intent.

While the discovery of the Bishop Museum manuscript casts no doubt on Mrs. Prendergast's authorship of the text of "Aloha 'Āina," neither does it confirm or deny Jose Libornio's role as musical creator. It does, however, offer a new set of possibilities and raises further questions about practices of musical collaboration and attribution within Hawai'i at the end of the 19th century.[7]

Submitted by C. K. Szego

Notes

1 Amy Ku'uleialoha Stillman, "'Aloha Aina': New Perspectives on 'Kaulana Nā Pua'," *HJH* 33 (1999) 83–99.

2 The spelling of "Aloha Aina" reflects the original document, which does not indicate vowel length and omits the *'okina;* MS MC Liliuokalani, Box 6.5, Bishop Museum.

3 A Joseph Libornio is named in court papers, and the apparent same individual, J. Libornio, is identified in the December 1891 records of the Privy Council of State. Libornio evidently stabbed a gentleman of Chinese ancestry out of romantic jealousy. During the legal process that ensued, Libornio required a Spanish interpreter, though documents also reveal that he spoke Hawaiian to his victim. He was found guilty of assault and battery with a weapon, sentenced to one year of hard labor, and fined one dollar. The Privy Council papers document a petition for the offender's pardon and restoration of civil rights, which were ultimately denied. The only evidence that might suggest a link to conductor/composer/arranger Jose Libornio is the location of the assault weapon—in a music box under a piano—found by

police in the assailant's upstairs room. It is wise to remember, however, that the offender could easily have been a male relative of the composer or no relation at all.

4 Copyright for I. Libornio's arrangement of "Maui Girl" was secured in 1892 by W. E. Reynolds in Hawai'i and the U.S.A., and again in 1897 by Wall, Nichols Co. of Honolulu. The only composition (as opposed to arrangement) found to date that is attributed to I. Libornio is "Leonora Gavotte," a solo piano piece published and copyrighted in 1892, also by Wall, Nichols Co.

5 The distinction between composition and arrangement is upheld by other J. S. Libornio publications. For example, if the phrase "by J. S. Libornio" is read literally, "Amistad (Pasodoble)" was copyrighted as a composition by Armstrong & Bacon in 1896. "Sweet-heart of the Long Ago" by J. Gordon Temple was copyrighted as a J. S. Libornio arrangement by E. W. Armstrong in the same year.

6 Stillman, "Aloha Aina" 86.

7 Least plausible is a scenario of misattribution: i.e., the music copyist indicating I. Libornio where J. Libornio was intended.

Response to Lydia Black's Book Review

In the last edition of the *Journal,* (*HJH,* vol. 37, 2003, 223–225), Lydia Black, *emerita* professor of anthropology, University of Alaska, Fairbanks, published an unfavorable review of my recent book *Hawai'i's Russian Adventure: A New Look at Old History* (Honolulu: University of Hawai'i Press, 2002), in which she did not recognize a single significant contribution the book makes towards better understanding a 19th century encounter between the people of Kaua'i and representatives of the Russian-American Company. The main focus of the book is a fort on Kaua'i that Hawaiians built starting in 1816. They called it by more than one Hawaiian name, and their main Russian-American Company ally, Georg Anton Schäffer, called it "Fort Elisabeth." Black appears to consider several main points of the book as "thin 'discoveries,'" including such crucial new information as the facts that Kaumuali'i, paramount chief of Kaua'i, had broken his 1810 alliance with Kamehameha *before* the arrival of Schäffer in 1816 (pp. 99–107); that Hawaiians did not build the fort in Waimea *for* the Russians (as Black continues to contend), but for themselves; that the fort carried ritual symbolism similar to heiau; and, that Kaumuali'i had the structure built on sacred ground as a part of his residential complex. She goes on to state that "there is little of adventure, or Russian, in the use the Hawaiians made of the original structure after Schäffer's ignominious departure." While I agree with her that the "Russian" aspects of this site have been overstated by previous historians (this is one of the main points of the book), her statement devalues, for example, one of the most important 19th century battles in the Hawaiian Islands, in 1824, that began at the fort (pp. 146–156). Her review also stands in stark contrast to the four other reviews I am aware of in the journals *Choice, The Contemporary Pacific, Historical Archaeology,* and *Oceania.*[1]

Black makes a noble but unnecessary attempt to defend the scholarship of two historians that I critique, Richard A. Pierce and Nikolai Bolkhovitinov. Although Black does not mention it, I offer praise to these historians for their contributions to Russian-American Company studies (see pp. 5, 20, 40–41), but I balance this praise with explicit examples and direct quotations where Bolkhovitinov and Pierce and other named historians chose to emphasize Russian agency and history and underemphasize Hawaiian agency and history (pp. 33–43). As a consequence of these critiques, Black claims that I single out Pierce and Bolkhovitinov as "Western chauvinists," an inflammatory term that I did not use and that I find most inappropriate. I recognize that constructing history is a process with inherent bias, and I certainly do not wish to condemn either man as being particularly chauvinistic. While Black states that she "is not competent to judge the author's presentation of purely Hawaiian political history," she somehow feels comfortable stating that Pierce and Bolkhovitinov "show excellent grasp of the internal Hawaiian politics of the time . . .".

Black also accuses me of "political correctness" and introducing "many errors not only of interpretation but also of fact." These are damning statements for any historical work, and given the vague nature of her declarations, they are difficult to defend. My sole recourse is to consider the only three distinct instances of supposed errors that she identifies, and that she proclaims she "chose at random." Any author who has attempted to summarize hundreds of published sources spanning such diverse areas of specialty as Russian history, Hawaiian history, the Pacific fur-trade, archaeology, and sociocultural anthropology, knows how difficult it is to keep errors of fact from creeping into a text, and I dreaded, as I read the review, some significant demonstration of such error. The three issues that she raised, however, were hardly egregious misrepresentations on my part, and demonstrate errors of fact and interpretation on her part. Although Black's intention in presenting these so-called errors seems to have been to discredit the entire book, I thank her for these specific comments, because they clarify the trivial nature of her discontent.

Her first point involves Petr A. Tikhmenev's book *Istoricheskoe obozrenie obrazovaniia Rossiisko-Americanskoi Kompanii i deistvii eia do nastoiashchago vremeni,* or *"Historical Survey of the Origin of the Russian-American Company and its Activities up to the Present Day,"* first published in Russian in two volumes (1861–1863). In my book's bibliography, I cite a 1978 translation by Richard A. Pierce and Alton S. Donnelly, published under a new title, *A History of the Russian-American Company.* Because the translated work was expressly derived from a Russian edition of 1888 (a fact that Black may have forgotten), I placed that date in brackets next to the date of 1978 in the citation. Black claims that I state that "Tikhmenev's book was published originally in 1888," which is simply her misinterpretation of the citation. She then implies that I was unaware of the earlier edition *even though I mention it in the text* (p. 36).

The second "error" that Black found "irritating" is my characterization of Otto von Kotzebue's vessel, the *Rurik,* as a Russian naval ship. She admits that the *Rurik* flew a navy flag, but, because chancellor Rumiantsev had funded the expedition, she tries to claim "Kotzebue acted as a private individual." Here, I cite Henry Kratz, translator and editor of *A Voyage Around the World with the Romanzov Exploring Expedition in the Years 1815–1818 in the Brig* Rurik, *Captain Otto Von Kotzebue,* by Adelbert von Chamisso (Honolulu: University of Hawai'i Press 1986, xii): "Even though Rumiantsev financed the expedition, the brig *Rurik* (more properly, *Ryurik*) was a vessel of the Russian Navy, manned by Russian naval men, carrying cannon; technically a man-of-war, it was entitled to the treatment accorded any other naval vessel when it called at foreign ports."

Finally, Black objects to my suggestion that Kamehameha used an interpreter to converse with Kotzebue (p. 35), and she correctly points out that both Kotzebue and Kamehameha spoke English. The man I refer to, Juan Elliot de Castro, certainly carried messages between Kotzebue and Kamehameha during the encounter, but I admit it would have been more justifiable to refer to him as a messenger than an interpreter. Black goes too far, however, when she ascertains "no translator was needed." This would assume that Kamehameha and Kotzebue *chose* to speak only in English to relay complex issues, and also ignores the following quotation relating to the encounter from Chamisso's journal (*A Voyage Around the World* . . . 116–117): "Our captain [Kotzebue] had arrived. The old warrior [Kamehameha] received him with cordiality. He understood protocol very well and knew how to act magnificently, impressively, and easily. Mr. Cook, a European who possessed his confidence, and who now had returned from the American ship to which he had been sent, *served him as interpreter* [emphasis added]."

With these three petty issues presented as her only evidence, Black proceeds to suggest that I suffer from poor training and a poorly qualified dissertation committee (this book is largely based upon my dissertation research). Over the last 20 years, I have researched issues of historical anthropology using archaeology, ethnohistory, and ethnology, in Alaska, Russian Fort Ross in California, Hawai'i, and New England, among other less relevant areas. My dissertation advisors were leading scholars in the anthropology of Russian-America: (Dr. Kent Lightfoot, University of California, Berkeley); Oceania, (Dr. Patrick Kirch, University of California, Berkeley); and ethnohistory (Dr. Stephen Greenblatt, currently holding the most prestigious John Cogan University Professor of the Humanities position at Harvard University). Black's vague references to "pseudo-scientific jargon" appear aimed at the book's brief theoretical sections, derived largely from the works of Marshall Sahlins, Fernand Braudel, and Antony Giddens, three of the most internationally recognized social theorists of the 20th century. In any case, I deliberately kept jargon to a minimum in the book (see my comments in the Preface, ix).

Despite my absolute protest of Black's lack of accuracy and scholarly balance in her review of my book, I close this reply by recognizing that she has had a long and distinguished career in Russian-American Company studies and Native Alaskan research. I have read many of her publications throughout the years with much enjoyment. It is a most unfortunate circumstance, and it is with deep regret, that I have been compelled to respond to her inequitable comments in this instance.

Submitted by Peter R. Mills
Associate Professor of Anthropology
University of Hawai'i at Hilo

Notes

1 F. Ng, *Review of Hawai'i's Russian Adventure: A New Look at Old History.* (Honolulu: U of Hawai'i P, 2002); *Choice,* December 2002, 40(4)524; Susan A. Lebo, Review of *Hawai'i's Russian Adventure,* in *The Contemporary Pacific,* Fall 2003, 15(2)486–489; Roger E. Kelly, Review of *Hawai'i's Russian Adventure,* in *Historical Archaeology* 2003 37(4)122–123; Leialoha Apo Perkins and Roland F. Perkins, Review of *Hawai'i's Russian Adventure,* in *Oceania* 2002 73(2) 147–148.

Book Reviews

Kahana: How the Land Was Lost. By Robert H. Stauffer. Honolulu: University of Hawai'i Press, 2004. x + 265 pp. Illustrated. Index. $38 cloth.

The history of land tenure in Hawai'i, especially during and after the events of the *Māhele* of 1846–1855, is a hot topic these days. A number of people have a particular interest in this issue because their ancestors received land through the *Māhele* either by award or purchase, and now that land is no longer in their hands, leaving them to ask, "What happened?" More recent studies have examined this issue in general, seeking to illuminate the process of the *Māhele* and its aftermath: Jon J. Chinen, Maivan Clech-Lam, Jean Hobbs, Lilikala Kame'eleihiwa, Marion Kelly, Ralph Kuykendall, Riley Moffat and Gary Fitzpatrick, Jon Osorio, David White, and John Wise. And there are a few studies of the changes in land tenure by those who participated in it, such as William DeWitt Alexander, John Lydgate, Jacob Brown, and Curtis J. Lyons. But just as we attempt to create a general description of the Hawaiian land unit known as the *ahupua'a* (land division), then find as we examine the hundreds of *ahupua'a* in Hawai'i that there is a plethora of variations; so, too, as we look at changes in land tenure of those same traditional land units in Hawai'i we find that each seems to have its own unique story that may not neatly fit into the general concept. A few historical studies of land tenure in particular areas have been done, such as Marion Kelly's study of nine *ahupua'a* in Ka'u Hawai'i, Jocelyn Linnekin's study of Keanae, Maui, and Jeffery Stover's thesis on La'ie, O'ahu. Now Robert Stauffer has refined his doctoral dissertation on the *ahupua'a* of Kahana, O'ahu, to present a tale that examines in detail the fate of all the lands in Kahana Valley that were set apart in the *Māhele,* and in so doing brings to light some very interesting events that while validating the common perception that most of the *kuleana* (land, property) awarded during the *Māhele* are no longer in the hands of the awardee's descendents, points out that some very creative methods were used to maintain control by the Hawaiian *kuleana* owners as well as those seeking to take control away from them.

Stauffer begins with a good detailed description of the *Māhele* process of 1846–1855 and how it was applied in Kahana Valley, both for the common people, the *maka'āinana,* and the chiefs or *ali'i.* Stauffer then describes two tracks the land privatization process took in Kahana Valley, one for *maka'āinana* and one for *ali'i.*

In Kahana Valley, 96 acres of the best lands were awarded in 34 *kuleana* claims to the *maka'āinana* living there, while the *ali'i,* Keohokulole, received title to the remaining 4,954 acres. To see that only 96 acres in that whole lush valley was being used, albeit by only 34 families, is surprising. In Stauffer's historical analysis of the population of Kahana Valley, and considering the size of the cultivated lands of the valley, I was chagrined by how few people apparently lived in what I would consider about the most salubrious and productive *ahupua'a* on O'ahu. Perhaps the carrying capacity of Kahana as well as the other lands of Hawai'i isn't as high as we thought. To really understand this I suppose a person would have to have been there to see what the land was capable of within the agricultural practices of the time. In many respects, chapter two leads one to conclude that the common folk with their small but productive fee simple *kuleana* fared better than the *ali'i* with their huge amounts of undeveloped and often unproductive land. Table 3 on page 83 is particularly illuminating in showing that the small acreage comprising the common people's *kuleana* truly was the most valuable land.

The government of Hawai'i under the control of the king and his ministers and advisors had a goal which they thought would benefit Hawai'i. However, the *Māhele* was not scripted. It was plowing new ground and evolved as problems were identified and dealt with. We need to be aware of the inexperience of those involved in planning and administering the *Māhele* process. Regarding hints of a conspiracy by foreign merchants and Christian missionaries to gain control of the land, I just don't see any real evidence of it in the events of the *Māhele* process. Stauffer goes on to suggest that for 50 years before the overthrow of the monarchy in 1893 Hawai'i was a de facto territory of the U.S. with 90% of the land owned or controlled by American interests, without considering the 984,000 acres of Crown land controlled by the monarch, the 1,495,000 acres of land controlled by the Hawaiian government, the best of which was sold largely to Hawaiians, and the 1,619,000 acres awarded to Hawaiian *ali'i* in the *Māhele* as their private property. In no description of the events of the *Māhele* do we see evidence of a conspiracy to defraud any person or group of their right to land ownership. While the *maka-'āinana* were one of the three groups with an interest in the land of Hawai'i under the principles established by the Land Commission, the common people were obviously not using one third of the land. So while their claims and awards amounted to a small percentage of the acreage of the land, that percentage did include the best lands. If the *kuleana* awards did not satisfy the *maka'āinana*'s desire for land, then the government offered its 1,495,000 acres for sale as described in the *Index of All Grants Issued by the Hawaiian Government Previous to March 31, 1886,* though this did not apply to Kahana specifically since the general title to the *ahupua'a* was awarded by the king to the high chief Keohokulole. This selling of hundreds of thousands of acres of the best government lands is described by Stauffer as being to haole (Whites), but a perusal of the list of grantees shows about 99 percent with Hawaiian surnames. As we lament the loss of these small, albeit valuable, *kuleana* little or no research has been done to document the fate of this much larger group of government lands sold mostly to Hawaiians. Nor do I see much attention given to the role of land acquisition by Chinese immigrants either by lease or by marriage. In Kahana, during the period being studied, the Chinese were an integral part of the community as leaseholders, owners, and farmers.

I could have understood land values and financial arrangements better in historic dollar values. I am used to thinking in terms of, say, the 1850s economy and prices, and Stauffer's large modern dollar figures I found to be confusing. Given the wildly fluctuating real estate values of recent years even these figures could become quickly obsolete.

In Kahana, the original *kuleana* holders by and large seemed committed to the *Māhele* process and the opportunities it offered and held on to their lands as best they could. Stauffer, by tracing the legal history of each *kuleana* in Kahana, describes the various ways that the *kuleana* holders used to keep control of their lands.

A major theme of the book is the description of the Non-Judicial Mortgage Act of 1874 and how it was used to wrest control of *kuleana* in Kahana from the original awardees and their heirs. Over time, as the *kuleana* owners needed cash they would take out a loan and use their *kuleana* as collateral. This new law allowed the lender to foreclose on the property for non-payment and have it auctioned off without having to go through the court system. Stauffer shows that there was great opportunity for abuse in this system which today we would probably consider unethical and illegal. It was definitely stacked against the *kuleana* owner. In Kahana Valley, from 1888 to 1903, 65 percent of the *kuleana* were taken this way. The Non-Judicial Mortgage Act of 1874, however egregious, played upon a fact of life we all have to deal with; when we borrow money we are expected to repay it. After reading Stauffer's detailed description of how well the Kahana *kuleana* owners used the new economic and financial system to preserve their titles I don't think we can use the excuse of ignorance of that system to explain how these folks found themselves in the precarious position of being victims of this law. Fortunately today, we have laws that see that we are treated fairly, but if we cannot repay a loan we still may have to forfeit our collateral.

These same exigencies were faced by the *ali'i* who though land rich were usually cash poor, having to generate income from often poor land without their traditional access to labor and tax revenues. Just like the common folk they saw borrowing on the land or selling it outright as a logical way to get the cash they wanted. Hence, many *ahupua'a* passed out of their hands.

The summary of the processes by which many Hawaiians lost control of the lands they had received in the *Māhele* begs the question of, if given the choice, what would the people have preferred: maintain the status quo as it was before the *Māhele* with unlimited access to the resources of the *ahupua'a,* but with often burdensome taxes of produce and labor, or the opportunity of fee simple ownership of the land they worked without the traditional demands of the chiefs? One of the major deficiencies mentioned by Stauffer for the failure of the *Māhele* to achieve its goal was that the government did not take the simple step of making these native lands inalienable which would have kept the land in the hands of the Native Hawaiians by law. I believe this option was discussed in the legislature at the time but was dismissed for a variety of reasons. Making native lands inalienable is part of the land tenure policy in other Pacific countries, such as Tonga, Samoa, and Fiji. The trade-off has been in development when investors with capital, usually non-natives, are concerned about the security of their investments when they cannot secure title to the lands they are investing in. I would like to see a dialogue between Native Hawaiians and Tongans, Samoans, and Native Fijians on the pros and cons of how their nations' land tenure systems have worked for them.

Another important theme described by Stauffer relates to the practice of Hawaiians getting together, pooling their resources, and buying an *ahupua'a* or another large tract of land. The Hawaiian *hui* or group purchase, with individuals buying shares, seems to be an attempt to replicate in many respects the situation that existed before the *Māhele.* The share-holders of the Kahana *hui,* which bought the title to the entire *ahupua'a* was established in 1874, and shareholders held the land outside their individual *kuleana* in common. Stauffer, correctly, I believe, describes the Kahana *hui* as a social statement, a move to return to a more traditional land tenure system that they were familiar with and seemed to work for them. Plus it gave them unrestricted access to all of Kahana's traditional resources.

The Kahana Hawaiians by and large resisted selling their *kuleana* to outsiders. Prior to 1887, none did. The eventual owner of most of Kahana, Mary Foster, was actually one-fourth Hawaiian and a staunch royalist. By the end of the century, however, many *kuleana* were held by disinterested heirs who usually did not live in Kahana Valley nor cared to. These are the people Foster, her agents, and others tracked down and made offers to. As the Hawaiian population gradually moved out, the rich lands of Kahana Valley were seen as underutilized by local businessmen who saw various opportunities and went after them. Through aggressive purchase of *kuleana* and *hui* shares by Mary Foster and her agents, the Kaneohe Ranch, Lincoln McCandless, William Wilcox, and various members of the Castle family, the Native Hawaiians of Kahana lost control of their valley. Stauffer examines all the methods used by these people to get control of the lands of Kahana.

Stauffer's story of Kahana is very interesting and illuminating. It adds important new dimensions to the dialogue on the evolution of Hawaiian land tenure. I think *Kahana: How the Land Was Lost* sets a high standard for research in a topic too often clouded by emotion and opinion and agendas.

Riley Moffat, Senior Librarian
Brigham Young University-Hawai'i

Inventing Politics: A New Political Anthropology of the Hawaiian Kingdom. By Juri Mykkänen. Honolulu: University of Hawai'i Press, 2003. xii + 248 pp. Notes. Bibliography. Index. $45 (cloth)

This book is a revised version of Mykkänen's Ph.D. dissertation in Political Science from the University of Hawai'i at Mānoa (Honolulu: "Locke in a Heathen Land: Cultural Construction of Politics on the Kingdom of Hawaii, 1825–1945," 1993.)

As Mykkänen's title suggests, he is influenced by an array of social theory attached to cultural "invention," and he applies this to Hawaiian political systems in the first half of the 19th century. Haunani-Kay Trask expressed contempt for this body of theory and considered it another colonialist tool used to make modern Hawaiian cultural values appear inauthentic ("Natives and Anthropologists: The Colonial Struggle," in *The Contemporary Pacific* 3(1): 1991: 159–167). Mykkänen obliquely addresses Trask's critique (p. 2), and is careful to use the idea of inventiveness as a cross-cultural process of adaptation employed by foreigners and Hawaiians alike. By drawing attention to the inherent imperfections in cultural translations, and the consequential tensions that affected processes of cultural mediation, Mykkänen conceives a fresh view of the roles played by chiefs, missionaries, *maka'āinana* and foreign residents in the fusion of indigenous and Western ideologies, including "politics." Although anthropologists and historians regularly study political organization within non-Western societies, Mykkänen takes the position that in the case of Hawai'i, "functionalist and quasi-functionalist understandings of politics have resulted in an unquestioned orthodoxy, and the whole concept of politics has been taken too much for granted" (p. 13). In order to rectify this, Mykkänen investigates the transposition and adoption of words like "government," "governing," and "politics" in Hawaiian culture, and exposes significant structural transformations in the meanings of autochthonous (and supposedly corresponding) terms such as *"aupuni," "ho'omalu,"* and *"kālai'āina."*

The author systematically examines relevant Hawaiian and English lexicon pertaining to politics in dozens of Hawaiian-English dictionaries written from the time of Captain Cook to the 1980s, and also presents quotations from missionaries and literate 19th century Hawaiians to contextualize the usage of various terms. This methodology is reminiscent of the compilation of the semiotic icon of the English language, the *Oxford English Dictionary* (see Simon Winchester, *The Professor and the Madman,* New York: Harper Collins, 1998), and the result is a detailed lexicography and historiography of Hawaiian political concepts. His analysis is also an insightful anthropology of culture contact that examines the fluid relationships between church and state in Hawai'i. Mykkänen thus invents a novel ethnography of 19th century Hawai'i, and the changing (and often ambivalent and paradoxical) alliances that were formed between missionaries and chiefs.

The "Introduction" is perhaps the weakest part of the book, not for a lack of theory, but for a lack of clarity. Mykkänen discusses the deconstruction of "savagery" in the writings of Enlightenment philosophers including Voltaire and Diderot, and connects this theme with other recent anthropological critiques surrounding Western portrayals of non-Western political systems. This, in turn, leads to his adoption of ideas pertaining to the "invention of tradition" *a la* Wagner (Roy Wagner, *The Invention of Culture,* (Chicago: University of Chicago Press, 1975); and Eric Hobsbawn and Terence Ranger, Eds., *The Invention of Tradition,* (Cambridge: University of Cambridge, 1983), in combination with other anthropologists and historians who have modified and applied these concepts in Pacific Island contexts, such as Greg Dening, Jocelyn Linnekin, Marshall Sahlins, and Nicholas Thomas. Although Mykkänen successfully demonstrates his familiarity with related theories and research, his introduction appears to be directed towards a relatively small audience of social theorists, and will likely alienate many potential readers before they reach the main substance of the book. Furthermore, the opening sentences in the book (p. 1) contain awkward grammatical structures, and the third sentence contains a clear grammatical error ("a steadily intensifying encounters"). These stylistic shortcomings provide an unfortunate first impression and foreshadow an awkward and often verbose writing style that makes the book unnecessarily challenging.

By the beginning of chapter one ("Natives and Foreigners: the Cultural Order of Hawaii's Early Missionization"), the merits of Mykkänen's work become more apparent. He opens with commonly discussed aspects of 19th century Hawaiian society (drawn from sources such as Beckwith, Kamakau, Sahlins, and Valeri), but he quickly proceeds into an uncommonly penetrating analysis of the traditional meanings attached to various Hawaiian words, including *"aupuni,"* referring to Hawaiian chants including the name chant of Kūali'i, the Kumulipo, and Kūkanaloa. Although this chapter could have been extended further into the past by discussing proto-Polynesian linguistic reconstructions, chapter one provides a traditional foundation similar to an "ethnographic present." From this perspective, Mykkänen begins to address the historical transformations of Hawaiian word usage, and corresponding conceptual changes, that accompanied the development of the Hawaiian monarchy.

I would quibble with the author over his representations of the 1824 insurrection on Kaua'i (p. 49–52) in which he repeats the missionary spin that the battle was a victory of Christianity over a "nativist rebellion" (p. 192). Mykkänen states that "Hoapili and another high-ranking Hawai'i chief, Kaikio'ewa, had a discussion with William Richards [Maui missionary] about Christian conduct of war and were advised not to kill captives: "It is not certain to what extent these orders were followed, but some of the chiefs certainly boasted of abstaining from even taking captives . . ." (p. 51). The figurehead of the rebellion was Kaumuali'i's son, Humehume, who had left the Islands for New England when he was approximately six years old, and returned with the missionaries in 1820 when he was 21. Hence, in terms of cultural mindsets, Humehume was one of the least native natives that could have led the rebellion, and the Windward chiefs consulted star positions, intentionally killed at least one captive chief, and were also reported by Kamakau and others to have wantonly defiled the bodies of the dead rebels (see *Hawai'i's Russian Adventure: A New Look at Old History* by Peter R. Mills (Honolulu: University of Hawai'i Press, 2002: 146–154). The missionary Hiram Bingham invented the idea that the battle was a victory of Christianity over a nativist rebellion. Like the 19th century Hawaiian chiefs who chose to adopt Christianity, Mykkänen uses the invented event to suit his own purpose.

Chapters two ("The Politics of Virtue") and three ("Culture in the Making: The Rise of Political Discourse") provide insightful anthropological studies of the culture of missionaries themselves, and how missionaries, Hawaiians, foreign merchants, and foreign governments employed various tactics to restructure Hawai'i as a polity. In chapter two, the author examines the tension that existed in New England between commercial liberalism in the merchant communities and the religious orthodoxy of Calvinism, setting the stage for the conflicts between merchants and missionaries in Hawai'i. The orthodox Calvinists were largely responsible for the creation of missionary societies such as the ABCFM, and were decidedly against many of the liberal ideas that accompanied secular capitalism. Mykkänen touches on the differences between orthodox Calvinism and a more popular reformed Calvinism that adopted emotional styles of Methodist and Baptist preachers (p. 66), but could have strengthened his thesis regarding the Great Awakening of 1837–1839 in chapter four ("Political Economy") by drawing more attention to the huge impact this transition had on the Hawaiian mission itself. Margaret Ehlke discussed this aspect of the mission, and this source would complement the issues touched upon by Mykkänen (see "Enthusiastic Religion and the Lives of Titus and Fidelia Coan, Missionaries to Hilo," by Margaret S. Ehlke, M.A. thesis, American Studies, University of Hawai'i at Mānoa, 1986).

By chapter three and leading in to the subsequent chapters, Mykkänen approaches the heart of his major contribution, drawing attention to the evolution of the concept of "politics" in Hawai'i. It is framed in an ongoing tension between merchants, missionaries, chiefs, and commoners to establish the roles of "church" and "state." Through the following chapters, the author translates Hawaiian language newspapers and other documents, and provides a historiography of the translation of political concepts. The year 1845 appears to be a pivotal time in Mykkänen's thesis in chapter five ("Natural Rights, Virtuous Wealth"), marked by the initiation of new ceremonial protocols and annual keynote speeches in Kauikeaouli's court (pp. 162–163). Among Mykkänen's findings are that the word "politics" and the concept of political activism were almost completely lacking in Hawai'i through the early 1830s, although "the notions of kingdom and government were frequently used" (p. 108). Likewise, Mykkänen finds that the words "government" and *"aupuni"* were not printed as equivalents until 1854 (p. 110). *"Kālai'āina"* also shifted conceptually from a meaning similar to political economy through land division to one of modern party politics and logistical aspects of running the government. Chapter six ("The Denouement") is a final impressive compilation of the etymology of various Hawaiian terms tied to politics (too many to cover here).

The author closes his work with a nine-page "Conclusion," which is more clearly written than the "Introduction," and perhaps should be read first by those who wish to get a better feel for what the book will be about. *Inventing*

Politics, despite some shortcomings, is an excellent piece of research with a robust methodology and thoroughly insightful analyses of the events that shaped 19th century Hawai'i.

Peter R. Mills
Associate Professor of Anthropology
University of Hawai'i atHilo

The Mysterious Death of Jane Stanford. By Robert W. P. Cutler, M.D. Stanford, California: Stanford University Press, 2003. x + 161 pp. Bibliographical references. Photographs. Appendices. Index. $29.95 cloth.

"Mrs. Stanford Dies, Poisoned" read the headline of the *San Francisco Bulletin* on March 1, 1905. Eye witnesses in Hawai'i agreed as to what happened, the doctors in attendance made a diagnosis of strychnine poisoning, chemists confirmed strychnine to be present in large amounts in the bottle of bicarbonate of soda from which she had been given a potion for stomach upset, and stomach contents and body tissues taken at an autopsy were positive for strychnine.

So what is the mystery Dr. Robert Cutler, almost a hundred years later, propounds in his 161-page exposé? There are mysteries enough to go around, but the most intriguing one from the perspective of a reasonably knowledgeable resident of Hawai'i is how it could be that virtually no one in today's California community of Stanford academia was even aware of how the cofounder of Stanford University died or that there is any mystery whatsoever! Dr. Cutler, a Stanford professor of neurology and neurological sciences, emeritus, readily admits that he came across the whole affair accidentally while working on another matter, magnesite mining. Having discovered the story, he queried his colleagues in the school of medicine, finding that they too were totally ignorant of the matter, and one, a lover of mysteries, encouraged him to delve further into the story. How is it possible that the faculty (and many others) of an institution of this caliber could overlook (or repress) the well-documented facts of the case and instead accept a medically preposterous explanation proposed from a distance of thousands of miles from the scene by the then president of Stanford University, Dr. David Starr Jordan? Could it be there was a constituency willing to believe that a diagnosis by physicians from a distant, exotic archipelago was most likely incompetent or even fraudulent, possibly conspiratorial, or perhaps it was all merely a ploy to gain notoriety? Dr. Culter addresses this question by extensively reviewing the qualifications of the Honolulu physicians and scientists with a conclusion much in their favor.

A preface sets forth Dr. Cutler's happenstance discovery of the story. The introduction provides a short history of the Stanford family, their son's death while they were traveling in Italy, and the founding of the Leland Stanford, Jr. University. Successful businessman and senator from California, Leland Stanford died leaving his wife Jane as the sole trustee. She is described by some in poetic verse as the mother of and moral guardian of California's children, but others found her to be an uneducated tyrant unfit to the task of directing the university, much less micromanaging its affairs.

As a good detective might, Dr. Cutler has divided the work into three parts. The first part in five chapters describes what is known about the events of her death, a description of a previous poisoning some six weeks earlier in San Francisco, the police investigation, witness accounts and later memoirs, the details of the inquest in Honolulu, and the arrival of Stanford's president, Dr. David Starr Jordan, and his party in Honolulu. These generally recognized "facts" have been gleaned from newspaper accounts, official records, archival material, and memoirs. The second part in four chapters discusses and analyses the theories, correspondence, press releases, accusations, and general confusion and misunderstandings on the part of the main characters: Honolulu physicians and scientists, the long time companions/servants/staff present and involved in the final events, witnesses, the detective agency's investigators, the police in San Francisco and Honolulu, and, most extensively, the machinations of Dr. Jordan. The third part has two short chapters. The first presents briefly what others have written about the character of Dr. Jordan. The summation chapter states bluntly Dr. Cutler's agreement with the finding that Mrs. Stanford died of strychnine poisoning and speculates on just how the entire matter seems to have mysteriously faded from public view. The U.S. mainland papers and the general public generally accepted that the death was due to a ruptured coronary artery or other cardiac disease as Dr. Jordan proclaimed. All of the materials are extensively cited and amplified for each chapter in the notes section following the main body of work.

I would suggest that in reading this fascinating, marvelously well-researched book that after the preface and introduction, one should then turn to the second and third appendices for a most important review of two critical events. One, the "Ross Affair," preceded the death of Jane Stanford and affected her greatly. This affair involved the firing of a professor of sociology and raised a national hullabaloo about academic freedom and freedom of speech, The other event also involved the firing of a professor, Dr. Goebel, a close confident of Mrs. Stanford and critic of the administration of

Dr. Jordan. The professor was dismissed soon after Mrs. Stanford died. He accused Dr. Jordan of attempts to bribe him in order to silence the professor's criticism and views on the cause of Mrs. Stanford's death. These events are essential for an understanding of the alienation between Dr. Jordan and Mrs. Stanford.

At least for myself, the large cast of characters was difficult to keep track of and required considerable rereading. In view of the vast bibliography and citations, I think it unlikely that any of the mysteries pertaining to the death of Jane Stanford will ever be resolved definitively. By the same token, the theories proposed as to why, by whom, and for what motive are tantalizing, some obviously impossible, and none completely satisfying. The best of mysteries, as in this case, I believe, are really those where readers must settle upon the answer that best suits their own fancy. For a follow-up, one might take a tour of the restored Moana Hotel in Waikīkī or perhaps even stay in room number 120 and perchance to dream of what it might be like to succumb to strychnine poisoning.

Alfred D. Morris M.D.
Cardiologist, Ret.
Honolulu, Hawai'i

A Date Which Will Live: Pearl Harbor in American Memory. By Emily S. Rosenberg. Durham; London: Duke University Press, 2003. x + 236 pp. Illustrated. Bibliographical references. Index. $24.95 cloth

Reworking the typed draft of his December 8, 1941, speech to Congress asking for a formal declaration of war, President Franklin D. Roosevelt pencilled out "a date which will live in world history" and made it "a date which will live in infamy"— altering the pedantic into the rhetorical, forever altering Americans' popular-culture association with the word "infamy" and also providing the root phrase for dozens of book titles.

For the first 50 years, the attack on Pearl Harbor was a seminal and singular event in American history, a "hinge of history," as Winston Churchill dubbed it, a moment beyond which the nation was altered. For Americans alive then, it is the moment the world changed into a frighteningly broad and unknowable landscape, but still one that could be tamed. For Americans alive since then, "Remember Pearl Harbor!" had the quaint resonance of "Remember the Alamo!" or "Remember the Maine!" It is a purely historical event, consigned to the dustbin, on a dimly realized par with the Norman Invasion or Paul Revere's Ride. And any deeply felt patriotic vibrations from the Pearl Harbor attack end at our borders. To the rest of the world, getting wrought up over this long-ago battle is a purely American pastime.

By the 50th anniversary of the attack in 1991, the attack on Pearl Harbor remained largely the province of the veterans who were there and rivet-counting military historians fixated on facts and technologies. There was a growing number of "revisionist" writers, mostly Republican, who seemed dedicated to blaming the success of the attack on either the sheer ineptitude or the evil calculations of Democrat President Roosevelt rather than crediting the Japanese military machine, but these were the voices of factless cranks with an agenda. When the 50th anniversary occurred, the emphasis among historians and veterans was scholarship and commemoration, combined with an old-soldier rapprochement with Japanese veterans of the attack. The vets of both sides discovered they had more in common with each other than with their own children.

During the decade between the 50th and 60th anniversaries of the attack, however, much of what we consider "history" in America underwent a radical change, rendering even the notion of scholarship itself as anchorless and defensive. Emily S. Rosenberg, a history professor at Macalester College, has attempted to distill the scholastic and political turbulence of the period in *A Date Which Will Live: Pearl Harbor in American Memory*. Although it's a slim volume, it is densely packed with ideas and observations about Pearl Harbor as a contested icon in our national mythology.

As the book makes clear, there was a veritable "memory explosion" during the 1990s, sparked largely by conservative groups seeking to "reclaim" history, a notion that literally redefined the abstract study into a salable product. The question posed was, "Who owns history?" A flood of memory products flooded the market, ranging from books such as *The Greatest Generation* to movies like *Saving Private Ryan* to entire television networks like the History Channel to Disney-designed historic theme parks to bizarre patriotic crazes like Civil War reenacting, all geared to culturally adrift Americans seeking solace in a calmly knowable past.

Even more sharply divisive were bitter debates over historical interpretation. Rosenberg notes that the Republican-led Congress, armed with conservative notions about "history standards," has led the attack on professional historical scholarship, seeking to replace history education that is broad-mindedly inclusive with another kind of teaching based on narrow definitions of patriotism. The ugliest battle was over the display of the nuclear bomber *Enola Gay* at the Smithsonian Air & Space Museum, when conservative lobbyists, with the sympathetic ear of Congress and armed with misinformation, scuttled a professional interpretation of the famous artifact. No less than House Speaker Newt Gingrich—a Ph.D. in history—drew the battle lines when he declared that the debate was "a reassertion by most Americans that they are sick and tired of being told by some cultural elite that they ought to be ashamed of their country."

Rosenburg makes a convincing and well-documented brief that this assault on culture, elitism, and professional scholarship mightily influenced the way Pearl Harbor was interpreted in the late '90s—and will be interpreted in the future. Another bitter fight erupted over whether to clear the reputations of disgraced Pearl Harbor commanders Admiral Husband Kimmel and General Walter Short. Congress was lobbied repeatedly on the issue and finally passed the buck to the Bush White House, who quietly tabled the notion.

Even so, there has been a recent explosion of "revisionist" texts about the attack, most laying the blame on Roosevelt, and all criticized for lacking data and original sleuthing. It is history by screed and wishful thinking rather than scholarship and reason, and sets the tone for the way history has mutated. Rosenberg notes, rather ruefully, that "Pearl Harbor" now calls to mind political perfidy and bureaucratic bungling as much as it does the Japanese sneak attack.

Her work winds down with the 60th anniversary of the attack in 2001, but there were two events that colored the commemoration. One was the big dumb movie called *Pearl Harbor,* that while historically inaccurate and artistically bankrupt, managed to reinsert the phrase into the consciousness of young Americans. The other was the 9/11 attacks on New York and Washington, a sudden, tragic, and evil event of such magnitude that the only cultural touchstone that put it in perspective was the attack on Pearl Harbor. Many newspapers simply used the word "Infamy!" in their headlines, making the cultural and historic connection part of modern times.

As President Bush wrote in his diary on September 11, "The Pearl Harbor of the 21st century took place today," and later explicitly expanded his political rhetoric to draw links between the Greatest Generation's "Good War" and the current fight against terrorism.

We live in interesting times. Rosenberg's meticulous study of the "memory icon" of Pearl Harbor, analyzing the shifting patterns of American thought on the uses of history in modern culture, ought to be required reading for all up-to-date historians and for those wondering why their grasp on history is slipping through their fingers.

Burl Burlingame
Honolulu Star-Bulletin

Pōhaku: The Art & Architecture of Stonework in Hawai'i. Coordinating Authors: David Cheever and Scott Cheever. Editors: Dr. Janine Shinoki Clifford, AIA and Frank S. Haines, FAIA. Photography: Douglas Peebles. Honolulu: Editions Limited, 2003. xi + 171 pp. Illustrated. Bibliography. Index. $39.95.

In Hawai'i, they surround us, quietly yet insistently shaping our perceptions of place and experience: *pōhaku*—Hawaiian stonework. We seek shelter within their stout walls, follow the paths they mark for us, and, standing in their shadow, reflect on the ancient heritage they represent. A collaborative effort involving contributions from more than 50 writers, *Pōhaku: The Art & Architecture of Stonework in Hawai'i* is devoted to the documentation and appreciation of stonework across all the Hawaiian islands from ancient times to the present. The book is arranged by building types: ancient sites, churches, government buildings, educational facilities, commercial structures, residences, pathways, and infrastructure, along with a chapter on stone quarries. The structures recorded here ranges from civic and religious buildings monumental in scale and importance through sober and forthright commercial structures to charming residences. But the built environment of Hawai'i includes far more than conventional architectural monuments. Fishponds, reservoirs, irrigation ditches, and retaining walls, works that mark the human manipulation of the natural environment, are included here as noteworthy components of the story of Hawaiian stonework. Within each chapter examples drawn from across the state are illustrated and described in short essays. Most of the essayists are architects, preservationists, or journalists, and the texts reflect their various expertise as well as their shared affections for the subject matter.

One of the challenges of a documentary effort like this is to keep the multiple short essays of so many different authors from becoming repetitious or worse, degenerating into a confusing babble of voices devoid of critical threads of continuity. The team responsible for producing *Pōhaku* deserves credit for meeting this challenge so well. Coordinating authors David Cheever and Scott Cheever, working with editors Dr. Janine Shinoki Clifford, AIA, and Frank S. Haines, FAIA, have produced a very thoughtful and readable study of the subject. Douglas Peebles's handsome color photographs provide the book's sustaining core. Peebles has a sensitive eye for photographing stonework; he captures his subject in telling details and odd photographic angles as well as in the standard general exterior views one associates with architectural photography. Text and image balance and amplify each other in an effective way, and this book is a pleasure to read.

If orchestrating the efforts of a team of writers is one challenge for the editors, conveying the rich complexity of stone's story constitutes a second challenge. In the built environment, everything is made intentionally of something, and that something—in this case, stone—has its own unique history, properties, and meanings for those who come into contact with it. Stone structures in Hawai'i have been fabricated out of volcanic basalt and sedimentary coral and sandstone. Rock was picked up off the ground (in a sense, harvested) as fields were cleared for agricultural use, quarried high and low across the Islands, and cut out of the offshore coral reefs. The chapter on quarries details the local origins of stone, but there is a global as well as a local dimension to the story of *pōhaku*. In the 19th century, granite arrived in Hawai'i as ballast blocks on board sailing vessels returning from China. Hawaiian sandalwood bound for Asian markets replaced the granite ballast stones in ships' holds, and the ballast blocks, in turn, were employed as paving stones for streets and sidewalks in Honolulu (examples still survive in the 1100 block of Nu'uanu Avenue). To balance the materialistic account of the subject, various authors recount the rich cultural history recorded in legends and local histories of *pōhaku*. Russell Oda, for example, contributes an essay about the Naha stone, a 7,000-pound block that now rests in front of the Hilo Public Library. Identified as probably the most famous ancient stone in the state, the legendary block reportedly supported not a physical structure but dynastic claims. Oda describes the stone's significance:

> [T]he sacred stone served as a platform to authenticate the Royal Naha lineage. If a male infant, positioned ceremoniously on the venerable stone, remained silent, it was proof of royalty, and he was destined to receive the title of prince, leader or king. If the infant cried, the status of commoner was immediately bestowed upon him. (p. 12)

One of this book's special pleasures is the connections among such disparate fields and disciplines as geology, ecology, architecture, history, and folklore (and this list could be expanded) the reader is invited to make as he or she moves from descriptions of an ancient *heiau* to an Anglican cathedral to bridges and culverts along the Hāna highway and the terrace walls of Doris Duke's Shangri La.

One theme that runs through the book deals with the significance and appreciation of permanence as a design virtue, a virtue increasingly missing in the built environment. In his introduction, David Scott, executive director of the Historic Hawai'i Foundation, notes:

> Stone is a building material that shapes future generations by its stamina and longevity. Building for permanence is today, I fear, a lost concept, a forgotten need. (p. x)

Today many of the uses for which *pōhaku* once served so well are handled by the artificial stone we call reinforced concrete. Cheap, easy to use, and durable, reinforced concrete is the global material of our time. But it is hard to imagine establishing royal legitimacy or building a haven called Shangri La with wheelbarrows of concrete. As Douglas Peebles's evocative photographs repeatedly seem to suggest, this must be considered our loss.

Dennis P. Doordan
Chairperson, Department of Art, Art History and Design
University of Notre Dame

Hawaiiana in 2003
A Bibliography of Titles of Historical Interest

Compiled by Joan Hori, Jodie Mattos, and Dore Minatodani, assisted by Joni Watanabe

Acson, Veneeta. *Waikīkī: Nine Walks Through Time: Exploring Historic and Contemporary Sites in Waikīkī.* Waipahu, HI: Island Heritage, 2003. xvii, 123 p. 2nd ed.

Aeder, Kirk Lee. *The Great Hawai'i Sports Journal: A Photographic Essay.* Waipahu, HI: Island Heritage, 2003. 172. p.

'Aha Pono-Native Hawaiian Intellectual Property Rights Conference 2003: Conference Summary. Honolulu: 'Īlio'ulaokalani Coalition, 2003. 16 leaves.

Allen, Thomas B. *Remember Pearl Harbor: American and Japanese Survivors Tell Their Stories.* Washington, DC: National Geographic Society, 2001. 57 p.

Arinaga, Esther Kwon. *Harriet Bouslog: Lawyer, Risk Taker, and Champion of the Underdog.* Honolulu: Center for Biographical Research, 2002. 7 p. (Biography Hawai'i: Five Lives: A Series of Public Remembrances). Also includes *Advocate for All Hawai'i* by Teresa Bill.

Ariyoshi, Rita. *National Geographic Traveler. Hawaii.* Washington, DC: National Geographic Society, 2000. 271 p.

Attack on Pearl Harbor. Edited by Thomas Streissguth. San Diego, CA: Greenhaven Press, 2002. 128 p.

At Hamilton Library, University of Hawai'i at Mānoa, Joan Hori is curator of the Hawaiian Collection; Jodie Mattos is a librarian in the Business, Social Science and Humanities Department; Dore Minatodani is a librarian with the Hawaiian Collection; and Joni Watanabe is a student in the College of Business Administration.

The Hawaiian Journal of History, vol. 38 (2004)

Beloff, Jim. *The Ukulele: A Visual History.* San Francisco: Backbeat Books, 2003. 127 p. Revised and expanded edition.

Birnsteel, Laurie. *Kahala: Growing up in Hawaii.* Indian Wells, CA: McKenna Pub. Group, 2002. 256 p.

Black, Cobey. *Hawaii Scandal.* Waipahu, HI: Island Heritage, 2002. 392 p. About the Massie case.

Brown, DeSoto and Linda Arthur. *The Art of the Aloha Shirt.* Waipahu, HI: Island Heritage, 2002. 96 p.

Buck, Peter H. (Te Rangi Hiroa). *Arts and Crafts of Hawaii.* Honolulu: Bishop Museum Press, 2003. xvi, 606 p. (Bernice P. Bishop Museum Special Publication, 45) Reprint of 1957.

Buke Mele o nā Hīmeni Hawai'i I haku a mele 'ia e nā kāhuli leo le'a o ka 'āina o nā Home Hawai'i Pono'ī = The Lyric Book of Hawaiian Choral Songs Composed and sung by the joyful-voiced native forest shells of Truly Hawaiian Homes. Compiled by Ed. C. Holstein, forward by M. Puakea Nogelmeier. Honolulu: Bishop Museum Press, 2003. xvi, 187, 21, 12 p. (Bishop Museum Classical Reprints in Hawaiian Language) Reprint of 1897.

Buke 'Oihana Lapa'au me nā 'Apu lā'au Hawai'i: He Alaka'i no nā Home Hawai'i i ka 'Oihana Kahuna, i Kūkulu a Ho'ola'a 'ia e nā Kūpuna o Hawai'i Lāhui no ka Make'e i ke Olakino = Book of Medical Practices and Hawaiian Prescriptions: a Guide for Hawaiian Homes in the Field of Expertise that was Established and Sanctified by the Ancestors of the Hawaiians for Preserving Physical Health. Edited by Thomas (Kamaki) P. Spencer, foreword by M. Puakea Nogelmeier. Honolulu: Bishop Museum Press, 2003. xvi, 120 p. (Bishop Museum Classical Reprints in Hawaiian Language) Reprint of 1895.

Century of the Tiger: One Hundred Years of Korean Culture in America, 1903–2003. Edited by Jenny Ryun Foster, Frank Stewart, and Heinz Insu Fenkl. Honolulu: Mānoa Journal: Centennial Committee of Korean Immigration to the United States: University of Hawai'i Press, 2003. 256 p. (*Mānoa Journal,* v. 14, no. 2)

Chang, Roberta. *Koreans in Hawai'i: A Pictorial History, 1903–2003.* Honolulu: University of Hawai'i Press, 2003. xv, 224 p.

Cheever, David, and Scott Cheever. *Pōhaku: The Art & Architecture of Stonework in Hawai'i.* Honolulu: Editions Limited, 2003. xi, 171 p.

Chinen, Jon J. *They Cried for Help: The Hawaiian Land Revolution of the 1840s & 1850s.* S.l.: Jon J. Chinen; Xlibris Corp. [distributor], 2002. 208 p.

Chinese Women Pioneers in Hawaii: a collection of stories written by ACUW members, relatives or friends honoring their pioneer women. Edited by May Lee Chung and Dorothy Jim Luke. Honolulu: Associated Chinese University Women, Inc., 2002. viii, 264 p. Includes portraits.

Christ United Methodist Church, 1903–2003: A Pictorial History = Kaeurisaeudo Yaeonhap Kamni Kyohoe 100-yaeon sajin yaeoksa, 1903–2003. Honolulu: Christ United Methodist Church, 2003. 256 p. In English and Korean.

Coffman, Tom. *The Island Edge of America: A Political History of Hawai'i.* Honolulu: University of Hawai'i Press, 2003. xv, 419 p.

Colburn, Bolton [et al]. *Surf Culture: The Art History of Surfing.* Laguna Beach, CA: Laguna Art Museum in association with Gingko Press, 2002. 1 v. (unpaged).

Columbia Documentary History of the Asian American Experience. Edited by Franklin Odo. New York: Columbia University Press, 2002. xiv, 590 p. Numerous references to Hawai'i.

Cordy, Ross H. *An Ancient History Of Wai'anae: Ka Moku o Wai'anae: He Mo'olelo o ka Wā Kahiko.* Honolulu: Mutual Publishing, 2002. xii, 164 p.

Creed, Victoria S. *Settlement Pattern for Waikapū, Wailuku District, Maui, Hawaii.* Kailua, Oahu, HI : Cultural Surveys Hawaii, 1993. 2 v.

Cook, Evelyn E. *100 Years of Healing: The Legacy of a Kauai Missionary Doctor.* Kauai, HI: Halewai Publishing, 2003. xxxiv, 255 p. About James W. Smith.

Cutler, Robert W.P. *The Mysterious Death of Jane Stanford.* Stanford, CA: Stanford General Books, 2003. x, 161 p. Case study and history of a murder in Honolulu.

Diamond, Luryier. *Images of Aloha.* Honolulu: Kamehameha Schools Press, 2003. ix, 198 p. Photographic history of Kamehameha Schools, photography by Luryier "Pop" Diamond.

Dias, Gary A. and Robbie Dingeman. *Honolulu Homicide: Murder and Mayhem in Paradise.* Honolulu: Bess Press, 2003. xx, 203 p. Case studies of investigations and history of police.

Dolim, Abel L. *Yesterday's Dragons: The B-17 Flying Fortress over Europe during WWII: A Navigator from Hawaii Recalls his 51 Missions Over Enemy Territory.* Newark, CA: Communications Concepts, 2001. ix, 154 p.

Dominion of the Hawaiian Kingdom. Honolulu: s.n., 2001. 1 v. (unpaged) + 1 CD-ROM. "Prepared for the United Nations' Security Council as an Attachment to the complaint filed by the Hawaiian Kingdom against the United States of America, 5 July 2001—David Keanu Sai, agent for the Hawaiian Kingdom."

Duus, Brian. *Federal Recognition of the Native Hawaiian Government with a Transfer to it of Territory Derived From the Ceded Lands.* Honolulu: University of Hawai'i, William S. Richardson School of Law, 2003. p. 470–515. From *Asia-Pacific Law & Policy Journal* 4.2 (Spring 2003). http://www.hawaii.edu/aplpj/

Earle, Timothy K. *Bronze Age Economics: The Beginnings of Political Economies.* Boulder, CO; Oxford: Westview Press, 2002. xi, 452 p. About Hawaiian chiefdoms.

Encyclopedia of Japanese Descendants in the Americas: An Illustrated History of the Nikkei. Edited by Akemi Kikumura-Yano. Walnut Creek, CA: AltaMira Press, 2002. xiii, 322 p. Includes Japanese in Hawai'i.

Engebretson, George. *Exploring Historic Wailuku.* Honolulu: Waterpark Pub., 2000. vi, 122 p.

Felipe, Virgilio Menor. *Hawai'i: A Pilipino Dream.* Honolulu: Mutual Publishing, 2002. xxiv, 212 p.

Forbes, David W. *Hawaiian National Bibliography 1780–1900. Volume 4 1881–1900.* Honolulu: University of Hawai'i Press, 2003. xiv, 791 p.

Gallery of Heroes: Honoring Hawaii's Medal of Honor and Distinguished Service Cross Recipients. Honolulu: Hawai'i Army Museum Society, 2001. 1 portfolio (unpaged).

Greenwell, Martha. *The Islands of Hawai'i.* Kamuela, HI: Hawaii Preparatory Academy, 2000. xiii, 58 p. Paintings by Martha Greenwell.

Hall, Dale E. *The Honolulu Symphony: A Century of Music.* Honolulu: Goodale Publishing, 2002. xvi, 224 p.

Halloran, Richard. *Sparky: Warrior, Peacemaker, Poet, Patriot: A Portrait of Senator Spark M. Matsunaga.* Honolulu: Watermark Pub., 2002. 259 p.

Hawai'i Data Book: A Statistical Reference to Hawai'i's Social, Economic and Political Trends. Edited by Robert C. Schmitt. Honolulu: Mutual Publishing, 2002. viii, 360 p.

Hawaiian Historical Society 2003 Calendar. Honolulu: Hawaiian Historical Society, 2002. 24 plates. Illustrated by photographs from the J.J. Williams Collection, taken in Hawai'i 1879–1926.

History, Heroes, and Untold Triumphs: Filipino Americans and World War Two: A Viewer's Guide to Accompany "An Untold Triumph: The Story of the 1st and 2nd Filipino Infantry Regiments, U.S. Army". Edited by Linda A. Revilla. United States: s.n., 2003. 1 v. (unpaged).

History of the Soto Sect in Hawaii. Honolulu: Hawaii Soto Mission Bishop's Office, 2002. 238 p.

Hopkins, Jerry. *Elvis in Hawai'i.* Honolulu: Bess Press, 2002. 88 p.

Imu, Adzes, And Upland Agriculture: Inventory Survey Archaeology in North Hālawa Valley, O'ahu. Edited by Leslie Hartzell, et al. Honolulu: Dept. of Anthropology, Bishop Museum, 2003. 2 v. in 5.

Japanese American Historical Experience in Hawai'i. Edited by Jonathan Y. Okamura. Dubuque, Iowa: Kendall/Hunt Publishing Company, 2001. 132 p.

Jensen, Dick. *Pearl Survivors: Eyewitness Accounts in Their Own Words.* Travelers Rest, SC: First Foundations, 2001. 100 p.

Johnson, Rubellite Kawena. *The Kumulipo Mind: A Global Heritage: In the Polynesian Creation Myth.* Honolulu: s.n., 2000. ix, 293, 14 p.

Kanaka Maoli Tribunal Kōmike. Kanaka Maoli Self-determination and the Case for Decolonization in ka Pae'āina (Hawai'i). Honolulu: The Kanaka Maoli Tribunal Kōmike, 1997. 1 v. (various foliations).

Kikuchi, William K., Dolores L. Kikuchi, and David Burney. *The Archaeological Excavations of The Makauwahi Sinkhole Site Site 50-30-10-3097 Ahupua'a of*

Pā'ā and Māhā'ulepū District of Kona, Island of Kaua'i. Puhi, Kaua'i, HI: Kaua'i Community College, 2003. viii, 140 leaves.

Kinro, Gerald Y. *Cup of Aloha: The Kona Coffee Epic*. Honolulu: University of Hawai'i Press, 2003. xii, 149 p.

Knudsen, Eric A. and Gurre P. Noble. *Kanuka of Kauai*. Honolulu: Mutual Publishing, 1999. 208 p. Rev. ed.

Kong, Sam. *Buckaloose: Kaimuki School Days with Israel Kamakawiwo'ole*. Honolulu: Mutual Publishing, 2002. 55 p.

Kupau, Summer. *Judicial Enforcement of "Official" Indigenous Languages: A Comparative Analysis of the Maori and Hawaiian Struggles for Cultural Language Rights*. Honolulu: University of Hawai'i, William S. Richardson School of Law, 2003. 77 p.

Landgraf, Anne Kapulani. *Nā Wahi Kapu o Maui*. Honolulu: 'Ai Pōhaku Press, 2003. 216 p. Photography, Hawaiian and English text, about sacred places of Maui.

Landis, Kenneth and Rex Gunn. *Deceit at Pearl Harbor: From Pearl Harbor to Midway*. USA.: 1st Books Library, 2001. xviii, 271 p.

Last Stand: The Vanishing Hawaiian Forest. Honolulu: Nature Conservancy of Hawai'i, 2003. 20 p. Includes history.

Lee, Blanche Kaualua L. *Don Francisco de Paula Marin: The Unforgettable Spaniard Who gave Hawaii The First Pineapple*. Edited by Norma Carr. Honolulu: B.K.L. Lee, 2002. 132 p.

Madsen, Daniel. *Resurrection: Salvaging the Battle Fleet at Pearl Harbor*. Annapolis, MD: Naval Institute Press, 2003. xii, 241 p.

Maly, Kepā. *Nā Honokōhau - Nā Hono i Nā Hau 'Elua (Honokōhau - Bays of the Two Wind-born Dews)*. Hilo, HI: Kumu Pono Associates, 2000. 2 v. (various pagings). Volume 1: A Report on Archival-Historical Documentary Research, and Oral History Interviews for the Ahupua'a of Honokōhau Nui & Iki. Volume 2: Oral History Interviews.

Maly, Kepā and & Onaona Maly. *He Wahi Mo'olelo no nā Ke'ei ma Kona Hema, Hawai'i: A Collection of Traditions, Historical Accounts and Kama'āina Recol-*

lections of Ke'ei, South Kona, Hawai'i; prepared for Kamehameha Schools. Hilo, HI: Kumu Pono Associates, 2002. 1 v. (various pagings).

Māmaka Kaiao: A Modern Hawaiian Vocabulary. Edited by Kōmike Hua'ōlelo. Honolulu: University of Hawai'i Press, 2003. 414 p.

Martial Law in Hawaii: The Papers of Major General Thomas H. Green, Judge Advocate General's Corps, U.S. Army. Project coordinator Robert E. Lester. Bethesda, MD: University Publications of America, 2000. 20 microfilm reels.

Mason Architects, Inc. *Washington Place: Historic Structures Report and Master Plan.* Honolulu, 2000. 1 v. (various pagings).

Matsuura, Richard M. *Rebel with a Dream from Hawaii: The Incredible Journey of Senator Richard M. Matsuura.* Hilo, HI: Orchid Isle Publishing Co., 2002. vii, 380 p.

Maui News, 1900–2000: 100 Years As Maui's Newspaper. Wailuku, HI: The Maui News, [2000?]. 48 p. "A glimpse of the past century as seen through the pages of Maui's Newspaper."

McDonald, Marie A. and Paul R. Weissich. *Nā Lei Makamae: The Treasured Lei.* Honolulu: University of Hawai'i Press, 2003. 200 p. Flowers and plants used in traditional lei making, with information and descriptions from traditional stories, and photographs of the lei.

McGregor, Davianna. *Prince Jonah Kūhiō Kalaniana'ole: Hawaiian Ali'i & Congressional Delegate.* Honolulu: Center for Biographical Research, 2002. 7 p. (Biography Hawai'i: Five Lives: A Series of Public Remembrances). Also includes *The First Election of ke Keikiali'i Kūhiō Kalaniana'ole* by Noenoe Silva.

Memorial Addresses and Other Tributes: Held in the House of Representatives and Senate of the United States, together with memorial services in honor of Patsy T. Mink, late a representative from Hawaii, One Hundred Seventh Congress, second session. Washington DC: U.S. G.P.O., 2003. iv, 160 p.

Moore, Susanna. *I Myself Have Seen It: The Myth of Hawai'i.* Washington, DC: National Geographic, 2003. 184 p. Hawai'i history, with personal recollections.

Morrison, Susan. *Kamehameha: The Warrior King of Hawai'i.* Honolulu, University of Hawai'i Press, 2003. xi, 85 p.

Mullins, Joseph G. *Hawaiian Journey.* Honolulu: Mutual Publishing, 2003. 128 p. Rev. and updated ed.

Mykkānen, Juri. *Inventing Politics: A New Political Anthropology of the Hawaiian Kingdom.* Honolulu: University of Hawai'i Press, 2003. xii, 248 p.

New Worlds, New Lives: Globalization and People of Japanese Descent in the Americas and from Latin America in Japan. Edited by Lane Ryo Hirabayashi, Akemi Kikumura-Yano, and James A. Hirabayashi. Stanford, CA: Stanford University Press, 2002. xxiii, 358 p. Includes Hawai'i.

Noyes, Martha H. *Then there were none.* Honolulu: Bess Press, 2003. vii, 109 p. "Based on the documentary film by Elizabeth Kapu'uwailani Lindsey Buyers."

Office of Hawaiian Affairs. *OHA's Strategic Plan 2002–2007.* Honolulu: Office of Hawaiian Affairs, 2002. 116 p.

Okimoto, Ken. *Exploring the Hāmākua Coast : A Pictorial Guide to the Plantation Era.* Honolulu: Watermark Pub., 2002. vi, 122 p.

Oral History of Robert Richards Midkiff. Honolulu: Center for Oral History, Social Science Research Institute, University of Hawai'i at Mānoa, 2001. 1 v. (various pagings).

Puna Hongwanji Mission: Centennial Celebration 1902–2002. Hilo, HI: The Mission, 2002. xi, 88 p.

Raymundo, Angeles Monrayo. *Tomorrow's Memories: A Diary 1924–1928.* Edited by Rizaline R. Raymundo. Honolulu: University of Hawai'i Press in association with UCLA Asian American Studies Center, Los Angeles, 2003. 280 p. Diary of a Filipino in Hawai'i.

Sandler, Rob. *Legends of Hawaii Golf: The First Century.* Honolulu: Exclusively Hawaii Publishing, 2003. 208 p.

Schweitzer, Sophia V. *Kohala 'Āina: History of North Kohala.* Honolulu: Mutual Publishing, 2003. 1 v.

Seiden, Allan. *Diamond Head: Hawai'i's Icon.* Honolulu: Mutual Publishing, 2002. 144 p.

Severns, Mike and Pauline Fiene. *Molokini: Hawai'i's Island Marine Sanctuary.* Waipahu, HI: Island Heritage, 2002. 159 p. Color photographs, includes some history.

Severson, Don R., Michael D. Horikawa, and Jennifer Saville. *Finding Paradise: Island Art in Private Collections.* Honolulu: Honolulu Academy of Arts: University of Hawai'i Press, 2002. xxxix, 355 p.

Silva, Kalena. *Princess Ruth Ke'elikōlani: Hawaiian Ali'i.* Honolulu: Center for Biographical Research, 2002. 7 p. (Biography Hawai'i: Five Lives: A Series of Public Remembrances). Also includes *Ruth Ke'elikōlani, Po'olua Child* by Rubellite Kawena Johnson; *Ruta Keanolani Kamu'olaulani Ke'elikōlani Kanāhoahoa: A View from Her Time* by Puakea Nogelmeier; *Ke'elikōlani Nui,* words & music by Kahauanu Lake.

Smith, Rex Alan, and Gerald A. Meehl. *Pacific Legacy: Image and Memory from World War II in the Pacific.* New York: Abbeville Press, 2002. 316 p.

Soehren, Lloyd J. *A Catalog of Moloka'i Place Names: Including Lāna'i.* Honokaa, HI: L.J. Soehren, 2003. xi, 254 p. "Compiled from the records of the Boundary Commission and the Board of Commissioners to Quiet Land Titles of the kingdom of Hawaii."

Stoddard, Tim. *Ho'ololi 'Āina: The Changing Landscape of Honouliuli.* Honolulu: Nature Conservancy of Hawai'i, 2002. 27 p.

Stone, Scott C. S. *Living Legacy: Outstanding Japanese Women of the 20th Century in Hawai'i.* Honolulu: Japanese Women's Society Foundation, 2002. 128 p.

———. *Yesterday in Hawai'i: A Voyage Through Time.* Waipahu, HI: Island Heritage, 2003. xiii, 121 p.

Testa, F.J. *Buke Mele Lahui: Book of National Songs.* Honolulu: Hawaiian Historical Society, 2003. xxiv, xiv, 112 p. (Hawaiian Language Reprint Series, Buke 2.) Facsimile reprint of 1895.

United Japanese Society of Hawaii. *Renkyo no Ayumi: United Japanese Society of*

Hawaii 40th Anniversary Publication. Edited by Patsy S. Saiki. Honolulu: United Japanese Society of Hawaii, 2000. 155 p.

Waddle, Scott. *The Right Thing.* Nashville: Integrity Publishers, 2002. x, 252 p. Regarding the Ehime Maru collision.

Warshaw, Matt. *The Encyclopedia of Surfing.* Orlando, FL: Harcourt, 2003. xx, 774 p.

Water for Life: The History and Future of Water on O'ahu. Honolulu: Honolulu Board of Water Supply, 2003. 1 v. (unpaged).

Westervelt, W.D. *Legends of Old Honolulu.* Forward by Glen Grant. Honolulu: Mutual, 2003. xiv, 282 p. Reprint of 1915.

Weyeneth, Robert R. *Kapi'olani Park: A History.* Honolulu: Kapiolani Park Preservation Society, 2002. 160 p.

Wichman, Frederick B. *Nā Pua Ali'i o Kaua'i: Ruling Chiefs of Kaua'i.* Honolulu: University of Hawai'i Press, 2003. x, 157 p.

Williams, Rianna M. *The King's Daughters Home.* Honolulu: s.n., 2002. 8 leaves.

Williams, Scott and Richard Nees. *Mo'olelo Ha'ikū: Archaeological Inventory Survey, Data Recovery, and Monitoring Investigations for the Interstate Highway H-3 within Ha'ikū Valley, He'eia Ahupua'a, Ko'olau Poko District, Island of O'ahu.* Honolulu: Ogden Environmental and Energy Services, 2002. x, 116 p.

Willmott, H.P., Tamotsu Haruo, and W. Spencer Johnson. *Pearl Harbor.* London: Cassell, distributed in the US by Sterling Pub., 2001. 208 p.

Wilson, Rob. *Reimagining the American Pacific: From South Pacific to Bamboo Ridge and Beyond.* Durhan, NC; London: Duke University Press, 2000. xix, 295 p. Cultural study, includes Hawai'i.

Yamashita, Bruce I. *Fighting Tradition: A Marine's Journey to Justice.* Honolulu: University of Hawai'i Press in association with UCLA Asian American Studies Center, Los Angeles, 2003. viii, 244 p.

YWCA of O'ahu Collection: 1900–1990. YWCA Archives Project. Honolulu: YWCA of O'ahu, 2001. 34 leaves.

Thesis and Dissertations

Bartlett, Rima Alicia. "Bringing the Bright Land into Being: Seeding and Feeding Space and Place in Hawai'i." Ph.D. dissertation, University College, London, 2000. 2 v. 151, 405. (Geography) About geographical names in Hawaiian.

Basham, J.J. Leilani. "He Puke Mele Lāhui: nā Mele Kūpa'a, nā Mele Kū'ē a me nā Mele Aloha o nā Kanaka Maoli." M.A. thesis, University of Hawai'i at Mānoa, 2002. xv, 184. (History) In Hawaiian, on Hawaiian patriotic songs.

Carney, Melissa Crimi. "The Kona Field System: An Interdisciplinary Investigation of the Human-Environmental Interactions that Caused the Death of Captain James Cook." M.A. thesis, Florida Atlantic University, 2002. 73. (Anthropology)

Chun, Allison A. "The Discourses (Re)constructing the Sacred Geography of Kaho'olawe Island, Hawai'i." Ph.D. dissertation, University of Hawai'i at Mānoa, 2002. xx, 477. (Geography)

Cottrell, Christopher Andrew. "Splinters of Sandalwood, Islands of 'Iliahi: Rethinking Deforestation in Hawai'i, 1811–1843." M.A. thesis, University of Hawai'i at Mānoa, 2002. v, 171. (History)

Cruz, Lynette Hi'ilani., "From Resistance to Affirmation, We Are Who We Were: Reclaiming National Identity in the Hawaiian Sovereignty Movement, 1990–2003." Ph.D.dissertation, University of Hawai'i at Mānoa, 2003. ix, 236. (Anthropology)

Huetz de Lemps, Paul. "Français Acteurs et Spectateurs de l'Histoire de Hawaii (1837–1898)." Thesis, Ecole Nationale des Chartes, 2001. 554. French actors and spectators of Hawaiian history 1837–1898.

Hunter, Charlotte Anne Tsali. "The C-Shaped Structures of Haleakalā National Park: Vernacular Architecture in the Hawaiian Islands." Ph.D. dissertation, Brown University, 2002. (Anthropology)

Imada, Adria L. "Aloha America: Hawaiian Entertainment and Cultural Politics in the United States Empire." Ph.D. dissertation, New York University, 2003. 350. (American Studies)

Inoue, Akihiro. "An Ethnographic Study of the Construction of Hawaiian Christianity in the Past and the Present." Ph.D. dissertation, University of Hawai'i at Mānoa, 2003. xiv, 308. (Anthropology)

Iwata, Taro. "Race and Citizenship as American Geopolitics: Japanese and Native Hawaiians in Hawai'i, 1900–1941." Ph.D. dissertation, University of Oregon, 2003. 321. (History)

Kinoshita, Gaku. "Storied Identities: Japanese American Elderly from a Sugar Plantation Community in Hawai'i." Ph.D. dissertation, University of Hawai'i at Mānoa, 2003. ix, 328. (Anthropology)

Kahakalau, Kū H. "Kanu of ka 'Āina: Natives of the Land from Generations Back. A Pedagogy of Hawaiian Liberation." Ph.D. dissertation, Union Institute and University, 2002. 276. (Education)

LaBarge, Andrea Louise. "Hawaii Government's Role in Japanese Ownership of Hawaii Hotels, 1970–1990." Ph.D. dissertation, University of Hawai'i at Mānoa, 2002. x, 264. (Political Science)

McBride, Christopher Mark. "The Colonizer Abroad: Island Representations in American Prose from Herman Melville to Jack London." Ph.D. dissertation, Claremont Graduate University, 2001. 232. (Literature) American writers visiting Hawai'i, including Mark Twain, Charles Warren Stoddard, Jack London.

McElroy, Windy Keala. "Variability in Poi Pounders from Kaua'i Island, Hawai'i." M.A. thesis, University of Hawai'i at Mānoa, 2003. xi, 121. (Anthropology)

Mironesco, Monique M. "Feminist Consciousness, Voice, and Empowerment: Women's Studies in Hawai'i." Ph.D. dissertation, University of Hawai'i at Mānoa, 2003. vii, 359. (Political Science)

Moran, Michelle Therese. "Colonizing Leprosy: Imperialism, Patients, and the Politics of Public Health in Hawai'i and Louisiana." Ph.D. dissertation, University of Illinois at Urbana-Champaign, 2002. 347. (History, European)

Nakamura, Kelli Y. "Murder, Rape, and Martial Law: A Dual-System of Justice for Japanese, 1928–1944." M.A. thesis, University of Hawai'i at Mānoa, 2003. xiv, 102. (History)

NeSmith, Keao. "Tūtū's Hawaiian and the Emergence of a Neo-Hawaiian Language." M.A. Plan B thesis, University of Hawai'i at Mānoa, 2002. 38. (Pacific Island Studies)

Nishimoto, Warren S. "An Oral History of the April 1, 1946 Tsunami at Laupahoehoe, Hawai'i: A Case Study in the Educative Value of Constructing History from Memory and Narrative." Ph.D. dissertation, University of Hawai'i at Mānoa, 2002. ix, 231. (American Studies)

Silva, Reinaldo Francisco. "Representations of the Portuguese in American Literature." Ph.D. dissertation, New York University, 1998. 398. (Literature) Includes Hawai'i.

Watson, Sandra Sachie. "The Transformation of the Landscape in Waimea, Hawai'i: Pre-Human Era to 1860." M.A. thesis, University of Hawai'i at Mānoa, 2002. viii, 89. (Geography)

Williams, Todd Austin. "Then and Now: A Comparison of the Attacks of December 7, 1941 and September 11, 2001 as Seen in the New York Times with an Analysis of the Construction of the Current Threat to the National Security." M.A. thesis, Ohio University, 2003. 115.

Selected Periodical References (Out-of-State Publications)

Articles in journals and magazines published in Hawai'i and the Pacific are selectively indexed in the Hawai'i Pacific Journal Index, at http://hpji.lib.hawaii.edu/

Amerasia Journal 29.2 (2003). Special issue on "Pedagogy, Social Justice, and the State of Asian American Studies." Includes: "Where I Live, There Are Rainbows: Cultural Identity and Sense of Place" by Alice J. Kawakami, 67–79; "Talking Story: A Virtual Interview with Christine Tanioka and JoAnn Wong-Kam" by Alice J. Kawakami, 81–90; "Our Own Liberation: Reflections on Hawaiian Epistemology" by Manulani Aluli Meyer, 139–164.

Borch, Fred L. "Comparing Pearl Harbor and '9/11': Intelligence Failure? American Unpreparedness? Military Responsibility?" *Journal of Military History* 67.3 (July 2003): 845–860.

Brown, Marilyn. "'Aina Under the Influence: The Criminization of Alcohol in 19th-Century Hawai'i." *Theoretical Criminology* 7.1 (Feb. 2003): 89–110.

Charlot, John. "Prophet of the Earth Overturned: Ke'āulumoku on Early Contact in Hawai'i." *Rongorongo Studies* 13.1 (2003): 20–36.

Clark, Herman Pi'ikea. "Ka Maka Hou Hawaii: The New Face of the Hawaiian Nation." *Third Text* 17.3 (Sept. 2003): 273–279.

Costa, Janeen Arnold. "Paradisal Discourse: A Critical Analysis of Marketing and Consuming Hawaii." *Consumption, Markets and Culture* 1.4 (1998): 303–346.

CR: The New Centennial Review 1.3 (Winter 2001). Includes: "Marshall Sahlins and the Apotheosis of Culture" by Victor Li, 201–287; "Response to Victor Li" by Gananath Obeyesekere, 289–298. Concerns Captain Cook in Hawai'i.

Ecological Restoration 21.4 (Dec. 2003). Includes: "Restoring a Part of Hawai'i's Past: Kaloko Fishpond Restoration" by Stanley Bond, Jr. and Richard Gmirkin, 284–289; "Native Hawaiian Collection, Use, and Management of Plants and Plant Communities within Hawai'i Volcanoes National Park" by Jim Martin and Laura Carter Schuster, 307–310.

Gibbs, Patricia L. "Alternative Things Considered: A Political Economic Analysis of Labour Processes and Relations at a Honolulu Alternative Newspaper." *Media, Culture & Society* 25.5 (Sept. 2003): 587–605.

Gould, L. Scott. "Mixing Bodies and Beliefs: The Predicament of Tribes." *Columbia Law Review* 101.4 (May 2001): 702–772. Concerns Native Hawaiians' legal status.

Grijp, Paul van der. "Configurations Identitaires et Contextes Coloniaux: Une Comparaison Entre Tonga et Hawaii." *Journal de la Société des Océanistes* 113.2 (2001/2002): 177–192. Text in French.

Grover, Gretchen G. "The Coast Guard's Pacific Colonizers." *Naval History* 16.4 (Aug. 2002): 43–47. Concerns U.S. attempts to colonize Pacific islands in the 1930s using Native Hawaiians.

History of Education Quarterly 43.1 (Spring 2003). Special issue on Asian-American educational history. Includes: "Introduction: Asian Americans and Educational History" by Eileen H. Tamura, 1–9; "Mandating Americanization: Japanese Language Schools and the Federal Survey of Education in Hawai'i, 1916–1920" by Noriko Asato, 10–38.

Hooper, Steven. "Making a Killing?: Of Sticks and Stones and James Cook's 'Bones'." *Anthropology Today* 19.3 (June 2003): 6–8.

Johnson, Greg. "Ancestors Before Us: Manifestations of Tradition in a Hawaiian Dispute." *Journal of the American Academy of Religion* 71.2 (June 2003): 327–346.

Johnston, Paul Forsythe. "A Million Pounds of Sandalwood: The History of Cleopatra's Barge in Hawaii." *American Neptune* 62.1 (2002): 5–44.

Journal of Pacific History 38.1 (June 2003). Includes: "Warfare and State Formation in Hawaii: The Limits on Violence as a Means of Political Consolidation" by Paul D'Arcy, 29–52; "Neo in Oceania: Foreign Vessels Owned by Hawaiian Chiefs before 1830" by Peter R. Mills, 53–67.

Jung, Moon-Kie. "Interracialism: The Ideological Transformation of Hawaii's Working Class." *American Sociological Review* 68.3 (June 2003): 373–400.

Kelly, Anne Keala. "A Kingdom Inside: The Future of Hawaiian Political Identity." *Futures* 35.9 (Nov. 2003): 999–1009.

Kelly, Marjorie. "Projecting an Image and Expressing Identity: T-shirts in Hawaii." *Fashion Theory* 7.2 (June 2003): 191–211.

Küchler, Susanne. "Imaging the Body Politic: The Knot in Pacific Imagination." *L'Homme* 165 (Jan.-March 2003): 205–222. Includes the Hawaiian sacred cord.

Ladefoged, Thegn N., Michael W. Graves, and Mark D. McCoy. "Archaeological Evidence for Agricultural Development in Kohala, Island of Hawai'i." *Journal of Archaeological Science* 30.7 (July 2003): 923–940.

Merry, Sally Engle. "Kapi'olani at the Brink: Dilemmas of Historical Ethnography in 19th Century Hawai'i." *American Ethnologist* 30.1 (Feb. 2003): 44–60.

Morgado, Marcia A. "From Kitsch to Chic: The Transformation of Hawaiian Shirt Aesthetics." *Clothing and Textiles Research Journal* 21.2 (2003): 75–88.

Parikh, Crystal. "Blue Hawaii: Asian Hawaiian Cultural Production and Racial Melancholia." *Journal of Asian American Studies* 5.3 (October 2002): 199–216.

Paxman, David. "'Distance Getting Close': Gesture, Language, and Space in the Pacific." *Eighteenth-Century Life* 26.3 (Fall 2002): 78–97. Includes Hawai'i.

Ruggles, Clives L. N. "*Heiau* Orientations and Alignments on Kaua'i." *Archaeoastronomy* 16 (2001): 46–82.

Sokolowsky, Brian William. "Photographs of Joseph F. Smith and the Laie Plantation, Hawaii, 1899." *BYU Studies* 41.4 (2002): 46–63.

Thompson, Lanny. "The Imperial Republic: A Comparison of the Insular Territories under U.S. Dominion after 1898." *Pacific Historical Review* 71.4 (Nov. 2002): 535–574. Includes Hawai'i.

Woodcock, Deborah. "To Restore the Watersheds: Early Twentieth-Century Tree Planting in Hawai'i." *Annals of the Association of American Geographers* 93.3 (Sept. 2003): 624–635.

World Archaeology 34.3 (Feb. 2003). Special issue on luxury foods. Includes: "Did East Polynesians have a Concept of Luxury Foods?" by Helen Leach, 442–457; "New Archaeological Insights into Food and Status: A Case Study from Pre-Contact Hawaii" by Patrick V. Kirch and Sharyn Jones O'Day, 484–497.

Chapters in Books

The following is the second annual list of book chapters on Hawaiian history, and includes chapters published 1993–2003

Asian/Pacific Islander American Women: A Historical Anthology. Hune, Shirley and Gail M. Nomura, eds., New York: New York University Press, 2003. Includes: "Constructed Images of Native Hawaiian Women," by Davianna Pōmaika'i McGregor, 25–41; "Redefining the Boundaries of Traditional Gender Roles: Korean Picture Brides, Pioneer Korean Immigrant Women, and Their Benevolent Nationalism in Hawai'i," by Lili M. Kim, 106–119;

"Passed into the Present: Women in Hawaiian Entertainment," by Amy Ku'uleialoha Stillman, 205–218.

Borgerson, Janet and Jonathan Schroeder. "The Lure of Paradise: Marketing the Retro-Escape of Hawaii." In Brown, Stephen and John F. Sherry, Jr., eds. *Time, Space, and the Market: Retroscapes Rising.* Armonk, NY: M.E. Sharpe, 2003. 219–237.

Churchill, Ward. "Stolen Kingdom: The Right of Hawai'i to Decolonization." In *Perversions of Justice: Indigenous Peoples and Angloamerican Law.* San Francisco: City Lights, 2003. 73–123.

Cook, Scott B. "Islands of Manifest Destiny: America in Hawaii." In *Colonial Encounters in the Age of High Imperialism.* New York: HarperCollins, 1996. 73–102.

Dieudonne, Fran, ed., "Hawai'i." In *The Pacific Islands and the Sea: 350 Years of Reporting on Royal Fishponds, Coral Reefs and Ancient Walled Fish Weirs in Oceania.* Encinitas, CA: Neptune House, 2002. 87–109.

Edles, Laura Desfor. "'Race,' 'Ethnicity,' and 'Culture' in Hawai'i: The Myth of the 'Model Minority' State." In Winters, Loretta I. and Herman L. DeBose, eds., *New Faces in a Changing America: Multiracial Identity in the 21st Century.* Thousand Oaks, CA: Sage, 2003. 222–246.

Feeser, Andrea. "Constance Fredericka Gordon Cumming's 'Picturesque' Vision: A Christian, Westernized Hawai'i." In Siegel, Kristi, ed., *Issues in Travel Writing: Empire, Spectacle, and Displacement.* New York: Peter Lang, 2002. 85–105.

Fenton, Steve. "Class Structures, Ethnic Formations: Malaysia, Hawai'i, Britain." In *Ethnicity, Racism, Class and Culture.* Lanham, MD: Rowman & Littlefield, 1999. 141–169.

———. "The Politics of Ethnicity: Hawai'i, Britain, Continental Europe." In *Ethnicity, Racism, Class and Culture.* Lanham, MD: Rowman & Littlefield, 1999. 191–211.

Gell, Alfred. "Hawaii: A Feudal Polity." In *Wrapping In Images: Tattooing in Polynesia.* Oxford: Clarendon Press, 1993. 275–278.

———. "Hawaiian Tattoo." In *Wrapping In Images: Tattooing in Polynesia.* Oxford: Clarendon Press, 1993. 278–280.

———. "The Distribution of Hawaiian Tattoo." In *Wrapping In Images: Tattooing in Polynesia.* Oxford: Clarendon Press, 1993. 281–294.

———. "The Corruption and Decay of Hawaiian Tattoo." In *Wrapping In Images: Tattooing in Polynesia.* Oxford: Clarendon Press, 1993. 285–287.

Halualani, Rona Tamiko. "Connecting Hawaiians: The Politics of Authenticity in the Hawaiian Diaspora." In Collier, Mary Jane, ed., *Intercultural Alliances: Critical Transformation.* Thousand Oaks, CA: Sage, 2003. 221–248.

Historical Ecology in the Pacific Islands: Prehistoric Environmental and Landscape Change. Kirch, Patrick V. and Terry L. Hunt, eds., New Haven: Yale University Press, 1997. Includes: "Pre-Contact Landscape Transformation and Cultural Change in Windward O'ahu," by Jane Allen, 230–247; "Hawaiian Native Lowland Vegetation in Prehistory," by J. Stephens Athens, 248–270.

Johnston, Patricia. "Advertising paradise. Hawai'i in art, anthropology, and commercial photography." In Hight, Eleanor M. and Gary D. Sampson, eds. *Colonialist Photography: Imag(in)ing race and place.* London: Routledge, 2002. 188–225.

Kaeppler, Adrienne L. "Hawaiian Art: From Sacred Symbol to Tourist Icon to Ethnic Identity Marker." In Merrill, William L. and Ives Goddard, eds., *Anthropology, History, and American Indians: Essays in Honor of William Curtis Sturtevant.* Washington, DC: Smithsonian Institution Press, 2002. 147–159.

Kashima, Tetsuden. "The Territory of Hawaii." In *Judgment Without Trial: Japanese American Imprisonment During World War II.* Seattle: University of Washington Press, 2003. 67–87.

Kenui, Cynthia Kanoelani. "*Na Kānaka Maoli:* The Indigenous People of Hawai'i." In Robinson, John D. and Larry C. James, eds. *Diversity in Human Interactions: The Tapestry of America.* New York: Oxford University Press, 2003. 93–110.

Liebersohn, Harry. "Images of Monarchy: Kamehameha I and the Art of Louis Choris." In Thomas, Nicholas and Diane Losche, eds., *Double Vision:*

Art Histories and Colonial Histories in the Pacific. Cambridge: Cambridge University Press, 1999. 44–64.

Mayer, Manu Aluli. "To Set Right: Ho'oponopono, a Native Hawaiian Way of Peacemaking." In Chew, Pat K., ed. *The Conflict and Culture Reader*. New York: New York University Press, 2001. 176–181.

Merry, Sally Engle. "Christian Conversion and 'Racial' Labor Capacities: Constructing Racialized Identities in Hawai'i." In *Globalization Under Construction: Governmentality, Law, and Identity*. Minneapolis, MN: University of Minnesota Press, 2003. 203–238.

———. "Legal Pluralism and Transnational Culture: The *Ka Ho'okolokolonui Kanaka Maoli* Tribunal, Hawai'i, 1993." In Wilson, Richard A., ed., *Human Rights, Culture and Context: Anthropological Perspectives*. London: Pluto Press, 1997. 28–48.

Scheiber, Harry N. and Jane L. Scheiber. "The Roles of Lawyers in a Civil Liberties Crisis: Hawaii During World War II." In VanBurkleo, Sandra F., Kermit L. Hall, and Robert J. Kaczorowski, eds. *Constitutionalism and American Culture: Writing the New Constitutional History*. Lawrence, KS: University Press of Kansas, 2002. 123–173.

Schodt, Frederik L. "A 'Staging Ground' in the Hawaiian Islands." In *Native American in the Land of the Shogun: Ranald MacDonald and the Opening of Japan*. Berkeley, CA: Stone Bridge Press, 2003. 157–184.

Stillman, Amy Ku'uleialoha. "Re-Membering the History of the Hawaiian Hula." In Mageo, Jeannette Marie, ed., *Cultural Memory: Reconfiguring History and Identity in the Postcolonial Pacific*. Honolulu: University of Hawai'i Press, 2001. 187–204.

Szego, C. K. "Singing Hawaiian and the Aesthetics of (In)Comprehensibility." In *Global Pop, Local Language*. Jackson, MS: University Press of Mississippi, 2003. 291–328.

Trask, Haunani-Kay. "Restitution as a Precondition of Reconciliation: Native Hawaiians and Indigenous Human Rights." In Winbush, Raymond A., ed., *Should America Pay?: Slavery and the Raging Debate on Reparations*. New York: Amistad, 2003. 32–45.

Wallace, Lee. "Sexual Encounter in Hawaii on Cook's Third Voyage." In *Sexual Encounters: Pacific Texts, Modern Sexualities.* Ithaca, NY: Cornell University Press, 2003. 38–56.

Wallace III, William Kauaiwiulaokalani. "Protecting the 'Sacred *Ipu*': Connecting the Sacred in Being Hawaiian-Christian in Hawai'i–A Personal Journey." In Iwamura, Jane N. and Paul Spickard, eds. *Revealing the Sacred in Asian and Pacific America.* New York: Routledge, 2003. 29–42.

Watson-Gegeo, Karen. "Language and Education in Hawai'i: Sociopolitical and Economic Implications of Hawai'i Creole English." In Morgan, Marcyliena H., ed. *Language & the Social Construction of Identity in Creole Situations.* Los Angeles: Center for Afro-American Studies, University of California, Los Angeles, 1994. 101–120. Includes history of pidgin.

Weinstein, Valerie. "Capturing Hawai'i's Rare Beauty: Scientific Desire and Precolonial Ambivalence in E.T.A. Hoffmann's 'Haimatochare'." In Herminghouse, Patricia and Ruth-Ellen Boetcher Joeres, eds., *Women in German Yearbook.* Lincoln, NE: University of Nebraska Press, 2002. 158–178.

Wiecek, William M. "Martial Law in Hawaii" In Chapter 2 "Sabotage, Treason, and Military Tribunals in World War II." In Ernst, Daniel R. and Victor Jew, eds. *Total War and the Law: The American Home Front in World War II.* Westport, CT: Praeger, 2002. 64–69.

Wilson, Robert. "Surfing Oahu's North Shore-'Eddie Would Go'." In *American Greats.* New York: PublicAffairs, 1999. 232–235.

Audio-Visuals

America's Darkest Day: Pearl Harbor. [s.l.]: Channel 1000, 2001. 256 min. Videocassette. Compilation of programs on the Japanese bombing of Pearl Harbor: *Pearl Harbor: America's Darkest Day, December 7th, Kamikaze, Kill That Zero! The F6F Hellcat at War.*

Arirang. Produced by Tom Coffman. Honolulu: Tom Coffman Multimedia, 2003. 111 min. Videocassette and DVD. Part 1: The Korean American journey; part 2: The Korean American dream. Documents the history of 100 years of Korean immigration to Hawai'i and the United States.

Big Island Flood November 2000. Hilo, HI: Center for the Study of Active Volcanoes, 2000. 15 min. Videocassette. Documents the Hilo floods of November 2000.

A Call to Serve. Producer, Eugene N. Tiwanak. Honolulu: St. Francis Healthcare Foundation of Hawaii, 2002. 11 min. Videocassette. Documents the history of St. Francis Healthcare System of Hawaii.

Coming to Hawaii: An Interview. Produced and written by Scott Culbertson. Honolulu: Public Broadcasting Service, 2003. 27 min. Videocassette. Profile of Hiram L. Fong.

Conquest of Hawaii. Produced by Melody Shafir, Jill Sharer, written by Susan Michaels. New York: A&E Television, 2003. 100 min. Videocassette. "The complete chronicle of Hawaii's history."

Daniel K. Inouye, An American Story: A Film. By Heather H. Giugni. Honolulu: Juniroa, 2003. 120 min. Videocassette and DVD.

Documenting Sovereignty: A Film. By Monique Yamaguchi. Los Angeles: Ordinary World Pictures, 2001. 22 min. Videocassette and DVD. Film makers Puhipau, Lurline McGregor, Leah Kihara, Heather Giugni, Kala'iokona Ontai discuss their work which focuses on Hawaiian history and culture.

Frontiers in Immigration: Okinawans in Hawaii. Produced by Sarah Fong, Joy Miyamoto. Hawai'i: Hawaii United Okinawan Association, 1998. 11 min.

Hali'a Aloha = A Fond Remembrance: Thomas Kananimauloa Maunupau, Jr. Nā'ālehu, HI: Nā Maka o ka 'Āina, 1998. 16 min. Videocassette.

Kaho'olawe: Ka Hā O Ko Mākou Mau Kūpuna = The Breath Of Our Ancestors. Producers, Jacqueline Langley, Mark Nitta. Honolulu: Kaho'olawe Island Reserve Commission and Hawai'i Pacific University, 2000. Presents the history of land use on Kaho'olawe.

Kāko'i. Nā'ālehu, HI: Nā Maka o ka 'Āina, 2003. 12 min. Videocassette. Demonstration of traditional Hawaiian techniques for flaking, grinding and hafting stone adzes.

Kamehameha the Great: Revolutionary, Reactionary, Reformer. Producers, Sean

Jung, Joshua Kitano. Kāne'ohe, HI: Kapunahala Elementary School, 2002. 11 min. Videocassette.

Kona Hema = South Kona. Nā'ālehu, HI: Nā Maka o ka 'Āina, 2001. 30 min. Videocassette. A historical and cultural tour of south Kona, narrated by residents of the area.

The Legacy of David Malo. Honolulu: Rotary Club of West Honolulu, 1997. 11 min. Relates the life of David Malo and the history of the David Malo Award.

Live from Pearl Harbor Highlights. Producer, Matt Ginsburg. New York: A&E Television, 2001. 50 min. Videocassette.

Made in Hawai'i, A Retrospective of Hawai'i Film Makers. Producers, Esther Figueroa, Richard Morse. Honolulu: Legacy Foundation of the Pacific, 2001. 335 min. Videocassette. Review of Hawai'i film and video, with interviews with film makers George Tahara, Dan Garab, Tip Davis, Heather Giugni, Meleanna Meyer, Victoria Keith, Tom Coffman, Ann Marie Kirk and Puhipau.

Maiki Aiu Lake. Producers, Joy Chong-Stannard, Craig Howes, Victoria Nalani Kneubuhl. Honolulu: Hawaii Public Television, 2002. 57 min. DVD. *Biography Hawai'i* series.

Oral History Project. Honolulu: University of Hawai'i, John A. Burns School of Medicine, Native Hawaiian Center of Excellence. Videocassette. Includes: Dr. Isabella Abbott. 2002. 80 min.

Pearl Harbor: Death of the Arizona. Produced by Kim Cachere, written by Eric Nelson. Bethesda, Maryland: Discovery Channel, 2001. Videocassette.

Tora, Tora, Tora: The Real Story of Pearl Harbor. Written by Laura Verklan. New York: A&E Television, 2000. 94 min. Videocassette.

A Tribute to Dorothy Kahananui Gillett. Written and produced by Esther Figueroa. Honolulu: Kamehameha Schools, 1996. 24 min. Videocassette.

A Tribute to Hawaii's Firefighters. Producers, Edgy Lee, Jeffrey Mueller. Honolulu: FilmWorks, 2003. 50 min. Videocassette. Presents the history of firefighting in Hawai'i.

Unsung Heroes of Pearl Harbor. Written by Norman Stahl, Joseph H. Alexander. New York: A&E Television, 2001. 50 min. Videocassette.

Voices of Our Kūpuna: World Conference on Hula, Hilo, Hawai'i, July 30, 2001. Nā'ālehu, HI: Nā Maka o ka 'Āina, 2003. 93 min. Videocassette. Winona Beamer, Pulu'elo Park and George Na'ope discuss their personal histories as masters of hula and chant.

The Hawaiian Historical Society

ORGANIZED 1892

THE HAWAIIAN HISTORICAL SOCIETY is dedicated to preserving historical material relating to Hawai'i and the Pacific and publishing scholarly research on the history of Hawai'i and the Pacific. The Society maintains a research library, publishes *The Hawaiian Journal of History* and limited-edition books, and holds regular lecture meetings. The Society is a not-for-profit membership organization funded by dues, contributions, book sales, an endowment, and grants for special projects.

Membership in the Society is open to both individuals and institutions and includes *The Hawaiian Journal of History, Na Mea Kahiko* newsletter, membership meetings, and discounts on publications.

____

NAME AS YOU WANT IT TO APPEAR ON MEMBERSHIP LIST

____

MAILING ADDRESS

____

CITY　　STATE　　ZIP

LIFE MEMBERS	ANNUAL MEMBERSHIPS HERITAGE CLUB	
☐ Founder $10,000	☐ Friend* $500	☐ Contributing $50
☐ Patron $5,000	☐ Associate* $250	☐ Regular (individuals) $40
☐ Benefactor $2,500	☐ Sponsor $100+	☐ Senior citizen (65+) $30
☐ Partner $1,000	☐ Corporate $250+	☐ Student (full-time) $20
		☐ Educational institution $40

Memberships at the $50 level and above are available for couples.
*Consecutive annual donations in these categories are credited toward a Life Membership

ENCLOSED ________________ DATE ________________

Hawaiian Historical Society
560 Kawaiaha'o Street
Honolulu, Hawai'i 96813
Telephone (808) 537-6271
Web site: http://www.hawaiianhistory.org